PACCAR

THE PURSUIT OF QUALITY

■ FOURTH EDITION ■

ALEX GRONER
AND BARRY PROVORSE

Documentary Media
Seattle, Washington

Copyright © 2005 by PACCAR Inc

All rights reserved—no part of this book may be reproduced in any form without permission in writing from PACCAR Inc, Bellevue, Washington.

First edition 1981

Second edition 1996

Third edition 1998

Fourth edition 2005

Documentary Media LLC
3250 41st Avenue SW
Seattle, Washington 98116
(206) 935-9292
email: books@docbooks.com
www.documentarymedia.com

Library of Congress Cataloging-in-Publication Data
Groner, Alex.
Provorse, Barry.
    PACCAR : the pursuit of quality / Alex Groner and Barry Provorse.—
4th ed.
        p. cm.
    Includes index.
    ISBN 0-9719084-7-8
    1. PACCAR—History. 2. Railroad equipment industry—United States—
History. 3. Truck industry—United States—History. I. Provorse, Barry,
1947– . II. Title.
HD9712.U54P323 2005
338.7'629224'0973—dc22   2005000898

Photo credits: Bethlehem Steel Co., pp. 23, 65; Joseph Daniels Collection,
University of Washington Archives, p. 39; Thomas Gleed family, p. 73;
Historical Society of Seattle and King County, pp. 10, 16–18; Charles M.
Pigott family, p. 68; Seattle Catholic Archdiocese, p. 15; Seattle Public Schools
Archive, p. 67; Sisters of the Order of Sacred Heart, p. 81; University of
Oregon Library, p. 57; University of Washington Library, pp. 8, 13, 14, 24,
85; Washington State Historical Society—Tacoma, p. 79

Produced by Marquand Books, Inc., Seattle
    www.marquand.com

Printed in China by C&C Offset Printing Co., Ltd.

PACCAR Inc

 Foden Trucks

A Division of **PACCAR** UK Ltd

PACCAR MEXICO

PACCAR
FINANCIAL

CONTENTS

The **PACCAR** Road . . . a Brief History

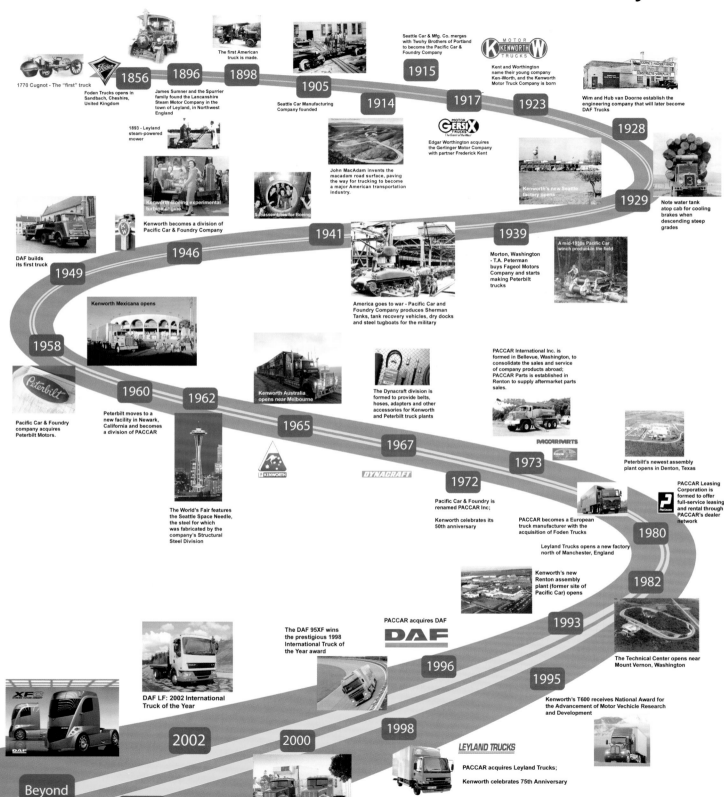

1770 Cugnot - The "first" truck

1856 Foden Trucks opens in Sandbach, Cheshire, United Kingdom

1896 James Sumner and the Spurrier family found the Lancashire Steam Motor Company in the town of Leyland, in Northwest England

1893 - Leyland steam-powered mower

1898 The first American truck is made.

1905 Seattle Car Manufacturing Company founded

1915 Seattle Car & Mfg. Co. merges with Twohy Brothers of Portland to become the Pacific Car & Foundry Company

Kent and Worthington name their young company Ken-Worth, and the Kenworth Motor Truck Company is born

1917 Edgar Worthington acquires the Gerlinger Motor Company with partner Frederick Kent

1923

1928 Wim and Hub van Doorne establish the engineering company that will later become DAF Trucks

1914 John MacAdam invents the macadam road surface, paving the way for trucking to become a major American transportation industry.

1929 Note water tank atop cab for cooling brakes when descending steep grades

Kenworth-Boeing experimental turbine engine

Kenworth becomes a division of Pacific Car & Foundry Company

Subassemblies for Boeing

1939 Morton, Washington - T.A. Peterman buys Fageol Motors Company and starts making Peterbilt trucks

A mid-1930s Pacific Car winch product in the field

Kenworth's new Seattle factory opens

1946

1941 America goes to war - Pacific Car and Foundry Company produces Sherman Tanks, tank recovery vehicles, dry docks and steel tugboats for the military

DAF builds its first truck

1949

1958 Kenworth Mexicana opens

Pacific Car & Foundry company acquires Peterbilt Motors.

1960 Peterbilt moves to a new facility in Newark, California and becomes a division of PACCAR

1962 The World's Fair features the Seattle Space Needle, the steel for which was fabricated by the company's Structural Steel Division

1965 Kenworth Australia opens near Melbourne

The Dynacraft division is formed to provide belts, hoses, adapters and other accessories for Kenworth and Peterbilt truck plants

PACCAR International Inc. is formed in Bellevue, Washington, to consolidate the sales and service of company products abroad; PACCAR Parts is established in Renton to supply aftermarket parts sales.

PACCAR PARTS

1967

DYNACRAFT

1973 Peterbilt's newest assembly plant opens in Denton, Texas

1972 Pacific Car & Foundry is renamed PACCAR Inc; Kenworth celebrates its 50th anniversary

PACCAR becomes a European truck manufacturer with the acquisition of Foden Trucks

Leyland Trucks opens a new factory north of Manchester, England

1980 PACCAR Leasing Corporation is formed to offer full-service leasing and rental through PACCAR's dealer network

Kenworth's new Renton assembly plant (former site of Pacific Car) opens

1982

1993 The Technical Center opens near Mount Vernon, Washington

PACCAR acquires DAF

DAF

1996

1995 Kenworth's T600 receives National Award for the Advancement of Motor Vehicle Research and Development

The DAF 95XF wins the prestigious 1998 International Truck of the Year award

DAF LF: 2002 International Truck of the Year

2002

2000

1998 J.D. Powers Award "Best In Customer Satisfaction" 2000: Kenworth T300 2001: Peterbilt 330

LEYLAND TRUCKS

PACCAR acquires Leyland Trucks; Kenworth celebrates 75th Anniversary

Beyond

2005 PACCAR celebrates its centennial.

FOREWORD

The fourth edition of *PACCAR: The Pursuit of Quality* chronicles the success of the company as it completes its one hundredth year of operation. It is a celebration of the many achievements recorded since the company was founded in 1905. During the past century, PACCAR has developed an unwavering approach for quality success. It is based on a philosophy of focusing on customer needs and providing the highest quality products to meet them. It combines management continuity with the dedication of thousands of hardworking employees to innovate on a daily basis. It is nurtured in a culture that combines integrity and the highest quality standards to establish a company that is respected as much for its ethics as for the products it manufactures and finances. PACCAR's consistent financial results are a measure of the resilience, flexibility, and stick-to-itiveness that define the core structure of the company. Hard work, imagination, and process excellence deliver superior shareholder results, with PACCAR recording a net profit every year since 1938 and a regular dividend payment since 1941.

The breadth of PACCAR patents and industry breakthrough technology spans the decades. A cohesive structure of innovative designs and sophisticated engineering, complemented by highly efficient manufacturing facilities, support services, and distribution centers, contributes to PACCAR setting the product and process quality standards its customers demand in their daily operations. Continuing investments in practical technology in all facets of the company ensure steady progress in manufacturing, financial services, and aftermarket customer support.

Independent, profitable distributor networks are a vital link to customers worldwide. PACCAR sells its products in one hundred countries. The aftermarket customer support operations—leasing, financing, parts, information technology—are integral components in the success equation.

Long-term partnerships with suppliers have resulted in a solid framework of innovation and reliability, which contributes to daily success.

Over the course of the last century, PACCAR has adapted to new industries, competition, and regulations. Steel fabrication, railcar design and production, commercial vehicle manufacturing, financial services, and innovative technology highlight the path of global growth, which PACCAR has embraced through the decades. Quality without compromise defines the company culture.

This book is a testament to the talent of thousands of dedicated employees, visionary directors, and loyal shareholders, all of whom have contributed to PACCAR's position as a leader in the many industries in which it serves its customers globally.

Mark C. Pigott
Chairman & Chief Executive Officer

CHAPTER ONE

WESTERN ODYSSEY

Along with about a sixth of the population of Ireland that emigrated in the wake of the potato famine of the mid-1800s went Michael and Anna Byrne Pigott. Seeking the brighter promise of America, they arrived in New York City in 1846, when Michael was just seventeen years old.

On June 27, 1860, in New York, Anna Pigott gave birth to a son, William. Not long afterward, the family moved to Hubbard, Ohio, where Michael Pigott could make good use of his taste for learning and his indefatigable penchant for work. He became the labor boss at the blast furnace of the Andrews & Hitchcock Iron Company.

William and his younger brother, Michael Jr., attended public and parochial schools in Hubbard for the requisite number of years. Then, as had many of their kin, they went to work for the iron company, Michael as a shipping clerk and William rising to the rank of salesman.

William's job helped open up new horizons as he traveled through various parts of Ohio, Pennsylvania, and New York to sell pig iron. Two things became crystal clear to him: first, that he needed to learn everything he could about the iron and steel business and, second, that he should use this knowledge in getting into the business on his own.

In the course of his travels, William Pigott met William D. Hofius, his senior by some eight years, but a young man with similar ideas. He was the son of Seth Hofius, one of the pioneers in pig iron manufacture in eastern Pennsylvania. William Hofius had given himself a thorough schooling in the business of making pig iron. He started by unloading ore with a shovel, at a blast furnace at Sharpsville, Pennsylvania, and loading pig iron by hand, as was commonly done at the time. His diligence brought him a promotion to the position of superintendent of a blast furnace at Black Rock, New York. Accumulating some capital, he bought an abandoned furnace that had been owned by railroad builder and financier Edward H. Harriman in eastern New York. Hofius moved from one such venture to another, ultimately becoming co-owner and operator of a blast furnace at Leetonia, Ohio.

Pigott decided that Hofius was a man from whom he had much to learn. When the opportunity presented itself, they became partners in the purchase of a blast furnace in Syracuse, New York. The venture proved more instructive than profitable. It was a failure—possibly the only business failure with which Pigott was associated in his lifetime.

Washington State Forest, 1890.

Henry Villard and the Northern Pacific cross the golden spike at Gold Creek, Montana, on September 8, 1883, bound for the West Coast.

— CALL OF THE WEST —

In the 1870s and the 1880s there was a tremendous push to get people to move to the West, and, most particularly, to the Pacific Northwest. Principally behind this campaign were railroad builders, who wanted the cities settled and farms staked out in order to increase the flow of goods between the East and West. Chief among these were Jay Cooke & Company, seller of government and railroad bonds, including those that helped build much of the Northern Pacific; Henry Villard, who took control of the Northern Pacific after the failure of the Cooke firm; and James J. Hill, a sound railroad man who built the Great Northern.

The cities, especially those vying for leadership in the Northwest, did what they could to further the campaign. They also outdid each other in proffering what favors they could to the railroads, a circumstance that the railroad builders used to their full advantage, often delaying decisions about routes until they had extracted the last ounce of benefits available.

Among the enticements the roads had for would-be settlers was land at very attractive prices. Congress had set aside huge grants of land to the railroads, as long as they continued building to the West at an appropriate rate. The railroad promoters printed and circulated pamphlets and books on the Northwest, and advertised splashily in eastern and midwestern newspapers.

"Millions and Millions of Acres," read one Northern Pacific Railroad ad, ". . . for Sale at the Lowest Prices ever offered by any railroad company, ranging most from $2.60 to $4 per Acre, for the Best Wheat Lands, Best Farming Lands, Best Grazing Lands in the World." Prices for land in Washington and Oregon ranged up to $6 an acre, but all were offered at a sixth down, with the balance payable in five annual installments, at 7 percent interest. The ad pointed out also: "These extremely productive Lands stretch out for 50 miles on each side of the Northern Pacific Railroad, and extend from the Great Lakes to the Pacific Ocean. An equal amount of government lands, lying in alternate sections with the Railroad lands, and FREE TO ALL, are open for settlement under the homestead, pre-emption, tree-culture laws."

An inspired newspaper article accompanying the advertisement made the prospect seem even more enticing:

> The best time to come to the GOLDEN NORTHWEST, either in MINNESOTA, DAKOTA, MONTANA, WASHINGTON, or OREGON, on the line of the Northern Pacific Railroad, is in the Spring . . .
>
> The breaking season extends from about May 15th to July 15th. Three horses or mules, each weighing from 1,200 lbs. upwards, or two yoke of oxen, constitutes a good breaking team for a sulky or walking plow . . .
>
> Good farm horses can be bought at from $100 to $150, according to size, etc. Cows are worth from $25 to $35 each, and working oxen from $80 to $125 per yoke. Standard makes of farm wagons cost $75 . . .
>
> The settler, opening a new farm, can always find plenty of work among his neighbors, after he has done his own breaking and back-setting and cut his hay . . .
>
> There is a combination of soil and climate in the Northern Pacific country which makes it the most reliable and productive wheat region in the world . . . It is as healthy a country as there is in the world . . . Settlers can find people of their own nationality at many points . . . , and the Land Department employs Norwegians, Swedish and German agents, who are ready to meet the emigrants . . . on their arrival.

The siren call of the West was one that could not long elude two such ambitious young men as William Hofius and William Pigott. With capital from Hofius and youthful enthusiasm from Pigott, they became co-partners in the purchase of the Trinidad Rolling Mill Company, at Trinidad, Colorado, on July 1, 1892. The two, thoroughly dedicated to their task, spent long hours to make this venture, known as the "black furnace," a success. After about three years, they were able to sell it at a profit to the Colorado Fuel & Iron Company, of Pueblo, Colorado. Pigott stayed on as superintendent of the mill, while Hofius moved to Los Angeles as the company's representative there.

Late in 1894 Pigott took some time out to return to Ohio and to marry Ada E. Clingan, of Hubbard. He brought her back to Colorado, and rarely thereafter did he allow himself to take that much time away from his work. Later, in seeking to persuade an associate to make an extended journey to China, Pigott expressed some of his personal views of the relative demands of work and home life. "You know," he said, "families get so they can get along without being too close. To illustrate that, I was working nights at the black furnace in Trinidad and, when I came home in the morning, as I came up the steps of my house, coming down the steps was a man with a little black bag. I was quite startled. And he says, 'It's a boy.' William had been born while I was working that night. I knew that William was coming but I didn't know that he was expected so soon."

In 1900, Ada Pigott was to give birth to a second son, Paul.

— SEATTLE —

Seattle and Tacoma were rivals in the 1880s and 1890s, each seeking to establish itself as the major seaport of the Northwest. As new railroads worked their way toward the Northwest, the importance of becoming their principal terminus was obvious to the two cities.

Both were located in an area rich in resources, but poor in people and the modern equipment and facilities to work and transport what the land offered. Tacoma realtors spent up to $5,000 a month for advertisements extolling their city in Eastern newspapers. The response was obvious in population growth, up from a mere 1,098 in 1880 to 36,026 in 1890. Part of the reason was surely the decision of the Northern Pacific Railroad to make Tacoma its main terminal in the West, with only a poorly served connecting line to Seattle.

Yet Seattle had some obvious attractions, too, for a westward-moving populace. Even while much of the lumber and wheat going to the Pacific was being exported from Tacoma, Seattle boomed, expanding its population from 3,553 in 1880 to 42,837 in 1890. And between 1890 and 1900, Seattle grew even more, to 80,671, while Tacoma gained barely 1,000 in population.

One reason for the continuing growth was James Hill's Great Northern Railroad. The line Hill laid out was 100 miles shorter than the Northern Pacific, had less total grade, and kept its steepest climbs in concentrated areas, where double-teamed engines could be used. It was more costly to build than the Northern Pacific, but less expensive to operate. And Hill's mastery of finance and marketing, as well as engineering, helped him complete the line without the financial turbulence that repeatedly beset the backers of the Northern Pacific.

Hill played the customary railroad builder's game of pitting one community against another as he selected the routes for his road. Judge Thomas Burke, one of the Northwest's leading lawyers, was the self-appointed champion of Seattle as the road's western terminus. So successfully did he plead the case that Hill not only chose Seattle, but he also hired Burke to represent him in negotiations with the city and its landowners.

When the first of the Great Northern's trains arrived in Seattle in July 1893, the only shadow that fell over the celebration and its Fourth of July oratory was the absence of business leaders from the East. For the nation was in the grip of a depression that counted fifteen thousand commercial firms, six hundred banks, and seventy-four railroads among its business failures. But Seattle itself was on its way. One of the failures was that of the Northern Pacific, which would be purchased, in part, by the city's good friend Jim Hill, and Seattle was about to become the railroad hub of the Northwest.

A newcomer who arrived in Seattle that same year was William Hofius, who left his job with Colorado Fuel & Iron to start his own business once again. Hofius saw an opportunity in serving the lumber industry with the iron and steel supplies it increasingly needed. As timber cutting moved back from the waterfront, where it was a relatively easy matter to skid logs with horse and ox teams into tidewater ponds, short logging railroads had to be built from the receding timberlines to shore transportation. And railroads, even short ones, required a great variety of steel equipment.

So he opened W. D. Hofius & Company, which dealt principally in rails, railway supplies, and various items of iron and steel equipment, representing manufacturers in the East and

Midwest. After a shaky start in the depression that followed the panic of 1893 and that slowed both investment and immigration to a trickle, business slowly improved.

Shortly after the birth of his first son in 1895, William Pigott moved to Seattle to join Hofius again as a partner and as vice president of the firm. But business again became slow and uncertain, and Hofius, feeling he had had enough of the West, returned East. Once there, he wired Pigott to sell out the inventory, mainly steel rails, close up the business, and come back East as well.

Pigott started to follow the instructions. The rails, German-made, could be used on logging railroads only, and it was there that Pigott concentrated his efforts. He met a logger named Mike Earle who was building a narrow-gauge railroad out of Port Angeles into the timber-rich Olympic Peninsula of Washington state. The project had all but bankrupted Earle, who told Pigott, "I might be able to use your rails, but I can't pay for them right now. I'll pay the freight on them. When I can, I'll pay you." The deal was made and the rails were sold. Earle later confessed that he had begged and borrowed every penny he could to get the rail line built, and the credit sale had saved him from ruin. Pigott and Earle became close friends, and continued to do business for years.

Perhaps a more fateful outcome of the transaction was that Pigott decided not to go back East. Instead, he convinced Hofius to return to Seattle. The two built up their product lines, and sales began to improve.

Then, in 1897, a gold rush came to the Yukon. When the steamer *Portland* arrived in Seattle from Alaska, local boosters let it be known that there was "a ton of gold" aboard. As word spread swiftly across the country, Seattle became the gateway to Alaska for the rush of eager gold-seekers.

Seattle waterfront, 1895.

Some Seattleites joined the rush. But many others more wisely stayed home to become the transportation, outfitting, and servicing center for those passing through. As in other boom towns, much of what they did and sold was chicanery or outright fraud, but this did not stop Seattle's business from booming. It became a shipbuilding as well as a shipping center, with its rail links to the rest of the nation and its firm hold on the sea traffic to Alaska.

W. D. Hofius & Company shared in the general prosperity. In 1897 it was advertising a variety of products and services in the local trade papers—"relaying and new rails, English fire brick, engines and boilers, steam pumps, iron water pipe, railroad spikes and supplies." By 1900 the *West Coast Lumberman* reported that "W. D. Hofius & Co. have opened a shop for the purpose of doing their own work. They report locomotives and steel rails moving slowly." And the following year the *Pacific Lumber Trade Journal* reported burgeoning sales in Shay logging engines, handled in Seattle by W. D. Hofius & Company, with an engineer engaged full time in selling and setting up the engines.

But by that year the two partners were not getting along very well. Hofius could be something of a martinet, who, by the account of one of Pigott's early employees, "used to sell

There were many logging companies in the Pacific Northwest by 1900, and their need for rail transportation equipment represented a large market for the region's railroad equipment manufacturers.

Pigott down the street but who, in a jam, went first to Pigott for help." Pigott, late in 1901, sold his interest to Hofius, who reorganized his company as the Hofius Steel & Equipment Company and continued to prosper, heading the company until his death in 1912.

— PIGOTT ON HIS OWN —

Early in 1902, Pigott organized his own business, the Railway Steel & Supply Company, which also dealt in rails, railway supplies, and steel, along with pig iron and coke. He took into the company as secretary his brother, Michael, who had just come to Seattle. William Pigott was the president and treasurer. The company rented offices in Seattle's Starr-Boyd Building. Pigott also owned a frame building on a 60-foot lot near the railroad. Half of this he rented to the Eagle Brass Foundry and the other half he used as a warehouse; later it was the shop of Railway Steel & Supply.

In response to what Pigott saw as substantial local demand, he decided to go into the business of building logging trucks, designed for the Northwest logging conditions, to be drawn by horses or oxen. Until that time, most of the trucks were built in Detroit and shipped to various local markets. A low four- or six-wheel unit, the logging truck, tethered to either end of a stack of logs, represented the precursor to the connected log car that was later to be developed by Pigott.

At the start of 1903, Pigott brought in as "active manager" D. E. McLaughlin, who had been assistant purchasing agent of the Northern Pacific Railroad in Tacoma. Others in the organization were W. T. O'Brien, salesman; W. C. Dickinson—shortly thereafter replaced by D. C. Schultz—, bookkeeper; and W. S. Bassage, stenographer. And in March F. A. Schidel, a boyhood friend from Hubbard, Ohio, came to Seattle and was made a warehouseman and shipping clerk.

With McLaughlin's arrival, plans were made to secure the needed machinery and equipment for building the trucks, and to use one end of the warehouse for that purpose.

Soon after his arrival William Pigott applied his talents to the benefit of the community. William Pigott (third from the right), Bishop O'Dea (fourth from the right), and committee members met in 1906 to plan the erection of Saint James Cathedral in Seattle.

There was considerable consternation when it was learned the necessary machinery would cost as much as $300, and it was only after some hesitation and calculation that Pigott decided to spend that amount for what seemed no more than an experiment.

The equipment, almost all of it secondhand, included a drill press, a forge, a machine for threading bolts and tapping nuts, a wood boring machine, a power-driven emery wheel for grinding chisels, and such hand tools as hammers, rasps, and tongs. The power tools were connected by belts and pulleys to a line shaft driven by an electric motor.

The company had no engineer or draftsman, but McLaughlin supervised the design and manufacture of the trucks and took charge of their sales. Pigott at times used his own considerable talents as a salesman, but he was chiefly engrossed in matters of finance, investment, and other affairs. The cars were sold on a contract basis, at a set price. L. Gilchrist, who had been with the Hofius firm, took charge of the shop as a "jobber," i.e., he purchased power and supplies and he furnished and paid for the labor. Something of a wizard at labor-saving tricks and unsparing in the use of the force of gravity or his own powerful shoulders, he got the maximum out of the equipment and his men, who received from 15 to 25 cents an hour.

In reporting the start of the new business, the *West Coast Lumberman* announced that Pigott "can supply a locomotive on demand, furnish track material or steel in any shape desired." Although Hofius was the local representative of the Lima Locomotive and Machine Company, which built the popular Shay locomotives, Pigott became the Seattle distributor of Climax locomotives.

When there turned out to be not enough logging car work to keep the shop busy, it was decided to take advantage of the considerable amount of building then going on in Seattle, and

Oxen were used in the 1800s to skid logs for up to a half mile, to reach water transportation to Pacific Northwest mills.

During the early 1900s, Railway Steel & Supply was the exclusive Pacific Northwest representative for the Climax Locomotive Company.

the company added structural steel members to its line. The machinery and equipment on hand in the shop proved adequate for the purpose. With its new products, Railway Steel & Supply entered into keen competition with the Hofius firm, as well as with the local Vulcan Iron Works. Bassage was put in charge of the new structural steel department, responsible both for sales and for purchasing and stocking inventory.

Aside from the machine work—drilling holes in steel, boring holes in wood truck bolsters, grinding tools on the wheel, operating the forge blower, and threading bolts and tapping nuts— a considerable amount of pounding and shaping had to be done by hand. Heavy iron or steel arch bars, along with iron parts for trucks, were heated at the forge and fashioned by hand on the anvil. Rivets were hammered by hand. Steel plates and structural forms, including I-beams of up to 18 and 20 inches, were shaped by hand with hammer and chisel. The finished work, however, was not crude, for it would compare well in appearance with similar parts made by machine many years later. The trucks were strong and durable, and the columns and girders went into many a Seattle landmark building.

For two years the company carried on an active business in building trucks and fabricating structural steel in its little shop. Inventory and finished products spread out into vacant fill land owned by the railroad, with free use given to Railway Steel & Supply. There they stored wheels, axles, and other truck parts, along with channel and I-beam stock, much of it in 66-foot lengths.

In June 1903, the company opened a branch office in Portland, with O'Brien in charge of sales. A small stock of supplies—rails, beams, chains, hand and push cars—was warehoused in Portland, while steel logging trucks, trade-named "Hercules," were available from Seattle. After a year, O'Brien purchased the supplies on hand and went into business for himself as the Railway Equipment Company. It was an amicable separation. O'Brien was the local agent for the Hercules trucks, and he and Pigott advertised jointly as "Agents for Irondale pig iron, Locomotives, Logging Engines, Rails, Frogs, Switches, Spikes, Bolts, Track Levers and Gauges, Track and Logging Jacks, Ship Spikes, Boom Chains, Shingle Bands, Wire Rope, Second hand Rails Bought and Sold . . ."

O'Brien operated his business successfully for a number of years. Eventually he was able to buy out complete logging railroads and outfits of different logging camps, and, in addition, he built a car and locomotive repair shop that made a variety of railway switching equipment.

— IRON AND STEEL —

The manufacture of iron and steel, like fertile soil or printer's ink, can get into the pores of a man. William Pigott, while engaged in various other manufactures, never foreswore his devotion to that industry. He saw iron- and steelmaking potentialities all around him, and as early as 1899 he was inquiring about the availability of needed raw materials.

Henry Hewitt Jr., president of the Wilkeson Coal and Coke Company, of Tacoma, wrote to Pigott that, in time, his firm would be able to supply very large quantities of coke. "You need have no fears," he assured Pigott, "any amount of coke can be got. However, on this coast, until

In the 1900s coal for steam, heat, and coke was mined from abundant seams in Washington. Here, miners prepare for their shift at the once prosperous Denny-Renton Clay and Coal Company mine.

In 1880, Puget Sound Iron Company constructed a smelter at Irondale, Washington. After a series of ambitious owners, including Western Steel Corporation, and investments in excess of $20 million, the smelter was acquired in 1913 by Pacific Coast Steel (two years after its merger with Seattle Steel).

other mines are opened, it will cost more money than coke elsewhere on account of the veins all being vertical and considerable dirt mixed in . . . on both walls,—consequently it has to be picked, crushed and washed, and one-third of the coal is lost. . . . However, if iron works should be started, making a sure sale for the coal or coke, I think present prices could be reduced."

Pigott was not alone in his visions of a major West Coast steel industry. Iron deposits in Oregon had aroused interest as early as 1861, and horseshoe nails and a pick had been fashioned from local ores the following year. A group of businessmen raised $500,000 to manufacture pig iron in 1865, and 6 tons of the metal were made when the Oregon furnace began operations in 1867. The Lake Oswego plant was rebuilt in 1888 and produced pig iron for the next six years, making total output since its founding some 93,000 tons, but the operation was abandoned in 1894 as uneconomical.

In the state of Washington a group of lumber and shipping operators organized the Puget Sound Iron Company near Port Townsend, Washington, some 40 miles northwest of Seattle, in 1880. They built the Irondale blast furnace, using nearby bog iron and local timber for charcoal, with a capacity of 4,000 tons per year. The furnace was enlarged and reached its maximum output of more than 10,000 tons in 1889. Then this project, too, was given up for the next eleven years.

In 1900 Homer H. Swaney, of Pittsburgh, sparked new interest in the idea when he had a study made of iron smelting on the Pacific Coast. In scarcely guarded terms, the Wellman-Seaver Engineering Company reported to him that the Irondale blast furnace could be repaired for some $25,000, that sufficient supplies of charcoal were readily available at low cost, that the quality of local ores was excellent, that the prospect of finding large local ore bodies was very good, and that the population of four million provided a substantial market for iron on the West Coast. In sum, they stated, "The plan of making iron and steel on the Pacific Coast is in our opinion a sound one." But they recommended that the blast furnace be rented for two or three years and the ore lands be leased on royalties, both with options to purchase.

Accordingly, Swaney acquired the Puget Sound Iron Company plant, along with a group of iron ore claims in British Columbia and in Washington. In 1901, he formed the Pacific Steel Company to operate the Irondale furnace experimentally, in order to determine whether successful iron operations could be maintained in the Pacific Northwest. Capacity of the furnace was increased to 60 tons a day. In the course of one year, over 6,000 tons of pig iron were turned out; foundries and machine shops from Alaska to southern California pronounced it first-class.

More ambitious plans then took shape. The Seattle Iron and Steel Company, with authorized capital stock of $6 million, in addition to $2 million to be raised through the sale of bonds, was incorporated in 1903 to take over and expand the properties of the Pacific Steel Company. A modern 250-ton blast furnace, basic open-hearth steelmaking furnaces, and rolling mills were projected for a site in Seattle. Heading a board of trustees made up of leading Seattle businessmen, Swaney was busily engaged in acquiring properties when he lost his life by drowning early in 1904 in the wreck of the steamer *Clallam.* The activities of Pacific Steel and of the new Seattle Iron and Steel Company came to a dead halt, and the properties were eventually disposed of through a receivership action.

Aware of all these developments, Pigott began his own activities in the steel business on a far more modest scale. Early in the 1900s he had bought land for the Northern Pacific Railroad for their line into the West Seattle area then known as Humphrey, and later as Youngstown. For himself he purchased an adjacent tract on the tideflats west of the Duwamish River. He bought a 12-inch steel rolling mill, secondhand, in the East, and took preliminary steps to build a small plant on his property to house it.

Pigott then stored his equipment while he entered into serious negotiation with his friend Judge E. M. Wilson, who owned and ran a steel mill at Lakeview, near Tacoma. Built as the Western Iron and Steel Company in 1895, the facility had three coal-fired furnaces, a 30-ton steel hammer, and 9- and 16-inch mills, turning out rails as their principal product. The project failed within a year, and Wilson was dispatched from Youngstown, Ohio, to straighten out the legal difficulties of the company. This he did, then he stayed on in Tacoma to take over the company itself as president and general manager.

In time, Pigott persuaded Judge Wilson to join forces with him in Seattle and sell the Lakeview real estate. On November 23, 1903, they incorporated the Seattle Steel Company, with Wilson as president, Pigott as vice president, and W. S. Burt as secretary.

Pigott wasted no time in moving ahead. Even before the incorporation, on November 11, 1903, the Seattle shipbuilding firm of Moran Brothers Company received this inquiry from Manning, Maxwell & Moore, of New York: "We are informed that Mr. Wm. Piggott [sic] who has an office . . . in our city, is about to associate with some other gentlemen that formed a company and . . . will want us to bid on a 5 ton electric traveling crane, and possibly other machinery, and perhaps a ladle crane. Can you give us any information regarding this party and his connection . . . ?" Kurt Moran replied promptly: ". . . we are very well acquainted with Mr. Wm. Piggott [sic]. . . . We have a very good opinion of him as a man, though we have no knowledge of his financial responsibility. We are inclined, however, to believe that he would be good for a limited credit. His reputation here is very good."

The first stock in the new company was sold to William Pigott—five hundred shares at

Judge E. M. Wilson was William Pigott's partner and president of Seattle Steel Company and later Pacific Coast Steel Company.

Below: Seattle Steel Company, 1906.

$100 per share, and a total of $100,000 in capital was raised. Wilson subsequently received substantially more in stock in exchange for the assets he contributed to the enterprise. The company purchased a rolling mill at Portland, Oregon, but it was never used, and was eventually dismantled.

Construction was begun early in 1904 on Pigott's 55 acres of land on the tideflats. It went ahead smoothly, and was completed in just over a year. Machinery and equipment were moved from Lakeview, and Pigott's 12-inch mill was installed.

The new plant quickly drew the attention of the trade and local press. In March 1905, *Railway and Marine News* reported, "The new rolling mill of the Seattle Steel Company at Humphrey . . . is rapidly approaching completion and will be in full operation within three or four weeks, giving employment to 70 skilled ironworkers and turning out 100 tons daily of merchant iron bars of . . . standard sizes. The buildings for the new plant are already completed and all of the machinery is on the ground, while the greater portion of it is already installed . . ."

The article went on to detail the eight frame buildings of the plant—scrap shed, heating room, rolling room, four stock buildings, and an office building, all of which comprised a total area of approximately 100,000 square feet. Also in the complex were an electric power plant, a five-ton electric crane, and a gravity water system by which water could be supplied from a standpipe on an adjacent hillside. There were five furnaces for heating scrap iron, the principal raw material to be used.

The plant started out with 140 employees and a monthly payroll of $10,000. Operations began on May 4, 1905, when the first merchant bars were turned out. The following day more than five hundred of the leading citizens of Seattle attended a special preview. The company had invited members of the Chamber of Commerce and the city's leading business and professional men to a reception at the plant, and had provided a special train to carry them on the Northern Pacific tracks. *Railway and Marine News* said the event marked "the beginning of a new industrial epoch."

By September, the *Seattle Sunday Times* was more extravagantly hailing the plant as "Seattle's Little Pittsburgh."

— BRANCHING OUT —

Never one to overlook a promising business opportunity, William Pigott became involved with still another new enterprise in the early months of 1904.

This one involved the construction of kilns for drying shingles and lumber, including the trucks and tracks for moving the wood products through the kiln. The leading spirit behind the enterprise was Frank E. Warman, of Indianapolis. Associated with him was V. C. Gilbreath, an engineer and draftsman, who had conducted studies of the kilns, determined the levels of heat and humidity, and familiarized himself with improvements that led to the most successful drying with the least fire danger.

Pigott was obviously impressed enough by their credentials and their proposals to make the necessary investment of funds. He undoubtedly had more to go on than was indicated by the *West Coast Lumberman*, which reported that "Warman . . . brings with him a splendid reputation, which, by the way, he does not need, as his face and general makeup soon convince even a stranger that he is alright." Warman stressed that the kilns would be a major improvement in getting timber products ready for the market, and would represent substantial savings to the lumber mills in drying time.

The North Coast Dry Kiln & Truck Company was incorporated with $25,000 in capital to manufacture the kilns, lumber trucks, and steel cars. Pigott became president and Warman the vice president and treasurer. The company acquired a Seattle site near track and water transportation, and started immediately to set up its plant.

The promoters were obviously correct in their assessment of market demand. By April 1904, even before operations started, there were orders for kilns on the books from three lumber companies in the area. By August orders were being filled for kilns measuring up to 104 feet in length, along with the trucks and cars used in their operation, and the company was soon reporting almost more business than it could handle.

It was a soul-satisfying time for the venturesome in the Pacific Northwest.

Seattle Steel grew to become one of the region's largest employers. Below, its rolling mill in 1907.

■

CHAPTER TWO

■

FOUNDER AND FOUNDING

What impelled William Pigott to organize the Seattle Car Manufacturing Company, a new enterprise, is a subject of conjecture, rather than of record. Regardless of motive, however, there was unquestionable logic in taking the step.

Some have surmised that Seattle Car's main purpose was to provide a market for the products of Pigott and Wilson's Seattle Steel Company. But the fact is that Seattle Car Manufacturing was established in February 1905, fully three months before the Seattle Steel mill was completed. And while it must have provided some comfort to have a ready and willing customer on hand, Wilson and Pigott were practiced businessmen, who surely were confident that a substantial market already existed for the products of their new business.

Others judged that Pigott's Railway Steel & Supply Company found itself in two widely differing businesses when it started to manufacture logging trucks, in addition to being the sales representative for other manufacturing firms. It was principally to separate these ventures, they believed, that Pigott felt a new business organization was called for. That made eminently good sense.

Or the principal motive may simply have been that Pigott—organizer, venture capitalist, champion of great enterprises for the Pacific Northwest—wanted the seed of one such enterprise for his very own. The railway supply company could not fill the bill, because it concentrated mainly on selling products that others made, mostly in other parts of the nation, and these products did not always fit the requirements of the Northwest logger. Seattle Steel might do, but Pigott was nominally the second man there, under Wilson's presidency. But this promising new field of building trucks to meet the needs of Northwest loggers might just prove to be the ticket he wanted.

As timber was being cut further and further back from the water, the loggers faced longer and longer hauls from the woods, either in animal-drawn vehicles or on logging railroads— some as short as a half mile—that they built and kept extending. Railway Steel & Supply was selling many loggers increasing quantities of rails and supplies. F. M. Raymond, the local representative for Climax locomotives, was headquartered in the company's offices, so that on occasion a complete logging railroad—tracks, locomotive, and logging trucks—would be sold in one transaction.

Skid roads, built of logs, were the accepted method of transporting giant timber from the forests of the Pacific Northwest in the 1800s.

Seattle Car Manufacturing was started on a far less ambitious scale than Seattle Steel. The total capitalization was only $10,000, with Pigott and Wilson each taking fifty of the $100 par common shares. The incorporation date was February 11, 1905, and the original incorporators were Pigott, who was president; his brother, Michael; Wilson; D. E. McLaughlin, who came from the Northern Pacific Railroad to become vice president of the new company; and T. G. Haywood, named manager. These and W. S. Burt made up the board of trustees.

The truck business, inventory, and machinery of Railway Steel & Supply was taken over by the new company, which also moved into the older company's offices in the Starr-Boyd Building in downtown Seattle. Some three months later the offices were moved to the new Alaska Building. Coincident with the start of the new firm, Railway Steel & Supply decided to discontinue one of its lines, the fabrication of structural steel. Its stock of goods was sold to Hofius, who was happy to be rid of a competitor in that business.

In June 1905, Seattle Car put up a small shop at Humphrey—later called Youngstown—in West Seattle, along the shore of Elliott Bay, on land leased from the Seattle Steel Company and adjoining its new mill. With no public transportation available to the plant, Pigott bought a horse and buggy for the trip, and later in the year acquired his first automobile, a Franklin. The first time he took the wheel of the car, Pigott drove it through a butcher's window, and he thereafter employed a driver. Some twenty workers who made up the initial crew fared less well with transport; but the following year a streetcar trestle was built to West Seattle, so that they had to walk only about a mile to the plant, crossing a bridge that spanned the tideflats.

The company built some horse- and oxen-drawn logging trucks, but quickly shifted its concentration to heavy-duty cars and trucks for the logging railroads. The principal early products were four-wheeled trucks used to transport logs from western forests by rail. As the product line gradually became more sophisticated, much of the output had to be tailored to the customers' specifications, since almost no two loggers wanted identical cars or equipment.

At the start, Seattle Car was more an assembling than a pure manufacturing industry, and various finished and semi-finished parts were obtained from widely scattered locations. Lumber and timbers, naturally, were purchased locally, and a number of steel shapes were bought from the Seattle Steel Company. The Griffin Wheel Company, of Tacoma, supplied bolts, nuts, and fasteners, while long plates were purchased from St. Louis, Missouri, and axles were acquired in the East.

Seattle Car Manufacturing Company operated continuously and at virtual capacity in its first two years. Indeed, it could not take on all the available business in logging trucks and logging flatcars because of the extreme shortage of capital and equipment. "Phenomenal industrial advancement has been made by the Seattle Car Manufacturing Company in one brief year's operation," wrote the *Pacific Lumber Trade Journal* in a glowing report in January 1906. "It has grown from a plant with a capacity of one car a day to a full-fledged car manufacturing industry with an output of ten cars each day, and these cars and the logging trucks have been of such a superior quality . . . that even this supply has been inadequate."

As a matter of fact, total sales in the active seven months of 1905 amounted to no more than $27,000, although net profit was a healthy 20 percent of sales. But more capital was clearly needed, and it was increased in mid-January 1906, to $100,000, or ten times the initial amount. The new stock was quickly subscribed and paid for. Pigott himself emerged with 355 shares, including 40 as payment for material contributed; Wilson had 250, William Hulbert 100, and various other subscribers—many of them the firm's customers in the lumber business—anywhere from 10 to 50 shares. Pigott was never one to hang on to control of a business through stock ownership. "His idea," a colleague once remarked, "was to 'build a business with other men's money.' But he retained a high sense of obligation or trusteeship."

Proceeds of the stock sale were used principally to purchase $50,000 in improved machinery and to build an addition of some 10,000 square feet to the shops. Orders started to arrive in more substantial quantities—twenty cars, for example, for the Chapman Timber Company, of Portland, Oregon; fifteen flatcars for the Northwest Log & Lumber Company, of Portland; twenty sets of logging trucks for the Coos Bay Lumber & Coal Company, of Marshfield, Oregon; and ten flatcars for the White River Lumber Company, of Enumclaw, Washington.

The company began to think in terms of providing various types of cars for main-line railroads, as well as loggers. They turned out a number of types and designs of wooden railroad cars in 1906, when shipments amounted to almost $240,000, and orders on hand at the start of 1907 totaled some $400,000.

— MONEY AND TALENT —

Pigott took a personal interest in all his employees, and he made it a point to look at the background and past work history of each of them before they were hired. He wanted to feel that they would be dedicated to the enterprise and its success, and that they were adaptable enough to grow with the company.

Some he had known through his earlier associations. The Plute brothers, Jerry and Joe, had worked under Pigott when he superintended the merchant steel mills of the Colorado

Seattle Car Manufacturing Company products of 1906, including flatcars, trucks, and boxcars, traversed wooden trestles connecting the Youngstown plant with the main lines in Seattle.

Fuel & Iron Company, at Pueblo, Colorado. He sent for them, Jerry to take charge of setting up the machinery and Joe to be leadman in the forge shop. He later hired as plant manager his wife's brother, T. S. Clingan, who had experience in steel industry management and who remained a key and trusted executive in Pigott enterprises for many years.

But two of his earliest management acquisitions were among those who would one day make the deepest impress on the company and its accomplishments. Oliver D. Colvin had been the Seattle representative of U.S. Steel Corporation and then vice president and general manager of the Snoqualmie Falls Power Company and later the Seattle-Tacoma Power Company. Colvin liked the prospects of the Seattle Car Manufacturing Company well enough to invest $25,000 in the business in the fall of 1906. He then took over as vice president and general manager of the car company, at which point McLaughlin left to join Wilson at the Seattle Steel Company.

Fred W. Chriswell was a mechanical engineer with an impressive background in innovative engineering. While with the New York Central he had designed the first all-steel passenger car. He also did a considerable amount of the design and engineering of cars for the New York City subway system and for London's famous Underground. Pigott, who liked to surround himself with "smart men, but not sharp men," wanted to build his sales staff around engineers who could sell and design equipment for a customer's needs. He hired Chriswell away from the American Car & Foundry Company in New York, to come to Seattle as his chief engineer, just as Colvin began to undertake his new duties. H. C. Jarvis was hired to assist in the engineering department.

The Seattle Car Manufacturing Company caboose, 1906.

With steel from Seattle
Steel and plentiful lumber
from Puget Sound mills,
Seattle Car Company built
wood-framed railroad cars
and cabooses. At left, car
construction in 1906.

It was not long after the first plant expansion took place that Seattle Car Manufacturing's business was again outstripping the plant's capacity to produce. Pigott felt that the time had come to again increase the capitalization, this time to $250,000. In March 1907, in a "Statement by the President"—essentially an investor's prospectus in those days before there was a Securities and Exchange Act—he wrote:

> Since the first of the year, in addition to orders already booked, as much more has been offered at profitable prices, which we have been unable to accept by reason of inadequate manufacturing facilities . . .
>
> The demand for logging trucks and flatcars throughout the timber section of the Northwest will inevitably increase for many years to come, and this alone warrants a large increase in . . . equipment and working capital . . .
>
> The demand of railroad companies for new equipment is now greater than the present works of the country can supply. The rapid increase of business reported by all railroads, the chronic shortage of cars, especially by roads doing business in this section of the country, and the era of railroad building this Puget Sound country is now witnessing, all are encouraging signs of a permanent and expanding local market for cars.

The statement went on to report that the company had purchased a 120-acre site near Lake Washington to the southeast of Seattle near the old coal mining town of Renton. They proposed to build there "a suitable plant with modern labor saving equipment" and employing no fewer than 250 men. It was pointed out that the company had sold a 40-acre tract near its present plant for $2,000 an acre, and that more land was being platted and sold for an average of $4,000 per acre. Seattle Car was thus in the process of making a tidy profit on its landholdings of almost 160 acres, purchased originally for less than $120,000. Pigott went on to announce the company's intention to offer not over 1,000 shares of stock at $100 per share, in order to raise up to $100,000 in new funds.

"While we believe a much larger sum could be profitably employed," said the statement, "a moderate investment will afford greater security to stockholders, and eliminate any *element of speculation* as to the permanent earning power of the company."

— TRIAL BY FIRE —

In the buoyant atmosphere of the Northwest, the new stock in the fast-growing company was readily subscribed to, but not all the money was immediately paid in.

The optimism soon appeared to be fully justified. Manager Haywood was chiefly instrumental in getting an order for two hundred boxcars, with a total capacity of 80,000 tons, from the Spokane & Inland Empire Railroad Company, a short line running from Spokane to the Palouse grain district. Haywood, confident that the order would be increased by fifty cars, ordered materials for the full two hundred fifty cars.

With working space for the large order becoming a problem, the company began construction of the new Renton plant, meanwhile building cars as rapidly as possible at the existing facility. This meant long working hours through the hot summer of 1907, often crowding men, materials, and finished goods into whatever space was available. By August between seventy-five and one hundred cars had been completed.

Few worked harder than engineers Chriswell and Jarvis. On the evening of August 12 they were on the job until midnight. At breakfast the next morning, after only a few hours of sleep in town, they learned that the plant, cars, materials, and nearly all machinery had been incinerated by a disastrous fire.

The fire had apparently broken out in the flooring of the middle shop, spreading quickly to the carshops and finished cars, then to the machine and logging truck departments, finally engulfing one million feet of high-grade lumber, valued at $40,000. With the tide out, little water was available, and efforts to dig a ditch through the tideflats were of no help.

Of the ultimate loss of $154,000, only $75,000 was covered by insurance. As a final blow, word came a few days later from the Spokane & Inland Empire Railroad that its order was canceled, since the cars had been needed to move the fall grain crop.

A few large pieces of machinery stood in the smoldering ruins, and these and all usable materials were moved to Renton, repaired, and installed in the new shops. But the trials of the Seattle Car Manufacturing Company were not yet over. In October, when the new Renton plant was ready to begin operations, the bank panic of 1907 broke on the financial world.

The unsuccessful market maneuvers of copper speculator Frederick Heinze triggered a series of failures of then-unregulated trust companies. Money tightened in New York, setting off a chain reaction of credit stringency across the country. Stocks collapsed, and depositors started a two-week run on banks, some of which failed. Businesses, without the lubrication of credit,

Fred Chriswell, Seattle Car's chief engineer, found the Youngstown plant in ruins the morning after the fire of August 12, 1907.

started to cut back. Among the hardest hit was the lumber industry, and the newly rebuilt Seattle Car Manufacturing Company found itself with nothing but canceled orders.

In order to preserve its assets and maintain a viable business, as well as to protect both creditors and stockholders, the company went into voluntary receivership. On November 9, 1907, the court appointed as receivers Pigott and Colvin. Their task was made easier by the forbearance of the principal creditors, chief among which was the Griffin Wheel Company, which furnished Seattle Car with wheels fitted to axles. Also among the creditors were some lumber companies, Seattle Steel, Scullin-Galliger Steel Casting Company, Railway Steel Spring Company, National Malleable Company, and Seattle Hardware Company.

Although the company had suffered substantial losses and its business had reached a virtual standstill, the receivers were able to report to U.S. District Court Judge C. H. Hanford that Seattle Car Manufacturing was in a basically solvent condition. Bills receivable amounted to almost $47,000, mostly secured by mortgages; accounts receivable, mostly collectable, were $16,000; inventory, including machinery and tools, was $174,000; real estate was $62,000, and construction improvements (buildings, water mains, railroad track and connections) were about $80,000; and unpaid stock subscriptions were almost $27,000. On the liability side were bills payable of $116,000, almost half of which represented the purchase price for land; accounts payable were $93,000; capital stock, including $89,000 in unsubscribed treasury stock, was $250,000; and net worth was some $35,000.

To help them keep the business running, the receivers asked the court's permission to buy about $7,000 in woodworking tools, already contracted for. And they reported that about half of the $130,000 in material and supplies could be converted into salable equipment if there were additional expenditures of $65,000 for new material and $27,000 for labor, and that the ultimate profit would be about 10 percent.

As business generally improved in the short-lived recession following the 1907 panic, Seattle Car was able to participate in the upturn. The plant itself was opened on February 1, 1908, and many of the previously canceled orders for logging cars were reinstated. In May an order

Already under construction at the time of the Youngstown fire, the Renton, Washington, plant was completed in 1908 while the company was in voluntary receivership.

was received for a number of flatcars and dump cars from Chin Gee Hee, regarded as the James Hill of Chinese railroading. Manufacturing was expanded to all types of railroad logging stock used in the logging industry. By October 1908, all of the company's debts were paid in full, and the court discharged Seattle Car from receivership.

In a letter prepared for the stockholders' meeting early in 1909, the management of Seattle Car described its tribulations tersely:

> Since the last regular meeting of the stockholders of this company we have gone through the experience of a fire which completely destroyed our shops . . .
>
> We completed the construction of our new shops at Renton . . . , put in roadbeds and tracks and established a water system for the protection of the property, expending in so doing $80,000. Machinery was installed costing us, including what we saved from the fire, $39,000.
>
> This fire disaster was followed by the panic in 1907, over half a million dollars worth of orders were countermanded, leaving us overstocked with $130,000 worth of material which we could not turn into money.
>
> On November 9, 1907, the financial pressure was so great that in order to protect the interests of the stockholders we went into the hands of receivers Wm. Pigott and O. D. Colvin, who served until they were discharged last October without compensation.

— THE RENTON PLANT —

With the start of operations at the new plant in Renton, not only was Seattle Car much better equipped to turn out its products, but the times were ripe for growth in both the lumber and railroad industries. The company kept pace by extending its manufacture to more types of equipment, particularly the railroad rolling stock that the logging industry sought.

Before the company was out of receivership, an effort was made to increase its capital resources through the sale of an issue of $100,000 in bonds. As of the September 30, 1908, trial balance, within a month of the discharge of the receivers, $27,000 of the bonds had been subscribed, including $5,000 to the Seattle Steel Company and $6,000 to Pigott himself.

At the same time there were additional subscriptions to the capital stock, notable among which were $10,000 to W. D. Hofius, $10,000 to Levi Ankeny, $5,000 to C. H. Cobb, and $2,500 to each of two timber firms, the Mason County Logging Company and the Western Washington Logging Company.

By December 9, 1908, the entire $100,000 bond issue had been distributed, including a total of $11,500 to Seattle Steel, $15,000 to Pigott's Railway Steel & Supply Company, $3,000 to the Hewitt-Lea Lumber Company, $1,000 to Westinghouse Electric & Manufacturing Company, and $8,500 to the Merchants' Protective Association. By January 31, 1909, a total of $232,084 in capital stock had been paid in, and another $8,041 had been subscribed to, for a total of $240,125.

Earnings were less favorable in those early start-up months. Seattle Car's "Statement of Loss and Gain" for the final months of 1908 and the first month of 1909 showed a surplus at the start of the period of $24,065, and of only $18,226 as of January 31, 1909. This would not only indicate a net loss of almost $6,000 for the period, but also that the company had lost some $10,500 during the year of receivership. Part of the expense for the last three months of 1908 was the cost of money itself, since $2,328 in bond interest expense accrued during the quarter.

But the company was confident that it stood on the threshold of much greater activity than it had ever experienced before. Haywood, who had been a leading figure in the aborted sale of

250 boxcars to the Spokane & Inland Empire Railroad Company, was put in charge of a satellite sales office in Portland, with a territory extending into northern California. In trade journals the company proclaimed toward the close of 1908, "We are rebuilding and equipping our new Works at Renton. Our capacity is greatly increased. We have facilities for getting out equipment second to none."

Pigott nonetheless sought to assure the shareholders that the company was by no means profligate with its funds. In the letter prepared for the 1909 stockholders' meeting, it was pointed out that the purchase of some $7,500 in woodworking machinery would virtually eliminate handwork in the woodshops. "For the iron working department we purchased and installed one triple bolt cutter, thereby reducing the expense at least one man per day." An electric power line to the Seattle-Tacoma Power Company at Renton would eliminate the cost of burning oil to produce power, for a monthly saving of $300 or more. And the company had abolished day labor in the woodworking and car building shops by installing the contract system, in which an individual contracted to do the painting and erecting of cars for a fixed fee. Seattle Car planned to extend the system into all its departments as quickly as possible.

"While the development of . . . new business in a new country is necessarily slow," the letter concluded, "the outlook for the development of a profitable business by this company is better today than at any time since we began operations."

New business turned out to be not so slow in developing. In 1909 Seattle Car received an order from the Northern Pacific Railroad for three hundred boxcars, the largest sale it had yet made.

— NEW PRODUCTS AND SERVICES —

Seattle Car's first important innovation for the logging industry was the "connected truck." At first the company, like its competitors, sold the railway trucks in sets, which would then be tied together by the customers by means of the logs themselves. Seattle Car's innovation was to tie the trucks together with strong lengthwise members, and install bunks to keep the logs in place and chocks to hold the ends securely.

The first purchaser was Lew Horton of the Northwest Lumber Company. The connected trucks were an immediate hit. They soon demonstrated their ability to haul the most massive logs ever placed on a logging railway, and like the trucks that preceded them, they were given the trade name of "Hercules." The connected truck quickly became the industry standard.

J. J. Donovan, one of the Northwest's leading lumbermen, was moved to write Colvin: "Your Hercules logging trucks are the best car for heavy logging that I have seen and we are now buying no other. My experience dates back twenty-five years, and I am familiar with . . . the trucks manufactured in Tacoma, Seattle and by ourselves. We have had them all more or less in our trains for the last ten years. . . . We have had less repairs and less trouble on account of hot boxes with your cars than any others."

Such praise served as balm to Pigott. It was his continued insistence that, regardless of what else might differentiate his firm's products from those of competitors, he wanted their quality to be second to none.

In keeping with its growing reputation for developing the most rugged products for the logging industry, Seattle Car in 1910 brought out all-steel, 50-ton logging trucks. The original had been previewed at the Alaska Yukon Pacific Exposition held in Seattle in 1909. The exposition had been planned originally for 1907, to commemorate the tenth anniversary of the discovery of

The railroad logging "truck" was the first product produced by Seattle Car Manufacturing Company.

Below: Seattle Car's most important early innovation was the "connected truck," introduced in 1909 for transporting logs.

Testing proved the connected truck not only laborsaving, but also safer for loggers than separated trucks.

Klondike gold in Alaska, but was put off for two years in deference to the Jamestown Tercentennial Exposition at that time. More than eighty thousand people came to see the wonders of the burgeoning Northwest, and James J. Hill was the principal speaker at the opening ceremonies.

To reflect more fully its enlarged capabilities, the company in 1911 changed its name to Seattle Car & Foundry Company. Before long the company's logging business was mainly in connected trucks, and very few detached trucks were any longer being built or sold. Another development in the same period was the skeleton logging car with air brakes, an important new safety feature.

As a demonstration of the adaptability of the connected truck and its advantages over the

The "Donkey Moving Car" was developed by Seattle Car at the suggestion of Pete Conacher, a customer, in 1912.

conventional flatcar for hauling logs, Seattle Car & Foundry built a number of such cars and equipped them with safety appliances to meet Interstate Commerce Commission and other safety laws. These cars were loaned to the Northern Pacific, Great Northern, and the Milwaukee railroads. As a consequence, this type of car was adopted for use on main-line railroads for transporting logs, and Seattle Car was also able to sell the lines a large number of its patented bunks and other specialties.

Many of these innovations were designed by engineer Chriswell, who, over the course of years, took out twenty different patents that he permitted or licensed the company to use.

Some ideas came to the firm from the outside, and if they showed promise they were acted upon. Pete Conacher, for example, came to Seattle Car in 1912, proposing to design a special car for carrying large donkey engines, which were mounted on heavy sleds especially adapted for use in forests and other remote locations. The company promoted the "Donkey Moving Car," and in time nearly every lumber camp had one of these special-purpose cars.

Seattle Car also entered into a contract with the Northern Pacific Railroad for car repair work. Continuing for more than fifteen years, this contract became unique in railroad annals, both in its long duration and in the number of cars serviced under it.

— THE OTHER BUSINESSES —

With Pigott devoting a major share of his time and attention to Seattle Car, most of his other business interests were left in the care of trusted business lieutenants or permitted to dwindle away.

The Railway Steel & Supply Company, which became less and less active as Seattle Car developed, underwent a name change in 1912 to become simply Railway Supply Company. The North Coast Dry Kiln & Truck Company continued to prosper; over the five-year period from the start of 1904 to the end of 1908, it averaged the sale of one dry kiln a week, in addition to such other equipment as kiln trucks, transfer cars, lumber trucks, and lumber stackers. To keep up with its expanding business the firm built a new plant in Seattle with triple the capacity of the old one, enabling it to ship a fully equipped dry kiln within twenty-four hours of the receipt of the order.

The place where Pigott continued to expend a major share of his effort and energy was in the iron and steel business. And he never left off dreaming about a great iron and steel industry that might one day be developed on the West Coast.

During the noon hour Pigott would frequently stroll along the waterfront, sometimes accompanied by Chriswell. He was deeply interested in the steel products that were being imported, chiefly from Europe, and his thoughts would turn to how the Northwest might fill those needs from its own resources.

Pigott's eye also remained fixed on the blast furnace at Irondale, established some twenty-five years earlier as the Puget Sound Iron Company, and later taken over by the ill-starred Homer Swaney's Pacific Steel Company, and then by Swaney's Seattle Iron and Steel Company. Following Swaney's death by drowning, the Irondale plant was purchased for $40,000 at a court sale in September 1906 by James A. Moore, of Seattle. The furnace was renovated, had its capacity increased to 80 tons of pig iron a day, and was put in blast as the Irondale Furnace Company in 1907. Some product was turned out for about a year, but when business recession slowed demand, the furnace was shut down in 1908.

No pig iron was produced at Irondale during 1909, but that October its backers incorporated a major new business venture, the Western Steel Corporation, ambitiously capitalized at $20 million. Moore was president of Western Steel, which set about acquiring extensive iron ore and coal properties in Washington, British Columbia, and as far afield as Nevada, along with limestone and dolomite deposits in Washington. One of its most valuable assets was an exclusive contract to be supplied with iron ore and pig iron by the Han Yeh Ping Iron and Coal Company of Hankow, the sole iron and steel company in China.

Pigott was not associated with this enterprise, although he was a close friend of Captain Robert Dollar, its vice president and head of the Robert Dollar Steamship Company, of San Francisco. The Dollar line had the lucrative contract to deliver the pig iron and ore from China to the Irondale plant.

The sponsors of Western Steel held high hopes for it to become the long-awaited major steel producer of the Northwest, and so it appeared to be in a glowing report prepared by J. A. Vandegrift, of the Equitable Bond and Certification Company. Equitable was retained to determine the value of the security behind an issue of $1 million in first mortgage bonds held by the Carnegie Trust Company, of New York. Vandegrift's report showed Western Steel held iron ore valued at almost $13 million; coal at $23 million; timber at $550,000; limestone and dolomite at $100,000; and real estate, including furnaces and mills, at $1 million. Against these assets was a capitalization of $15 million in common stock, $5 million in preferred stock, and $2 million in mortgage bonds, leaving a surplus of some $15.5 million. The properties, said the report, "contain the necessary raw materials to operate an iron and steel plant of 1,000 tons daily capacity for over one hundred years," in addition to the resources available through the Chinese contract, which extended to mid-1918.

The Robert Dollar
Steamship Company
delivered the first of
25,000 tons of Chinese
iron ore to Western
Steel's dock at Irondale,
Washington, on July 1,
1910.

Western Steel had other plans and projects under way. It had two 25-ton basic open-hearth furnaces for steelmaking, and was building a third, along with two ingot heating furnaces. It had a 22-inch and a 14-inch rolling mill, and was installing a 9-inch mill, for rolling steel ingots into various shapes. It built a foundry to make car wheels, its own ingot molds, and other castings. It installed horseshoe machines with a capacity of 750,000 pounds a month—making it the only horseshoe factory west of Chicago. The company planned a by-product coking plant with a daily capacity of at least 300 tons of coke, to replace the charcoal that the Irondale furnace had used previously in iron-making.

The forecast was that the plant would have an overall capacity of 200,000 tons of steel products per year; a ready market seemed to exist for this output, since the projected steel consumption of the three Pacific Coast states for 1910 was 3 million tons.

The blast furnace was blown in during the spring of 1910, and the first cargo of Chinese ore and pig iron arrived there on July 1. Plans called for the use of half Chinese and half domestic ore, but the furnace's charge actually consisted of two-thirds Chinese and one-third local ores. A total of 25,000 tons was imported during the remainder of 1910. Coke was purchased, pending construction of the ovens, and the old charcoal kilns were abandoned. Both local and Chinese pig iron were combined with scrap to feed the open-hearth furnaces. The steel was then rolled into billets and finished shapes.

As in the past, both the pig iron and the steel turned out to be of very good quality. But, also as in the past, the company operated for barely a year and then became insolvent. Western Steel had overextended itself in acquiring undeveloped properties, and market demand was

Seattle Steel was renamed Pacific Coast Steel following the merger of the two companies in 1911. Above, the Youngstown mill in 1914.

slow in making itself felt. Receivers took over Western Steel, and they shortly disposed of the various raw material properties.

Meanwhile in May 1909 the Pacific Coast Steel Company, of California, was incorporated, and a new open-hearth furnace and rolling mill were built at South San Francisco. Pacific Coast Steel entered into talks with Pigott and Wilson with a view toward consolidating their iron and steel enterprises, and merged with Seattle Steel on July 15, 1911. Wilson was named president of the expanded Pacific Coast Steel Company and moved to the San Francisco Bay area. Pigott remained as vice president and general manager of the Seattle operations.

At the end of 1913, Pacific Coast Steel purchased the Irondale plant of the defunct Western Steel Company. The rolling mill equipment and open-hearth furnace were subsequently moved to the Seattle plant site, but the blast furnace was permitted to fall into disrepair. A 40-ton open-hearth furnace was erected at the Youngstown plant in 1914, and three others were added over the next few years.

William Pigott (sitting second from the right) and members of the U.S. Chamber of Commerce traveled to China in 1910 to promote and better understand possibilities for East-West trade.

— CHINA CONNECTIONS —

In the closing years of the nineteenth century and the early years of the twentieth century, China and her hundreds of millions of people were still a largely untapped and unexplored source of trade for the United States. Internationally minded businessmen on the West Coast were conscious of the potential, few of them more so than Robert Dollar, whose steamship line already plied China's waters in search of trading and shipping opportunities.

Dollar helped convince the Chinese Chamber of Commerce of the treaty ports that it would be to their benefit to cement closer relationships with West Coast business leaders. The Chinese Chamber decided to invite the associated Chambers of Commerce of the U.S. Pacific Coast to send a delegation of representative business leaders on a tour of China. Of the twenty-two men and fifteen women named to make up the delegation, three were Seattleites, one of whom was William Pigott.

The trip was made in 1910, and Pigott had an opportunity to meet government officials of the old regime not long before the revolution set up a Chinese republic under Sun Yat-sen. Pigott nevertheless was able to lay the groundwork for future business relationships in China. Toward the end of 1912, he sent Chriswell on a four-month trip to China, Japan, the Philippines, Java, and other centers to look into sales prospects there. Seattle Car & Foundry, at one time represented in the Orient by the Dollar Steamship people, had made occasional shipments to the Far East, but had never tried seriously to compete with European manufacturers in seeking major car orders in Asia.

The Japanese were great imitators, and they attempted to copy the connected logging car from rough plans left behind by Chriswell during his 1912 journey. Only after they failed did they consider placing an order with Seattle Car & Foundry. In 1914 Chriswell was asked to meet with Japanese officials in Yokohama and from there they were to travel to Formosa to survey the Airtran Railway.

After nearly being lost at sea during a typhoon, Chriswell and his Japanese hosts arrived in Chi-lung. From there they traveled in chairs carried by Chinese coolies to the city of Kazi. Chriswell inspected the railroad that ascended to an elevation of nearly 8,000 feet and passed through sixty-two tunnels. "It was a narrow gauge road and the tunnels were not big enough to get this big timber through," observed Chriswell. "The Japanese cars had not allowed clearances enough for curves, so all of the cars would go off the track. Most of their time was spent putting the cars back on the track." Chriswell returned to Seattle with an order, this time for fifty narrow-gauge connected truck cars designed to transport timber out of Formosa's Arisan Forest.

As Pigott's own wealth, influence, and reputation grew, he became involved in a large number and wide variety of civic, religious, and political activities. None, however, commanded his interest and attention as much as international affairs.

In 1909 he was named chairman of the Foreign Industrial Trade Commission of the Manufacturers' Association of Washington State. Active in Alaskan affairs, he was a trustee of the Alaska-Yukon-Pacific Exposition, held in 1909; was a principal advocate in Washington, D.C., of the Alaska Railroad; and organized and financed the Seattle campaign for home rule for Alaska. But he saved some of his greatest enthusiasm for the National Foreign Trade Council.

At a National Foreign Trade convention in 1914, the National Foreign Trade Council was created by a group of business leaders to work on the extension of American commerce abroad. Pigott's close business friend James A. Farrell, president of the U.S. Steel Corporation, was named president of the new Council, and Pigott became one of the original thirty members, as well as president of its Pacific Coast Council. Pigott's paper on China trade was read at the convention and included in the printed record.

Invitations to West Coast businessmen to attend the National Foreign Trade convention in New Orleans in 1916 were sent out by Pigott, who sought to assure participants that their time would be well spent. "The discussions will be confined to the application of proven principles of sound foreign trade to the problems now before the nation. Little time will be given to reiteration of theories. Every opportunity will be afforded for practical discussion by the delegates."

Pigott's interest in international affairs also extended to a membership in New York City's India House, a club devoted to the promotion of foreign trade. He contributed a painting of a ship from the windjammer days, and it was hung on the club's walls.

Pigott probably joined India House at Farrell's urging. Others in Pigott's wide circle of business acquaintances included John D. Ryan, of Anaconda Copper; Martin Egan, of the investment banking firm of J. P. Morgan and Company; Howard Elliott, of the New Haven Railroad; and James Hill, of the Great Northern. When out-of-town notables came to visit Seattle, Pigott would usually be on the reception committee. Henry Barbour of the Lackawanna Steel Company once observed that Pigott probably had the widest acquaintanceship among business leaders of anyone in the United States.

He occasionally appeared as a spokesman for business. When the Federal Trade Commission held two days of hearings in Seattle in August 1915, Pigott was one of the witnesses who gave his views. He advocated a tariff commission to study the actual conditions that American

manufacturers faced in overseas trade, more flexible tariffs, and a broader and more comprehensive policy of extending trade.

Seattle Car's first sale to China was a passenger car for the Sun Ning Railway in 1908.

    On another occasion Pigott was a dinner speaker and took the opportunity to upbraid a University of Washington professor who had referred to the nation's businessmen as a "capitalistic class." Indignant, Pigott said: "Think of it—a man paid by the state to instruct our youth going out making speeches and attempting to create a class in this country of ours, arousing animosities, when he ought to be attending to work for which he is paid. . . . While the politician and demagogue have been doing their work, the businessmen of the nation have gone to sleep. . . . We must change our position and our views with respect to businessmen. There's no man in my company's employ in whose family and welfare I am not interested. I work as hard as the hardest worker among them, and I am often kept busy when they have quit their work for the day."

    It was once suggested to Pigott that he take the nomination for U.S. Senator, but he declined, pointing out that he had offered his support to Senator Miles Poindexter, who had been a staunch friend of Northwest business. Pigott's endorsement was sought by others seeking office, and he once regretfully turned down a candidate's request for support as Seattle port collector because he had already endorsed someone else.

Pigott's concerns outside of his business were wide-ranging, and encompassed educational, civic, and religious, as well as political matters. He was appointed to the Seattle School Board in 1908 and later served as its president. He pushed for the organization of a Department of Vocational Training, for which he recommended the use of first-class tools and equipment and saw to it that they were installed at Broadway High School. In 1914 the governor of Washington named him to chair a commission charged with drafting a first-aid amendment to the Workmen's Compensation Act. In 1916 he was a delegate to the National Democratic Convention in St. Louis, where Woodrow Wilson was nominated for the presidency—just as Hofius much earlier had been a delegate to the Democratic Convention that nominated Grover Cleveland for the first time.

In 1916 Pigott was elected president of the Manufacturers' Association of Seattle. At that time, *The Timberman,* a trade paper, said, "The association has ambitious plans . . . for the coming year and under the direction of Mr. Pigott it is certain to enjoy a prosperous future."

— THE PRODUCT LINE EXPANDS —

The Seattle Car & Foundry Company grew as the Northwest logging industry grew. In the eight years from 1910 through 1917, the company built an average of 656 railway and 107 industrial cars per year, mostly to handle logs. Of the 840 railway cars manufactured in 1910, for example, 300 were boxcars for the Northern Pacific, but most of the remainder were cars and trucks designed to transport logs.

A 1913 company catalogue boasted that the firm "not only competes on an equal footing with the East for the trade of the Pacific, but has extended its field successfully into Alaska, British Columbia, China, and all other sections of the Orient." A partial listing of products designed and built "in its commodious, modern and efficient plant" included flatcars, boxcars, logging cars, logging trucks, air-equipped connected trucks, logging bunks and chocks, gondola cars, caboose cars, camp cars, industrial cars, contractors dump cars, push cars, quarry cars, track construction cars, and tram cars.

The breadth of product helped make the company the principal supplier of rolling stock for West Coast railroads, and particularly for Northwest logging railroads. By 1920, the company had built more than seven thousand logging cars, all of special design, with a total value of some $10 million.

The timber industry apparently gave great credibility to the company's claims for the products. A long discursive ad that appeared in the *Timberman* in 1911 discussed the safety, efficiency, and low-cost results to be obtained with the "new Skeleton Logging Car or Connected Air Brake Truck, equipped with Hercules Bunk and Chock stands." Said the ad: ". . . it saves human lives and material. The air brake eliminates the danger in operating the trains; the bunk and chock the danger in discharging the load, and the open design reduces the danger in working about the car while loading. The saving in material is shown in the weight of the cab, which is 30 percent less than standard equipment of the same capacity. . . . Thirty percent more cars can be handled on the return haul with the same motive power . . ." Helping bear out these claims was the fact that many of the early cars and trucks operated well into the 1960s and connected truck cars into the 1970s.

One of the company's early specialties was the refrigerator car, built of steel and northwest wood. In time, thousands of these were manufactured. The early refrigerator cars had a capacity of 70,000 pounds, and the interiors were arranged to handle beef halves suspended from any of

Camp car interiors were not plush, but they were efficient.

Below: Seattle Car & Foundry Company began manufacturing camp cars in 1913 as part of its expanded rail product line.

three trolleys riding on tracks that extended the length of the car. The trolleys were arranged so that the beef could be moved directly from the cooling room into the car, or switched from one to another. Cooling in the car was provided by iceboxes at each end.

For the loggers working patches of timber isolated from railroads and water, the motor truck became a favored means of transportation. To accommodate the great length and weight of typical Northwest logs, a trailer was essential for use in conjunction with the motor truck. Chriswell designed a two-wheeled trailer in response to a single order received in 1915. It was completed but the order was canceled, and the trailer was put into storage until later that year when it was sold to a trucker named Brickstrom. He returned the trailer to Seattle Car a short time later with broken wheels and instructions to Chriswell to rebuild it with Jenkins roller bearings and deluxe springs and equip it with rubber tires. If these conditions could be met, Brickstrom assured Chriswell that he would purchase a second trailer, and a new product was born at Seattle Car.

The trailer was progressively improved and its use soon became so widespread that it came to be known as the "Universal Trailer." Seattle Car & Foundry cooperated with the Kelly-Springfield Motor Truck Company in developing a truck and trailer adapted to this service. Most of the one thousand or so two-wheeled trailers were still in use decades later, with pneumatic tires eventually replacing those made of solid rubber.

The early years of World War I brought increased calls by the European participants for a wide variety of goods manufactured in the United States. In 1915 Seattle Car & Foundry was invited to submit a bid on fifteen thousand freight cars that the Russian government was seeking to buy for use on the Siberian railroad. The size of the order was subsequently reported to have been increased to forty thousand freight cars. Chriswell, returning from a trip to New York,

The refrigerator car was one of several specialty cars produced by Seattle Car as the Renton plant's capacity was expanded in 1909.

reported that the Russians, after protracted negotiations, would not offer satisfactory terms to American car builders.

In time, the Russians began placing orders for part of their freight car needs with a number of American car builders: two thousand with Canadian Car & Foundry Company, two thousand with American Car & Foundry Company, two thousand with the Eastern Car Company, and several thousand with Pressed Steel Car Company. In mid-1915 Colvin journeyed to Petrograd, and there engaged in negotiations for about a year. He returned with a contract for one thousand cars to be built at the Seattle plant.

— GROWING PAINS —

The expansion of William Pigott's enterprises into major Seattle industries, sometimes spectacular and almost always taken for granted, was not without many of the problems normally attendant on such growth. Pigott himself never lost a personal interest in his employees, their work, and their welfare. Where machines could replace brute strength in doing jobs, he usually installed them. Seattle Steel was one of the first plants in the United States to have full electrical operation, and it was the first steel mill in the country to go on an eight-hour day.

The "Universal Trailer," designed by Seattle Car & Foundry in 1915, was a new and successful means of transporting logs from the Pacific Northwest forests.

Seattle Car dealt with a union known as Federated Employees, and had to meet what were then demanding provisions of tough labor contracts. A proposed labor contract in 1917, for example, called for an eight-hour day, then a novelty in industry generally; time and a half for work on Sundays and legal holidays, such as Washington's Birthday, Decoration Day, and Labor Day; three-stage grievance procedures; access of union business representatives to yard and plant "when necessary providing . . . they . . . do not in any way interfere with or cause men to neglect their work"; and a requirement that employees take out a union card after three days. Among wage rate increases sought were those for machinists and electricians, from 55 cents an hour to 62½ cents; for bolt threaders, from 27½ cents to 35 cents; and for wheel borers, from 35 to 45 cents.

Another sign of Seattle Car's industrial maturity was the use of institutional advertising, or ads that made little or no mention of the company's products. Toward the end of 1914 an ad in the *West Coast Lumberman* was devoted entirely to extensive quotes from the First National Bank of Seattle's "Digest of Trade Conditions." The writer observed that, "For the past two or three years, because of the constantly changing and irregular business situation, the resourcefulness of almost every business man has been taxed to the limit to keep his own particular business operating on an even keel and in a fairly satisfactory manner." But in recent weeks, the text noted, there had been an unparalleled situation in world history of growth in the financial and commercial power of the United States. This was marked by a sharp increase in total money in circulation, the ad said, while per capita circulation rose in a year from $35.03 to $37.31, a new record.

The bright conclusion of this analysis stated, "In confirmation of the foregoing, the past few days has [*sic*] witnessed a marked increase in the number of inquiries for lumber and shingles enough to cause the logger and lumberman to look forward to 1915 with smiles of joyous anticipation." Seattle Car & Foundry then ended the ad by wishing to all the compliments of the holiday season.

Two months later Seattle Car ran an ad with the poetic heading, "The Arch of the Setting Sun," in which it gave its corporate blessing to "two great Expositions held in California this year" and urged "all whose eyes may chance to fall on this page to support by their attendance and kindly words the efforts of those who have borne the burden of making them successful."

The company pointed out that the nature of its business made it impractical to show its products at these fairs. It nevertheless extended "a cordial invitation to any who may be interested in the class of cars, trucks and general railroad equipment which we manufacture, to investigate by personal visit or by correspondence our lines and our facilities."

Seattle Car & Foundry's buildings were connected by boardwalks, and its heavy equipment was set on pilings driven into the Renton, Washington, bottomland.

CHAPTER THREE

PACIFIC CAR & FOUNDRY

The Twohy brothers of Portland, Oregon—Judge John and James F.—came from a family with a long tradition of railroad building in the Northwest. They cleared rights-of-way, shaped road beds, and laid track for the Canadian National Railroad, the Northern Pacific, and the Southern Pacific, among others.

In 1910 they formed the Twohy Brothers Company, which was soon engaged in a wide variety of other work. It was characteristic of the uneven times that a firm would be prepared for another line of endeavor when business slowed in its first. In a 1915 ad in the *Timberman,* the Twohy Brothers Company boasted, "Repairing and Construction—Facilities unequalled by any shop on the Pacific Coast—We make a specialty of repairing locomotives, cars, steam shovels and logging donkeys—We also like to submit you figures on all kinds of tank work, boiler work and heavy forging."

To do their rail contracting, it was necessary for them to have various types of railroad cars, and for these they erected a repair shop in Portland. The shop was larger than they needed for their own cars, so they sought outside work to keep it busy. They arranged with their salesman to have him run the plant and to build logging cars, as well as sell them.

The Twohy brothers thus became Seattle Car & Foundry's only West Coast competitors in the logging car business. At first the competition was negligible. The Twohys built their first logging trucks in 1912—six for Simpson Lumber of Coos Bay and a half dozen for another Oregon logging company owned by J. H. Chamber. But the business soon expanded. Later in 1912 they opened a branch office in Vancouver, B.C., and their long-standing relationship with the railroads helped them get car orders from the rail lines.

Toward the end of 1916 the Union Pacific Railroad divided its order for 400 steel underframe boxcars equally between the Twohy firm and Seattle Car. A few months later the Southern Pacific gave each of the firms orders for 150 all-wood boxcars. The Twohys then began construction of a boxcar factory, planning to spend $50,000 on changes in the plant and nearby tracks.

William Pigott and John Twohy had been well acquainted for a number of years. About this time Judge Twohy, sensing that his resources might prove inadequate for the heavier volume of production, made the first overtures to Seattle Car with a view toward combining the enterprises.

Seattle Car & Foundry merged with the Twohy Brothers Company, of Portland, Oregon, on September 4, 1917, to form Pacific Car & Foundry Company in Renton and Portland. Shown is the Portland plant.

T. G. Haywood acted as negotiator between the two firms. A principle of consolidation was agreed upon and a new enterprise, Pacific Car & Foundry Company, was formed on July 1, 1917, capitalized at an even $1 million. Seattle Car's net worth had increased from its capitalization of $250,000 in 1911 to something over $600,000 by 1917. The initial agreement was that its stockholders were to receive six thousand of the ten thousand shares of $100 par common stock in the new company; the Twohy Brothers firm would get three thousand; and the remaining one thousand shares were to be turned over to T. S. Clingan as trustee, until more precise values of the properties could be determined.

The formalities of the merger were not carried out until August 1917, and it was almost the end of the year before the final valuation of assets was agreed upon. Seattle Car held the meeting of trustees designed to wind up its affairs on August 8 and the meeting of stockholders on August 20. At this meeting it was voted to make the formal proposal to turn over its assets to Pacific Car in exchange for stock in the new company, to authorize the trustees to attend to the necessary details, to make a pro rata distribution of the company's stock to the old company's shareholders, and to hold some stock in reserve in the Seattle Car treasury to meet such undetermined liabilities as taxes that were yet to fall due. Similar resolutions were voted by the Twohy firm.

In conjunction with the meeting, Seattle Car stockholders owning the bulk of the shares signed an agreement and consent to the formation of the new company, which was to have seven directors: the two Twohy brothers; Judge Twohy's son, Robert E.; Clingan; Colvin; Pigott; and Wilson. Signers and their holdings in Seattle Car stock were Pigott, 1,050 shares; Colvin, 337½ shares; Wilson, 316 shares; W. M. Hulbert, 100 shares; Patrick McCoy, 50 shares; Mason County Logging Company, 25 shares; W. S. Burt, 22 shares; D. E. McLaughlin, 15 shares; M. E. Smith, 10 shares; and Eva Colvin, 5 shares. This totaled 1,930½ shares that the company had issued and outstanding.

A month later, at a special meeting of the trustees of the new Pacific Car & Foundry Company, the proposal of the two merging firms was accepted. A resolution was passed naming James F. Twohy the company's attorney-in-fact for the purpose of conducting business in the state of Oregon.

The Twohy Brothers Company property was finally determined to be worth $350,892. Seattle Car contributed to the new company assets worth $649,108, making the total just $1 million. In order to reach this precise figure, Seattle Car declared a dividend of $49,592 and paid it into its own treasury, in anticipation of an indeterminate amount of unpaid debts. The distribution of stock in the new company was in a somewhat more generous proportion to the Twohy Brothers, giving them 3,700 shares, as against 6,300 for Seattle Car.

On December 15, 1917, the trustees of Seattle Car decided to distribute only 5,746⅘ shares to their stockholders and to turn the remaining 553⅕ shares over to Clingan, as trustee for the company and its shareholders, providing a substantial reserve for obligations that might become payable.

Some four years later, on June 20, 1921, the Seattle Car trustees noted that their company's indebtedness amounted to approximately $66,000, against which it still held the $49,592 dividend that had been paid into the treasury. The trustees further authorized the officers to sell 250 shares of the Pacific Car stock held back, using the proceeds to pay debts as they fell due, and to distribute the remaining 302⅕ shares to Seattle Car stockholders. The company was later assessed $4,079 in additional income taxes for 1917; after paying this amount, there was still

Judge John Twohy addressed the Portland crew of the newly formed Pacific Car & Foundry Company in 1917.

some $22,000 worth of Pacific Car stock in the treasury, and it was voted in February 1923 to distribute this to shareholders and dissolve Seattle Car.

The new Pacific Car & Foundry Company, meanwhile, set about its business. Pigott was named president at a meeting of trustees on September 6, 1917; James Twohy was elected vice president and treasurer; O. D. Colvin, vice president and general manager; James E. McInerny, who had been with the Twohy firm, secretary; and T. G. Haywood, director of purchases.

Late in November, Seattle Car and Twohy Brothers assigned to Pacific Car the contracts for each of them to manufacture two hundred boxcars for the Union Pacific. The trustees voted to furnish a $160,000 bond that the Union Pacific Equipment Association requested before making an advance payment of almost that amount on the cars.

A committee was named on December 7, 1917, to study the matter of officer compensation. A week later the board voted to pay Colvin $550 per month; James Twohy, $300 per month; Haywood, $350 per month; McInerny, $200 per month; F. W. Chriswell, $250 per month as chief engineer; and H. B. Wilkinson, $225 per month as general auditor. It was also voted to pay an annual retainer of $1,000 to Hulbert's law firm, Ballinger, Battle, Hulbert & Shorts.

The board decided on December 15 that the company should vote a semi-annual dividend amounting to 3 percent of the par value of the stock, payable every January 1 and July 1, the first such payment to be made on July 1, 1918.

In the operations area, a Greene electric furnace was installed at the Renton plant. To provide adequate capital needed to run the plants, the officers were authorized to establish a line of credit of $300,000 with Seattle and Portland banks.

One of many capital improvements at Pacific Car's Renton plant immediately after the 1917 merger was the installation of a new Greene electric furnace in the foundry.

The joining of the two disparate groups into a single entity was not without some of the frictions that might have been expected. James Twohy and McInerny were authorized to sign checks, but either Pigott, Colvin, or Clingan had to countersign them. At a meeting of trustees on November 18, 1917, Colvin moved that James Twohy look into the advisability of moving the purchasing department from Portland to Renton. There was a prolonged discussion of this proposal at the December 7th meeting, and finally James Twohy moved that Haywood continue as director of purchases at Portland, but that A. E. Saul be moved to Renton to handle purchasing activities under Haywood's supervision. But a week later this compromise was knocked out and a new one put in its place. E. T. Fehnel, who had been with the Twohy firm, was appointed acting director of purchases, with offices in Renton, while Saul was to remain at Portland and report to Fehnel.

There was an even more acerbic exchange with regard to the manner of keeping inventory records. The minutes of the June 17, 1918, meeting of trustees, in attorney Hulbert's office, stated: "Mr. Clingan in making report previously asked for by the President, Mr. Pigott, advised that records of the Car Company's stock of materials on hand had been faulty and that intelligent buying could not have resulted from such condition. It was moved, seconded and carried, that the quantity system formerly used by the Seattle Car & Foundry Company for keeping costs of records be reinstalled. . . . The President appointed a committee of Mr. Chriswell, Mr. Haywood and Mr. Fehnel to supervise the taking of inventories of materials at Renton and Portland."

Even with all the activity attendant on the start of a new company, Pigott was unable to forgo his penchant for forming new business enterprises. He incorporated the Pacific Coast Forge Company to supply railroads with track spikes and bolts, along with other machine forgings. A plant was put up on property he owned on the Duwamish Waterway in southwest Seattle. Key employees of "the Car Company" subscribed to the stock.

— WARTIME CAR BUILDING —

On April 6, 1917, less than three months before the organization of the Pacific Car & Foundry Company, the United States entered the war on the side of the Allied powers. Although U.S. troops were not committed to combat until 1918, procurement activities of all kinds were stepped up rapidly in the United States. In the winter of 1917–18 Pacific Car sent Chriswell to take charge of an office opened in Washington, D.C., to seek out government business.

Judge Twohy was familiar with a number of political figures in the nation's capital, and he made frequent trips to Washington. It was common knowledge at the time that the Railway Administration was laying plans for the purchase of 100,000 freight cars. It was also common knowledge that the country had excess car-building capacity. The railroads had gone on a buying splurge in 1906, ordering 250,000 cars, a figure not matched before that time or up to the war years. The shops had been expanded and, in Chriswell's words, "Every shop was hungry for business."

The director general of the Railway Administration was William Gibbs McAdoo, who was also President Wilson's son-in-law. Judge Twohy was acquainted with McAdoo, and he made an appointment for himself and Chriswell. "Well, judge," the director general began, "what can I do for you?" Twohy responded by painting a word picture of the great Northwest, its industries and its opportunities. After some fifteen or twenty minutes of that, McAdoo asked, "Well, judge, what is your proposition? What do you want?" Twohy then turned to Chriswell and said, "Fred, what was our plan?"

Chriswell explained that Pacific Car could start building wooden cars the very next day. Although the government's plan was to build steel cars, there was some question about the availability of enough steel. And Chriswell pointed out that his company could build cars without seriously affecting the pinched steel supplies. "All right," said McAdoo. "You go down and see Mr. Vulcan. He is in charge of the engineering end."

Chriswell then went to see Vulcan, who had been head of the Baldwin Locomotive Works. He was unable to sell the idea of wooden cars, but he did get Pacific Car placed on the list of bidders for steel cars. Compensation was to be made on the principle of cost plus 5 percent, based on minimum bids.

Pacific Car first was awarded an order for one thousand of the cars, and shortly thereafter for another one thousand. This meant car building on a dimension and in a time frame that was new to the company and both its component units. But they started to prepare the plants immediately.

Judge Twohy insisted that half of the cars be built at the Portland plant, so both plants had to undergo major expansion programs. An entirely new erecting shop was built at Portland, and Renton added a paint shop and expanded the erecting shop, steel plant, runway, and foundry. New machinery was added to both shops during the second half of 1918.

So hasty was the effort that the company's management moved ahead with capital purchases without getting prior board approval, and the action was approved in a somewhat

The U.S. Railway Administration purchased two thousand boxcars from Pacific Car to meet increased transportation requirements brought about by America's involvement in World War I.

chiding resolution introduced by Judge Twohy and passed by the board. Twohy also moved that the government order be handled on a separate basis from the standpoint of operation, finance, and auditing, and that it be placed under the direct charge of Pigott and Chriswell, who had returned from his Washington assignment. This motion, too, was carried. At the same meeting, Hulbert, who had replaced James Twohy on the board temporarily, resigned so that Chriswell might be named a trustee.

About this time some major new management acquisitions were made by the company. H. N. Curd, hired as plant manager, was instrumental in organizing production on an assembly-line basis. When the completed program got under way, a new car was being rolled out of the Renton plant every hour. The other addition was John Purse, an expert in matters of auditing and finance. Purse had done an exemplary job in putting the Washington-Oregon district of the Emergency Fleet Corporation on a sound financial and accounting basis. Pigott asked him to join Pacific Car during the period of rapid expansion. Purse was named general auditor and assistant to the president, at a salary of $5,000 a year, plus bonuses as the board determined. He remained with Pacific Car until early in 1922.

To help finance this mounting activity, the board authorized an increase in the company's line of credit from $300,000 to $500,000. It still became necessary at times to engage in unorthodox stratagems to acquire needed funds. In October 1918, Pigott loaned the company $100,000, for which Colvin and McInerny gave him the company's note—an action ratified by the board a few days later. And treasurer McInerny asked that James Twohy and Purse be made a committee to confer with him on financial matters.

On the whole, the government order proved profitable, both from the standpoint of earnings and that of the modernization of the plant that it occasioned. Part of the earnings were not realized until claims against the government for excess cost were settled some years later. These negotiations were undertaken jointly by the car builders as a group, and in February 1921 Pacific Car & Foundry turned over its power of attorney in the matter to an executive of the American Car & Foundry Company, C. S. Sale, a name that was to become significant in the future of Pacific Car.

Sale settled Pacific Car's claim against the U.S. Railway Administration in about two months. The company received $84,240, plus $2,360 in interest, or 48 percent of what it had sought.

— POSTWAR HARD TIMES —

Shipbuilding had always been a very minor industry in the Pacific Northwest, but the start of hostilities in Europe soon changed that. So rapidly did both wood and steel shipbuilding expand that it soon became second only to lumbering among the region's principal industries, employing 50,000 men at its peak. It also brought in substantial capital investment and nourished secondary industries that served the shipyards and their workers.

Among those who joined the rush for wartime orders were the Twohy brothers. In the spring of 1918 they acquired the Erickson Engineering Company, renamed it the Seattle North Pacific Shipbuilding Company, and began a vigorous program of building vessels. They got orders for ten ships from the Emergency Fleet Corporation, laid the keel for the first in mid-June,

Pacific Car & Foundry proudly displayed its products in Portland's 1918 Rose Parade.

and launched it eighty-four days later, a record for a new yard. They soon had two others built, including a 9,400-ton steel ship that was completed in only eighty-one days.

The shipbuilding program continued after the signing of the Armistice on November 11, 1918, and in 1919, when the U.S. Shipping Board predicted optimistically, "A new industry has been created and bids fair to remain an important feature of our commercial structure." But this was not to be. By mid-1920 employment in the industry had dropped from its peak of 385,000 to just 75,000.

The Northwest was hit even harder. Orders for 146 ships were canceled, and employment dropped to under 1,000 by 1921. Logging camps and lumber mills in Washington laid off 15,000 men as the price of native lumber dropped sharply. The state's total industrial payroll was cut in half.

For Pacific Car & Foundry Company, however, greater stringency in the economy simply meant more aggressive efforts to find new business and tighten controls over costs.

One product that helped tide over the period of fewer car orders was the truck trailer that Chriswell had developed and he and others had improved. The *West Coast Lumberman* early in 1919 noted that "the now famous 'Universal Trailer' for auto trucks . . . has not only revolutionized logging in the West but has increased the possibilities of the motor truck as well. . . . So great has become the demand for this equipment in other fields as well as logging that a special trailer department and organization has been established." At the same time Pacific Car added another new department for the repair of locomotives and locomotive wheel replacement.

The trailer had established itself firmly for lumbering during the war when the Army helped compensate for the scarcity of railroad equipment by using trucks and trailers to haul spruce for aircraft production. Fifty-two of the Universal Trailers were used, and their large capacity made possible the hauling of sizable portable sawmills to timber tracts, saving extra hauls and the construction of stationary mills. On one occasion a truck and trailer transported a 25-ton log, 24 feet long and measuring 99 inches in diameter at the butt end.

Pacific Car put its engineers to work to modify the trailers for other uses. In California the Spreckles Sugar Refining Company used a number of them to haul sugar beets over the sandy soil with loads as high as 30 tons. Another development was a gravel and grain dump body affixed to a trailer for hauling and easy unloading of heavy bulk materials. But early in 1920 Pigott recommended that the company policy should be to concentrate on logging trailers, while keeping in touch with other types of development.

The company's Portland shop concentrated on such railroad car business as it could get after the war. It first took on a repair contract for the Union Pacific Railroad. This was followed in 1920 by an order from Pacific Fruit Express Company for 200 steel underframe refrigerator cars. Next an order came in for 1,033 insulated refrigerator cars. Since savings of $15 per car could be realized by building them at Portland, heavy punches and other equipment were shipped to the Oregon plant. To help supervise the work, two members of the engineering staff, Thales Gyllenflecht and Alex Thompson, were asked to spend much of their time in Portland. There was then another order for 957 cars; thereafter the Portland plant became a virtual specialty shop for building refrigerator cars, which used the region's own wood products. But the Renton plant continued as a diversified shop in the fields of car and truck building and manufacture of steel castings.

In all these wide-ranging activities, Pigott continued to insist that the company's quality standards be maintained. Because customers in this industry had long memories and might come back for new orders only after the passage of several years, this unwillingness to

Pacific Car developed new products, such as a bulk haul trailer, to keep its plants busy after World War I car building concluded in 1919.

compromise quality served Pacific Car well. Some of the larger customers were never off the books, with their new orders coming in before the old were completed. In all, some 3,500 refrigerator cars were built in the early 1920s, and 4,000 cars were repaired.

Early in 1919 the Pacific Car board resolved to call a special meeting of stockholders to consider an increase in capitalization from $1 million to $1.5 million. The meeting was called for June 30, adjourned for lack of quorum to July 10, adjourned again to July 31, and still again to August 15. The matter of increasing capitalization was subsequently dropped.

There were a number of changes among board members and executives in the early postwar years. Haywood resigned from the board in 1919 and young Robert Twohy came to an untimely death. They were replaced by McLaughlin and James Twohy. In November Purse asked that he be relieved of his duties as assistant to the president and paid a reduced salary of $300 a month. Curd, the general manager, was appointed assistant to the president, while Chriswell was named acting sales manager and Fehnel assistant sales manager, both with responsibilities for traveling, handling inquiries, selling, and estimating.

In January 1921 Pigott advised the board that he could no longer devote the time to his duties that he considered necessary, and asked to be relieved as president. The trustees acceded to his wishes and named Judge Twohy president, Curd and Colvin vice presidents, and McInerny secretary and treasurer. The following month Judge Twohy resigned from the board because of his continued absence from Seattle. He was replaced by Curd. But Judge Twohy was returned to the board six months later.

Some time earlier, in November 1919, when the first pinch of postwar economic contraction was felt, Pigott requested that his own salary be cut to $250 per month. The board voted the reduction, and also authorized Pigott and McInerny to sell at their discretion some $100,000 in Liberty Bonds to which the company had subscribed at various times during the war period.

This reining in of expenses, however, did not keep the company from voting the customary Christmas bonuses to women employees, ranging from $10 to $50 and totaling $600. The trustees also recommended that Curd be paid half of his expenses for moving from Tennessee to Seattle, and that Chriswell be given a special payment of $1,200 for his work on the development of logging trailers. In September 1920 the board set aside 10 percent of net earnings, after taxes and payment of a 6 percent dividend, as a bonus for key employees.

By the start of 1921 the pinch was being felt again, and the company followed an ultra-conservative policy of cutting back expenses. They started with a 10 percent reduction of pay for all salaried personnel, except that the cuts for Curd and Colvin were greater than 10 percent.

The cutting fever spread during the next few months. In April 1921 the board approved a report by Curd that called for a reduction in salaried personnel, only partial operations of the Portland plant, elimination of some land rents, and a reduction of 10 percent in shop wages at Renton, to go into effect May 1.

— RETURN OF PROSPERITY —

William Pigott was by nature an organizer and builder of enterprises. When his companies made little or no money, he tended to watch and husband whatever funds they had. When they prospered, his instincts led him toward using their profits for further growth.

He rarely expressed his thoughts in this manner, but it may have been by a word, a gesture, or a grimace that he transmitted these sentiments to his associates. And he was probably chiefly responsible for the fact that the dividend voted by the board in September 1920 was never actually paid, on the premise that the company's funds would not warrant it.

The Twohys, on the other hand, always seemed to be in need of money and wanted to have their enterprises supply it. So it was probably they who were behind a resolution passed by the board in June 1921 to rescind the earlier 6 percent dividend action and to pay a dividend of 8 percent. The trustees at the same meeting approved the sale of $115,850 face amount of Liberty Bonds for $104,478, since the interest paid by the bonds was considerably less than the 7 percent the company paid on its indebtedness to the Dexter Horton Bank.

The following year another dividend, this time of 6 percent, was declared. The board also voted that 10 percent of the earnings after taxes and the dividend payment be disbursed to a selected group of employees, as determined by a committee consisting of the Twohy brothers, Pigott, Curd, and Clingan.

Pigott also had a reputation for fairness, which came into play when he was asked to mediate disputes within the company. Colvin, for example, had entered on the books in 1919 a charge of $29,000 against the Twohy Brothers Company to cover a loss sustained on orders taken over from the Twohys. At the same time, Colvin entered another charge against Twohy Brothers of $20,000, the amount awarded as damages by the city of Portland because of the construction of a viaduct on their factory site. Pigott looked into both matters and held that there was no substance to either. The first charge could not be satisfactorily substantiated as a claim, he said, and the second was an event that predated the merger. Pigott did find, however, that a resurvey of the Portland plant site showed it to be two acres short of the twenty acres it was said to contain, and he recommended that the Twohy Brothers account be charged $4,800, or $2,400 an acre. The board followed all his suggestions.

In another controversy, Haywood claimed that he had been promised one hundred shares of Pacific Car stock, either by the company or by Judge Twohy, for his work in connection with

Hot rivets were used to join steel shapes into Pacific Car & Foundry railcars. At left, part of the Car Company crew in 1923.

the consolidation of the two firms. Haywood also said he had been given some promises in this regard in talks with Pigott. Curd, Clingan, and Fehnel were appointed as a committee to examine these claims. At a special board meeting some six months later, in June 1922, the matter was discussed but not acted upon. Finally, in November 1922, the trustees voted that the treasurer pay Haywood $2,500 in settlement of his claims against the company, the two merging firms, Pigott, and Judge Twohy.

In the spring of 1922 both McInerny and Purse resigned their offices in the company. Curd named W. S. Bassage secretary-treasurer to succeed McInerny, and J. Browne to Purse's former post of auditor. He also changed Chriswell's designation from acting sales manager to sales manager, and appointed F. T. Falco district sales manager, with headquarters in Portland. The board approved all these appointments.

A special meeting of stockholders was called for October 2, 1922, to amend the Pacific Car bylaws to add a "chairman of the board of trustees" to the list of officers and to provide for the election of an executive and finance committee. After two adjournments, the shareholders voted the bylaw changes. The duties of the new chairman of the board were to include presiding at all meetings of stockholders, trustees, and the executive and finance committee.

At a special meeting of trustees on November 13, 1922, Pigott was unanimously elected to the new position of chairman of the board. Though he had been an interested stockholder, this was the first office he had held in the company for almost two years. Other members named to the executive and finance committee were Clingan, Curd, and the Twohy brothers.

At this time, Pacific Car & Foundry was doing an increasing amount of profitable business.

As a consequence of a postwar scarcity of suitable horses and of men willing to drive them in the western logging camps, the company undertook experiments with a gasoline-powered logging tractor. The huge rear wheels were 11 feet in diameter, with rims 20 inches wide. Tests were carried out in the fall of 1923 on the property of the Fruit Growers Supply Company, but it was found that the round wheels were less suited to the work than were the crawler tractors already making headway in the field.

But business was booming in the company's other lines. In February 1923, "with relation to the borrowing of money for the purpose of carrying on the increased amount of business now on the books and in contemplation," the president or either vice president were authorized to borrow, in aggregate, up to $1 million. Ten percent of earnings for the last half of 1922 was again set aside for employee bonuses, and the compensation for the company's law firm was increased to $1,500 a year.

At an adjourned meeting of the board in November 1923, there was a discussion of a settlement with Chriswell of his claims with regard to certain patents he had taken out and assigned to the company. Chriswell had offered to take $10,000 in full settlement, and Pigott and Curd were appointed as a committee to make the necessary arrangements with him.

The year 1923 was by all odds the peak of the company's car business. Profits were approximately $750,000, which was three-quarters as large as Pacific Car & Foundry's total capitalization. On the motion of James Twohy, the board of trustees in December 1923 voted a dividend of 22 percent on the company's capital stock, "to be payable at the convenience of the Treasurer."

Pigott appeared to possess an uncanny knowledge of the direction the business was about to take. In a letter to Chriswell written in May 1923, he predicted that the company's car business would drop by a third in 1924 and 1925. He told his manager to plan on such a decline,

Odd, but original, this innovative log hauler —the "Galloping Goose"— was developed by Pacific Car in 1923.

Page 63: The development of special purpose logging equipment by the Car Company contributed to its prosperity during the early 1920s.

ASAHEL CURTIS
A 1882.

and Pigott added that he would himself assume the responsibility if he was proved wrong. The company's car business actually dropped by slightly more than a third, from fifteen hundred cars in 1923 to nine hundred the following year.

— IRON AND STEEL —

Iron and steel production never left Pigott's mind and did not too often leave his conversation. Seattle businessmen became familiar with his special interest and preoccupation. When a Nevada mining company wrote to ask the Seattle Construction & Drydock Company whether they had any interest in a high-grade iron ore deposit, the inquiry somehow found its way into Pigott's hands.

Nothing came of this, just as very little happened when Pigott acquired the Oswego furnace, near Portland, for the Pacific Coast Steel Company. An effort was made to rehabilitate the facilities, but work was soon stopped. The high cost of assembling the needed raw materials kept the plant from being put into operation.

The Pacific Coast Steel Company, however, experienced steadily increasing demand for its products. Under the impetus of war in Europe, its steelmaking capacity grew to 125,000 tons a year, and the rolling mills at San Francisco and Seattle added structural shapes to their existing production of merchant steel and concrete reinforcing bars. Among the raw materials used were Chinese iron ore and the considerable quantities of scrap iron and steel that accumulated on the West Coast.

Entry of the United States into the war gave western iron production an impetus it might otherwise never have had. The scarcity and high price of pig iron on the West Coast made it feasible even to rehabilitate and start up the rusting blast furnace at Irondale, which had stood cold since 1911.

The Irondale furnace was blown in on September 10, 1917, and, except for short periods, it remained in continuous production until February 27, 1919. It used the stocks of Chinese and domestic ore shipments remaining from the days of the Western Steel Corporation, along with ore shipped from British Columbia and mill cinder from rolling mills at Lakeview and Seattle. Coking coal supplies came from the Wilkeson-Carbonado field in Washington State, and limestone flux from the quarries at Roche Harbor on Washington's San Juan Island. Total production for the period was 22,316 gross tons, mostly pig iron but also including small amounts of foundry iron for special needs. Average daily output was 56 tons, and the best single day's production, on February 18, 1918, matched the furnace's capacity of 80 tons.

The average cost of producing iron was close to $40 a ton, an uneconomic figure under ordinary market conditions. The high costs were chiefly the consequence of the large amounts of coke used and its high price at the time, as well as heavy labor expense. After the furnace shut down in 1919, it was dismantled, not to be used again.

None of this dimmed Pigott's enthusiasm for the industry that was his first love and remained his major interest. In 1920, after discussing matters of raw material supply with steelmen, mining men, and officials of the Department of Commerce, he went to China to study the availability of needed materials. While the Japanese had a hold on a large part—as much as three-fourths—of Chinese ore, Pigott found, there were still more supplies available. And, looking into what turned out to be a rather clouded crystal ball, he reported, "The more I saw of it, the more I was convinced that it will be many a day, if ever, before Japan or China can compete successfully with the United States in the manufacture of steel."

William Pigott returned to China in 1920 to meet with agent Harold Dollar and continue his study of China's iron industry.

Pigott did hold out some ray of hope, however, for the future of industry in the Orient. ". . . while the Orientals are highly intelligent and technically capable," he wrote, "they lack the virile physical and mental forces . . . and cannot produce comparative results in steel. Later on they will no doubt install more up-to-date labor-saving machinery, and therein lies their only salvation."

He was astonished to learn that the Tata Steel and Iron Company, in India, was making pig iron for the incredibly low figure of $13 a ton. "This," he said, "can be attributed to a great extent to foreign management."

His final conclusion was not much different from his starting premise, which is to say he remained convinced that a viable steel industry could be established on the West Coast. For this purpose he deemed it best to arrange for part of the ore supply to come from China and part from the Pacific Coast, to find an assured source of coking coal in the Northwest, and to install a by-product coking plant and a blast furnace on Puget Sound. He wrote: "With the necessary capital and organization, I believe we could produce pig iron on Puget Sound on a sound commercial basis of cost, and probably cheaper than it could be produced in China at present."

He remained in touch with Chinese business acquaintances and occasionally dealt with them, purchasing quantities of iron ore and pig iron, as well as seeking quotations on considerably larger quantities, e.g., 2,500 tons a month for a period of years.

In 1923, having closely reviewed the investigations made by others, he decided to make a much more thorough study on his own. He organized a syndicate, which he called the Puget

Sound Steel Company, to engage in his study. He sent a note to a number of business acquaintances, saying:

> The establishment of an iron and steel plant in the Puget Sound area has been discussed for many years . . . , but nothing positive has resulted and no plant has been erected. The failure has been due in part to the fact that many of the plans were too ambitious, and because the sponsors in many instances had not been actively identified with the iron and steel business and were not familiar with the problems involved.
>
> It is now believed that some of these handicapping factors may be eliminated if a project to build a moderate sized blast furnace plant . . . be substituted for the more pretentious combination of an iron and steel plant. It is also believed that the chances of success are greater if the various interests representing the holdings of raw resources, the existing iron and steel plants, and the industrial users of pig iron take an active part . . .
>
> The proposal has been made that a group of business men directly concerned with this matter meet the partial expense of a comprehensive investigation of the subject . . . and that the cooperation of the University of Washington be secured . . .
>
> This letter is being sent to persons who are believed to be directly interested in seeing a basic industry established tributary to the Pacific Northwest in the hope that they will . . . become associated in this investigation.

The response was not very encouraging. Most of those who received the letter politely expressed their interest, but declined to take part in financing the study. "I have considered it carefully from the point of view of the Seattle Hardware Company and I do not believe that it is a matter for them to share in just now," wrote C. H. Black, whose firm had once shown forbearance in pressing its claim against the fire- and panic-ridden Seattle Car Manufacturing Company. Others showed similar aloofness. So Pigott decided to press ahead and finance the investigation at virtually his own expense. He obtained the assistance of Joseph Daniels, a University of Washington professor and metallurgical engineer, who later became the leading historian of Pacific Coast steelmaking efforts.

Pigott did manage to get help from one source. At a meeting of the trustees of the Pacific Car & Foundry Company, he brought up the subject of the research work he and his associates were carrying on. After some discussion, James Twohy moved that the board appropriate $2,500 to help Pigott carry out the investigation.

— HONORS AND APPOINTMENTS —

Pigott probably deserved better treatment at the hands of his friends and business acquaintances. When others felt that a job needed doing, he was frequently the one called upon to do it, and he gave unstintingly of his time and energy if the cause was one he believed in. And if he was not accorded similar treatment, he did receive his full share of recognition and awards.

Edward Hurley, as chairman of the U.S. Shipping Board during World War I, appointed Pigott director of wood ships for the Northwest district. Taking the assignment seriously and at face value, Pigott devoted nearly all his time to it for the duration. He opened an office in Washington, D.C., for the convenience of Northwest businessmen, and a number of them made it their headquarters in the capital.

In 1922 he accepted the job of state chairman of the National Irish Relief Committee, and the following year he was made the state chairman of the American Committee for Relief of German Children. In the fall of 1923 he also took on the chairmanship of the United Parishes Campaign of Seattle. Earlier that year he had done yeoman work in helping the Missionary Sisters of the Sacred Heart raise funds to complete a much-needed new and expanded orphanage. For this he was decorated with the insignia of Chevalier of the Crown by King Victor Emmanuel III of Italy.

In 1924 Pigott created a trust fund to help indigent prisoners on their release from jail. Generous to a fault in his own philanthropies, he once expressed his philosophy of giving in this way: "Don't talk about somebody being worthy. None of us is very worthy. If they need help, give it to them."

His business principles often found expression in the pronouncements of the Pacific Foreign Trade Council, which he had founded and continued to guide as its president. The Council's Statement of Principles of Business Conduct included the following:

One of William Pigott's many community responsibilities was the Seattle School Board, which elected him president in 1914. Pigott (on the right) was first elected to the board in 1910.

U.S. Secretary of Labor Jim Davis visited with William Pigott (front row, left), William Pigott Jr. (top row, right), Scott Clingan (front, right), and area labor leaders at Pacific Coast Steel in 1923.

- Representations of goods and services must be truthfully made and scrupulously fulfilled.
- Business men should render restrictive legislation unnecessary by conducting themselves so as to deserve and inspire public confidence.
- Equitable consideration should be given to capital, employees, and the public . . .
- Waste in any form is intolerable . . .
- We should adhere to the policy of maintaining an excellency and permanency of service.
- Business is entitled to a fair profit and a safe reserve, commensurate with risks involved . . .
- Understanding is developed as a reward of unceasing study of facts; by utilization of statesmanship in construing international policies; by ability to eliminate prejudicial propaganda, . . . by a willingness to be open-minded . . . , and by an adherence to good principles and conduct meriting confidence.

On his own Pigott once told the Council, "The greatest contribution to humanity is the opportunity afforded others to become actively engaged in lucrative employment. . . . I believe that to assist in and be engaged in the industrial growth and activities of life that furnish employment whereby people can find useful work at commensurate compensation is the most worthwhile and honorable work that men can do. You can get along without nearly everything else except good health and bread."

In time the conflicting business aims of Pigott and the Twohy brothers—one to keep funds in the business and the other to distribute earnings to the owners—reached a state that bordered on impasse. The Twohys, in financial trouble and with a lawsuit with the Southern Pacific on their hands, were pressed for cash. As one way out, Judge Twohy suggested selling the company to an organization such as American Car & Foundry Company, then busily engaged in a program of acquiring car building plants throughout the country.

This was not a solution very much to Pigott's liking, but he was a staunch advocate of peace in the business family, and indicated his willingness to go along. American Car & Foundry reacted favorably to the initial overtures, and negotiations got under way.

Chriswell, who had once worked for American Car as chief draftsman and chief estimator, was another who did not like the idea of selling out, and he remonstrated to Pigott. "I don't like to do anything to hurt the old judge," Pigott told him. "Can you think of any way to do it without going into American Car?"

Chriswell thought there was a way, and he wrote out a proposal. His suggestion was that the company be dissolved, its cash used to pay off the interests of the Twohys, and that the business then be started up again by the Pigott interests. "Well, we'll see what comes of it," Pigott said.

Nothing came of it. Not only were negotiations with American Car already well along, but Pigott remained convinced, as he had written to Chriswell earlier, that the railcar manufacturing business was about to turn sharply downward.

On August 30, 1923, Pigott and Judge Twohy made a detailed offer of sale to American Car & Foundry Company. American Car was to form a new company, which was to take over the assets of Pacific Car & Foundry and in exchange was to give shares of various classes of its stock, mostly preferred, to stockholders of Pacific Car. American Car was given ninety days to accept the offer, and the transaction was to be consummated within thirty to ninety days after the acceptance, unless both sides agreed to an extension.

The talk, usually conducted by or with the guidance of lawyers for the two companies, went on for weeks, as various details were clarified or worked out. On October 26, a "fair value" having been agreed upon for the land, buildings, and other fixed assets of Pacific Car, Pigott and Judge Twohy wrote to American Car, stating that the company's net assets as of September 30, 1923, were $2,188,480.84. In November, American Car asked for an extension of time in which they might accept the proposal, and Pigott wired them on November 22, extending the period of American Car's option to the end of 1923. Then, on December 29, American Car exercised its option and accepted the proposal.

The first official notice that Pacific Car shareholders had of any of these transactions was in a letter sent to them on December 22, in which details of the proposed sale were outlined. The unissued stock in Pacific Car's treasury was sold to shareholders, pro rata at par, so that all 10,000 shares of the company's stock were then issued and outstanding.

A group of major stockholders—Pigott, James Twohy, Wilson, Clingan, McLaughlin, and Bassage—wrote to Judge Twohy, as president, requesting a special meeting of shareholders. The meeting was to consider and act upon three proposals—the sale to American Car; an increase in the company's capital stock from ten thousand shares of $100 par value to fifteen thousand shares of $100 par value, or from a total of $1 million to $1.5 million; and a change in the corporate name to Seattle Pacific Investment Company. The change of name would make available to American Car the name of Pacific Car & Foundry Company for their new enterprise, if they chose to use it. And the increase in capitalization would more fully reflect the value of the company's fixed assets and working inventory, and perhaps simplify the exchange for stock in American Car's new company.

On January 1, 1924, the special meeting was called for January 18. This meeting and a special meeting of trustees were held and adjourned over and over again until March 21. Meanwhile, negotiations between the firms continued on a number of points. A principal negotiator for American Car was C. S. Sale, the executive who had reached the settlement of Pacific Car's claims against the federal government for excess costs in its wartime manufacturing program.

The Twohys remained concerned about how much cash they could expect for their holdings and how soon they could get it. After some discussion of this subject at a trustees' meeting on February 5, Judge Twohy and Pigott sent a telegram to Sale, saying: "Minority stockholders representing one third total stock . . . raise following point: Pacific Company is guaranteeing everything in this transaction, including posting of bonds or securities, and are turning over this business and its control to the new company without any guarantee whatever either as to dividends or redemption of preferred stock. They are willing to go ahead, as are we, provided American Company will advise who they propose to nominate as officers, directors, and what salaries to be paid and who will direct the general policies of the new company."

This wire received a satisfactory reply, and other details were worked out as well. Finally a take-over scheme designated "Plan C" was devised, its principal purpose being to arrange

Begun in 1895, American Car & Foundry built railcars of every description, including refrigerator cars, by 1920.

the deal in a way that would minimize tax problems of the Pacific Car shareholders. Plan C provided the following:

First, all the stock of Pacific Car would be endorsed for transfer and turned over to Pigott and Judge Twohy, or to a bank, pending final consummation of the sale.

Second, Pacific Car would change its name, so that the new company could assume the former name.

Third, the new company would be organized with 6,000 shares, worth $600,000 of Class A 6% cumulative preferred stock, of $100 par value; 18,000 shares, worth $1,800,000, of Class B 7% cumulative preferred stock, of $100 par value; and 36,000 shares of no par value common stock.

Fourth, Pacific Car would transfer to the new company all its assets and goodwill, and the new company would assume all Pacific Car liabilities.

Fifth, the new company would issue to Pacific Car shareholders, pro rata, (1) enough of the Class B stock to cover $1,500,000 in assets—$1,000,000 in fixed assets and $500,000 in "active" inventory, or inventory on hand to fill present and prospective orders; (2) enough of the Class A stock to cover $500,000 in additional inventory, cash, and receivables, less liabilities; and (3) two-tenths of a share of common stock for each share of the Class B preferred so issued.

Sixth, American Car would purchase for cash $200,000 worth of Class B preferred and up to 15,400 shares of common stock, at some nominal value, in the new company.

Seventh, Pacific Car would indemnify the new company against any tax liability for prior years or any liabilities not shown on the books at the time of closing the transaction.

In addition to the above conditions American Car agreed that, "The preferred shares to be not entitled to vote so long as there be no default in the payment of dividends thereon, but if for two successive years there shall be no payment of dividends on the preferred shares, then voting rights (share for share with the common stock) to attach to the preferred shares, and to continue until the payment of all accumulated dividends on the preferred shares and until the payment of dividends on the preferred shares shall be resumed or provided for."

Under continuing pressure from those stockholders who felt that American Car should offer more guarantees to the preferred shareholders in the new company, Pigott on February 25 wired Sale: "Under original plan stockholders here expected to realize quickly upon cash and liquid assets of company. We approve Plan C upon understanding that we may declare dividends out of cash and liquid assets prior to closing deal and further that the American Company will guarantee redemption of the Class A stock as outlined in your plan." Sale immediately responded that there would be no objections to such dividends if the assets involved in the transaction were not impaired. But, he added: "Concerning guarantee of redemption of Class A stock by American Co. this is not acceptable to us as we said when the matter was previously discussed. Plan C proposed primarily to help you solve your tax problem and if not acceptable to you on that basis alone we shall be glad to revert to Plan A. Regard it highly important you definitely decide which plan you desire and advise us."

The following day Pigott and Judge Twohy replied: "Referring your wire . . . we accept Plan C. Trustees meeting March 7, stockholders meeting March 10."

Both meetings were adjourned to March 12, when Pigott named a committee to be chaired by T. S. Clingan and James Twohy. On March 13, their report said that Pacific Car's net assets would total about $2.5 million at the time of the sale, and that they believed a dividend for all such assets in excess of $2 million should be declared and paid. Since a large part of the company's funds were tied up in inventories, however, there would not be enough cash for this purpose. They therefore recommended a dividend of 35 percent on the capital stock, or $350,000, prior to the consummation of the American Car transaction, and that the new company sign notes for any balance and turn them over to the Dexter Horton Bank, as trustee for the Pacific Car stockholders.

The trustees followed the recommendation and declared the 35 percent dividend. The final approval of Plan C by trustees and stockholders came at meetings held on March 21. At the same time the name of the company was changed to Seattle Pacific Investment Company, and the trustees and officers were authorized to take the necessary steps to make the name change official.

As if to underscore the fact that Pacific Car & Foundry Company was to remain a going business, Chriswell reported to the March 21 meeting of trustees on new orders that had been obtained. These included the construction of 100 connected truck logging cars for $121,300 and 125 steel frame stock cars, for $205,640, both for the Western Pacific Railroad Company, along with 50 connected truck logging cars, for $72,500, for the Polson Logging Company.

The sale of Pacific Car & Foundry Company had its closing on March 31, 1924. The only change from the details of Plan C was that shareholders would get three-tenths of a share of common stock of the new company, rather than two-tenths, for each share of Class B preferred they received. Slightly more than one-fifth of the B preferred and common stock was to be held in escrow to handle any undisclosed liabilities, under the indemnification provisions of the plan.

The new company was organized under the old name of Pacific Car and Foundry Company, and American Car named eight of the fifteen members to the board. Seattle Pacific Investment Company held its organization meeting on April 17, having filed the appropriate papers with the state of Washington and with King County officials. At this meeting a number of members of the board of trustees resigned and were replaced by representatives of American Car, which thus took over control of the last official vestige of the old Pacific Car & Foundry Company.

— YOUNG PAUL PIGOTT —

William Pigott's two sons, in order, were named William and Paul. William was born in Colorado during his father's tenure with the Colorado Fuel & Iron Company in 1895. Paul was born in 1900, five years after the Pigotts had moved to Seattle. William and Paul attended public grammar school and Broadway High School in Seattle. Paul left home to attend and graduate from Culver Military Academy in Culver, Indiana.

William Pigott Sr. had an insatiable drive to succeed as an entrepreneur, with his outside interests limited to his family, church, and community. T. S. Clingan had an uncle's interest in the well-being of William and Ada's children, and through him they learned to love and be proficient at a wide variety of sports.

Paul excelled at both golf and tennis. Along with bird hunting and fishing, these activities became an inseparable part of his identity.

After graduating from Culver, Paul attended Stanford University, where he studied metallurgical engineering. Just prior to his graduation, Paul learned of his father's decision to sell Pacific Car & Foundry. William Jr.'s interests were always with Pacific Coast Steel, but Paul had always regarded Pacific Car as a kind of family affair, and he greatly resented the fact that it was leaving the family. His previous summertime experiences, with such inconsiderable tasks as a sorter and counter of nuts and bolts at the company, now appeared to head nowhere. Later, as a minority stockholder, Paul cast the one lone, but unremarked, dissenting vote against the company's sale to American Car & Foundry.

In 1924, soon after receiving his degree from Stanford, Paul married Theiline McGree, his college sweetheart. "I thought that I was going into the wilds in Seattle. I would probably come back with a feather in my hair," recalled Mrs. Pigott; yet she and Paul established their first home in Seattle.

William Jr. became employed by, and represented, the family interest in the Pacific Coast Steel Company. Paul, on his return to Seattle, chose a job outside the family business and went to work as a sales engineer for the Wallace Bridge and Structural Steel Company. He later rose to the rank of vice president, but as John McCone, Paul's close friend, recalled, "Paul wanted to be his own entrepreneur." Clearly, Wallace Bridge would not provide Paul's answer.

Paul Pigott (right) with his banker, adviser, and friend, Thomas Gleed.

CHAPTER FOUR

THE AMERICAN CAR AND FOUNDRY YEARS

The first meeting of trustees for the new regime in Pacific Car and Foundry Company was held in the company's Seattle offices on April 17, 1924. It was a session at which the lawyers were obviously in charge, with various trustees playing a kind of game of musical chairs—resigning, leaving the meeting while some necessary business was being transacted, being re-elected, and sometimes resigning again. The final outcome was that the Seattle Pacific Investment Company turned over all its capital stock to the new Pacific Car and Foundry in exchange for the bulk of Pacific Car's preferred stock and notes, as had been agreed earlier.

Most of those elected as officers of the company also resigned at this meeting, and were replaced by those who were to serve more permanently with the company. These included Lucius T. Carroll, president, who was to hold that office as long as American Car retained its interest in the company; William M. Hager, board chairman; W. S. Bassage, secretary and treasurer; and H. N. Curd, vice president. The latter two were holdovers from the old Pacific Car & Foundry Company.

The trustees thereafter were to hold their meetings in New York, while the annual meetings of shareholders would continue to be held in Seattle. Carroll presided at the first of these annual meetings on June 19, 1924, and Bassage acted as secretary. The meeting formally approved the actions of trustees in effecting the organization of the new company. Elected trustees were William Pigott, John Twohy, T. S. Clingan, and E. M. Wilson, representing the interests of stockholders in the old company; and Hager, J. M. Buick, H. W. Wolff, G. R. Scanland, and C. S. Sale for American Car.

The organization meeting of this new board was held in New York, and only the five trustees from American Car were present. They elected the same officers, with the addition of Horace Hager as a vice president. Appointed to key operating positions were Curd, general manager; J. Browne, auditor; Milo C. Shands, assistant secretary; Chriswell, sales manager; E. T. Fehnel, assistant sales manager; C. P. Sander, assistant general manager; G. M. McBride, purchasing agent; and K. C. Boehmer, assistant purchasing agent. J. E. LeBlanc was appointed assistant treasurer to replace Curd in that office, and LeBlanc and S. C. Williams were named assistant secretaries.

In 1931 Alex Finlayson, Pacific Car and Foundry's metallurgist, developed Carcometal, a strong, lightweight steel, for casting.

There was thus enough continuity for the company to maintain its normal operations, and indeed a great many of the employees were only vaguely aware that a change in ownership had taken place. The company continued to develop its specialties—refrigerator and insulated cars, and the logging equipment line. But, as Pigott had predicted to Chriswell, the railcar business turned down rather sharply in 1924 and 1925, and fewer and fewer logging cars were being ordered or built, progressively through the 1920s. So pronounced was the railcar slowdown that the Portland plant was soon closed down.

While there was some railcar business, however, Pacific Car continued to get its share, right into 1929. In 1928 the company was filling an order for 1,000 refrigerator cars from the Pacific Fruit Express Company. In April of 1929 it was announced that Pacific Car and Foundry would build 50 flatcars for the Western Pacific Railroad, for hauling tractors, heavy machinery, and forest products. Later in the year Pacific Car announced that it had completed 166 cars of an order for 500 automobile freight cars for the Northern Pacific. While auto hauling was a good source of business, it was symptomatic of a major change taking place in the national lifestyle, as motor vehicles began to take on a major share of overland transportation, once the almost exclusive province of the railroads.

To help keep the shops busy, the company fabricated a large number of steel bridges and structural steel buildings. It frequently fashioned huge steel elements for this work. For one Seattle bridge, at West Garfield Street, the company built two 65,000-pound girders, each 88 feet

After its acquisition by American Car and Foundry in 1924, Pacific Car, in addition to building railcars, pursued the structural steel business.

long and 10 feet deep, and the two were joined and riveted in place by the steel erector, Wallace Bridge and Structural Steel Company, where Paul Pigott was employed. To further vary its line of products, Pacific Car also added a drop forging department, and undertook sheet metal and galvanizing work.

In September 1924, the trustees ruled sternly that any contract for the purchase of material would have to be approved by the president or board chairman. The board then gave its after-the-fact sanction to a ten-year contract for oxygen requirements entered into by Curd and Bassage. The trustees thereafter did not appear to keep a heavy hand on the company's operations.

The company's financial operating results and balance sheet stayed healthy enough at the start. Net income for 1925 was $371,000, enough to pay preferred stock dividends, as well as a substantial dividend on the common, and still leave a surplus of $124,000. Current assets of $1,462,000 were more than ten times the current liabilities of $137,000 at the end of the year, reflecting the firm's considerable liquidity. Total assets were $2,355,000, including a plant and property account of $882,000.

In 1926 the company's net income slipped to $210,000, still sufficient to cover the preferred dividend requirements of $140,000. But in 1927 profits plummeted to $30,000, so that the trustees had to dip into the earned surplus, creating a deficit in that account, in order to pay preferred dividends. Although earnings seesawed during the remainder of the 1920s, Pacific Car continued to pay the preferred stock dividends regularly into 1930, and even used its earned surplus at times to redeem some of the preferred.

With business continuing at a relatively low plateau, little thought was given to plant expansion, and the value of the plant and property account continued to decline as depreciation reserves were set aside and some of the company's real estate was sold. The board first took up the matter of disposing of unused real estate at its December 1924 meeting. A resolution authorized the president and secretary to contract for the sale of seventeen lots adjacent to the Renton plant for cash or installment payments. In 1926 the same officers were empowered to sell six lots and their buildings in Renton, as well as more than ten acres of land. The executive committee in 1929 passed a resolution authorizing the sale of eight lots in Renton to Linde Air Products Company for $3,500.

There were minor shifts among officers and directors in the 1920s. James Twohy was named a vice president, to be headquartered at Portland, in 1924. At the annual meeting of stockholders in February 1925, Judge Wilson was not among the trustees elected, and the new name added was that of C. J. Hardy, who was to become president of American Car and Foundry some years later. Late in 1925 the board voted to increase the number of trustees from nine to thirteen, and Wilson, Carroll, Noah A. Stancliffe, and Horace Hager were voted in as additional members. James Twohy and W. J. Harris were elected trustees by the board to fill two vacancies in 1928, but Twohy withdrew his name in 1929 and the board named Curd a trustee.

Leading figures of the old Pacific Car attended stockholders' meetings very irregularly. William Pigott Jr. was at the 1925 annual meeting, while Paul Pigott was represented only by a proxy. In 1926 both Paul and William Pigott Jr. attended the meeting along with James Twohy, while William Pigott and the William Pigott Company submitted proxies. From the 1927 through the 1930 meetings, none of the Pigotts attended in person, but sometimes they had proxies. Paul Pigott attended the 1931 meeting. William Pigott himself never attended any of the shareholder meetings under the American Car and Foundry banner.

William Pigott devoted his attention principally to steelmaking activities after the sale of Pacific Car. Even before that sale was consummated, Pigott was writing letters to Northwest businessmen to acquaint them with the studies he was making with regard to establishing a major steel industry in the region, and seeking to enlist their active participation.

> We hope to determine *once and for all* whether or not there is within reach of Puget Sound the necessary Iron Ore and Coking Coal in quality and quantity to produce Pig Iron and Steel at a cost that would warrant investment.
>
> We will not begin this investigation with the idea that it *can* or that it *cannot* be done, but will simply assemble accurate figures and data that can be considered reliable and final. . . . If Pig Iron (the basis of all steel operations) cannot be produced on Puget Sound in competition with Eastern and Foreign Producers, we should dismiss the matter from our minds . . .

These letters received a substantially less enthusiastic response than those he wrote to potential suppliers of coal, coke, limestone, and other needed raw materials as the intensive investigation got under way in April 1924. From then until October 1925 he had surveys made of those materials and their distribution, of the market, of by-product coking operations, and of the overall economic prospects. A typical reply to his inquiries was that sent by John S. McMillin, president of the Tacoma and Roche Harbor Lime Company, who wrote to Pigott in April 1925:

> I thank you for . . . asking . . . the writer's opinion as to what should be . . . a fair estimate for limestone delivered at Seattle or Tacoma in cargo lots of thirty to one hundred tons . . . a day over a period of five or ten years. We understand that your inquiry is tentative and you are not asking us to quote at this time and in fact it would be impossible to make quotations on any such quantity of stone . . . without consideration of all details and careful analysis of transportation problems. . . . Speaking in the most general way, however, we believe that limestone in that quantity and of high quality could be delivered on board barges alongside dock at Seattle or Tacoma for approximately $3.00 per ton . . .

The letter went on to state that the lime company was interested in using iron barrels, provided prices could be reduced substantially by the establishment of a sheet mill on Puget Sound, and asked whether any such move was contemplated. None was, of course, unless it could eventually be fitted in with Pigott's larger plan.

Toward the end of 1925, however, it became evident that the larger plan itself was not feasible. The studies showed that the state of Washington had adequate quantities of limestone and coking coal. But no large bodies of iron ore had yet been developed, and there was considerable doubt that adequate supplies could be found. It became increasingly clear that the iron ore resources of Washington and the Pacific Coast had been greatly overestimated by optimistic businessmen and promoters. While Pigott was finally willing to concede that the time had not yet come for a major blast furnace installation to be operated profitably near Seattle, he remained unwilling to dismiss the prospect from his mind. He stayed in touch with any development that might have a bearing on the problem.

Pacific Coast Steel
Company products
reflected the needs
of the rapidly growing
West Coast.

While indulging in these dreams, Pigott was much more interested in building up his
adopted Northwest than in amassing more personal wealth. Indeed, it was for him an expensive
preoccupation, as his fervor at times tended to outpace his sound business reasoning. The
wonder was that he and others felt that the West, with investments of millions, could compete
against a huge and growing eastern and midwestern steel industry, with established markets
at home and abroad, with the rich ore veins of the Mesabi range, and with its capitalization
in the billions.

Where Pigott's fortunes prospered most was in the Pacific Coast Steel Company, which
fashioned steel without depending on local sources of ore or pig iron. By the end of September
1927, the company's assets in Washington and California stood at almost $13 million, and the
surplus account alone was well over $3 million. With five or six hundred employees, Pacific
Coast Steel disbursed more than $1 million a year in payrolls, and another $2.25 million for
supplies. Its four open-hearth furnaces had a combined capacity of 400 tons of steel a day, and
the company kept installing more equipment—a 2,500-horsepower motor to drive its largest
rolling mill, an overhead runway to handle raw materials, and more than a dozen cranes,
ranging from 5 tons to 75 tons in capacity.

The steel company was big enough and successful enough to have attracted the attention
of the giant Bethlehem Steel Company, which in the 1920s had already acquired the Buffalo,
New York, plant of the Lackawanna Steel Company and two coal and mining companies near
Johnstown, Pennsylvania, but which had no West Coast facilities. With that in mind, they began
conversations with Pigott in 1929.

Some years earlier, in September 1925, Pigott had placed his own interests in Pacific Coast

Steel, along with all his other securities and real estate, into the William Pigott Company, a newly organized holding company. The corporation was given broad powers to deal in stocks, bonds, and government and other securities; to buy and sell personal property and real estate; to form subsidiaries; to execute contracts; to borrow or lend money; and to enter into partnerships, among other endeavors. William Pigott and his two sons were named trustees, and William Pigott was elected chairman and Paul the secretary. The capital stock consisted of 20,000 shares of $100 par value for a total of $2 million. William Pigott subscribed to 19,998 shares, and his sons to one share each.

The assets that Pigott transferred to his holding company included $100,000 in stock of the Seattle Steel Company; $714,000 in common stock, $714,000 in preferred stock, and $133,000 in bonds of the Pacific Coast Steel Company; $85,000 in stock of the Pacific Car and Foundry Company; and real estate valued at $233,000.

The William Pigott Company did very little, except to make minor changes in the family's finances and to distribute payments to the owners. William Pigott was voted a salary of $2,000 a month as president and treasurer and Paul a salary of $50 a month as secretary. One property, the Nettleton Lumber Company, was authorized to pay $500 a month to Ada Pigott, William's wife, to be charged to his account. One piece of beach property was deeded to Ada, and also charged to William's account. Other than this there were some minor sales of real estate and stock, and the payment of annual dividends to stockholders from the investment earnings.

Following the sale of Pacific Car, Pigott kept at least as busy as ever in his philanthropic, civic, and organizational activities. Some of these were directly in the public eye, others known to only a handful.

He took a leading part, for example, in a 1924 campaign to defeat an anti–private-school bill that had been put forward by members of the Ku Klux Klan. In this effort he had the help of the *Union-Record,* to whose editors he wrote, "Our greatest compensation is realized in the fact that our most substantial support came from the big, broadminded, liberal and intelligent men and women of the State of Washington—regardless of religious belief and fraternal association."

At the request of a local justice of the peace, Pigott contributed $1,000 to create a trust fund to help indigent prisoners on their release from jail. In setting up the fund, Justice C. C. Dalton explained, "In many cases . . . unfortunate men and women charged with minor offenses . . . may be slightly punished . . . or . . . placed on parole. In some instances the defendant may be required to leave the city . . . to the house of some friend or relative. In many instances they are turned loose on the street without a penny and told to be good."

When local Catholic sisters acquired some land and built a frame building for an orphanage, Pigott declared, "It is not only inadequate, but it is a fire trap. You need a modern fireproof building. Count on me for the first and last $50,000. Get the money and build it." It was built, in part with added contributions from Pigott. After it was completed, he felt the chapel was inadequate, and had one built. Few people were aware of these benefactions until he was made a Knight of St. Gregory, the highest honor the Pope could bestow on a layman.

A good part of his energies were expended on behalf of the National and Pacific Foreign Trade Councils. At Boston, attending the National Foreign Trade convention in 1924, he worked hard to bring the following year's meeting to Seattle. Chicago was the chief competitor. Pigott conferred with heads of transcontinental railroads and trans-Pacific steamship companies to gain their cooperation, special fares, and stopover privileges. With the strong support of not only the

William Pigott donated the money for building the chapel at the newly completed Sacred Heart Orphanage, "In memory of my Mother, Anna."

Seattle Chamber of Commerce, but also of the Chambers of every major city on the West Coast, Pigott won out.

The 1925 convention was deemed a major success in influencing the more rapid development of American foreign trade. In an editorial, *Marine News* said of Pigott: "In bringing the convention here, he struck a mighty blow on behalf of Northwest prosperity and progress. If we had 50 more William Pigotts in this part of the world, it would mean unprecedented growth."

As head of the Pacific Foreign Trade Council, Pigott chaired annual gatherings in Tacoma; Portland; San Francisco; Los Angeles; and Victoria, B.C.—attended by delegates from more than a dozen foreign countries and by eight trade commissioners of the U.S. Department of Commerce.

— **THE DEATH OF PARTNERS** —

On a single day in 1927—November 22—death took Judge John Twohy and Judge Elliott M. Wilson, who had been the principal partners of William Pigott in the two major enterprises of his business career. The board of trustees of Pacific Car and Foundry Company passed resolutions stating their sense of loss and conveying these sentiments to the families of the bereaved.

William Pigott, 1860–1929

Less than two years later, William Pigott was stricken with a heart attack on July 12, 1929, while visiting Vancouver, B.C., to preside as chairman of the Pacific Foreign Trade Council. His two sons came to his side, but his wife was on her way home from a trip to Europe. She arrived in New York on July 18, and arrangements were considered to fly her to Vancouver—no casual undertaking at the time, just two years after Charles Lindbergh's "lone eagle" flight across the Atlantic. But on the following day, July 19, Pigott died at the age of sixty-nine.

Memorial tributes came in from many quarters, and collections of them were printed in local newspapers. Included were statements from the Rt. Rev. E. J. O'Dea, Bishop of The Catholic Diocese of Seattle ("Seattle has lost an outstanding and patriotic citizen, the business world a progressive and forceful leader and the church a loyal and exemplary member."); Mayor Frank Edwards ("His acts of charity will linger long in the history of Seattle. Mr. Pigott also was an outstanding figure in the steel industry and was admired by the big steel men of America."); Judge George Donworth ("William Pigott had in his character an unusually strong business capacity and push, happily combined with a kindly, lovable and sunny disposition."); Alberto Alfani ("I had for him a great admiration and respect, particularly for his good works among the sick, the poor and the orphans."); John Isaacson ("During twenty-two years' business dealings with Mr. Pigott I developed a strong personal friendship and most sincere admiration for his many fine qualities. He was a builder, a man of unusually high honor and integrity.").

Trustees of the Seattle Chamber of Commerce stood in silence, and adopted a resolution eulogizing Pigott.

Perhaps the most extravagant memorials came from his associates in the Pacific Foreign Trade Council. "I regret exceedingly that we are not to have Mr. William Pigott with us at the annual convention of the Pacific Foreign Trade Council this year," said Robert Dollar, "but his memory will be cherished because of the great good he has accomplished." At the meeting itself, which took place in Seattle and where twenty-three foreign countries were represented, Pigott was eulogized as the "father of the Council . . . the president since its inception. . . . Without him it is doubtful whether the Council would have survived its earlier stages, but under his guidance it has grown to usefulness and service."

Wrote the *Marine Digest* of his work in the Council: "He had no personal aim to serve. It was wholly an unselfish and patriotic labor. . . . In brief, he labored to make his world better than he found it, and he succeeded."

The William Pigott Company proved to be an excellent vehicle to conclude the unfinished business of his lifetime. William Pigott Jr., as vice president, presided at a special meeting of the company. Paul Pigott transferred to his mother a half interest in his one share of the company's capital stock, and Ada Pigott thus became eligible to succeed her husband as a trustee.

In November the company acted to consent to the sale of Pacific Coast Steel Company to the Bethlehem Steel Company, authorizing William Pigott Jr. to sign the needed documents. The transaction was concluded early in 1930, Bethlehem thus becoming the owner of the first and largest steel mill in the Northwest as well as Pacific Coast Steel's San Francisco and Los Angeles facilities.

Ada Pigott and her two sons then agreed to liquidate the assets of the William Pigott Company. In the stock distribution, Ada Pigott became the majority owner, with 9,999½ shares, while William Jr. had 4,999½ and Paul 4,999.

When William Pigott's will was admitted to probate it showed an estate of $2.3 million, the largest within the memory of King County court officials. He left half the estate—$1.15 million— to his widow, and the balance to be divided between his two sons, except for $25,000 in specific bequests. These were $15,000 to the "afflicted and distressed," to be distributed by Mrs. Pigott; $5,000 to be distributed among the women employees of the Pacific Coast Steel Company; $2,500 to women employed in Pacific Coast Steel's San Francisco office; and $2,500 to the women employed in the Pacific Car and Foundry office.

As for other appropriate objects of his bounty, Pigott wrote in a 1927 codicil to his will, "I make no further bequests . . . as I have made certain gifts to institutions and people during my lifetime. It is my desire to keep the industrial concerns in which I am a stockholder intact . . . , believing that the establishment and maintenance of industrial activity whereby men and women find regular employment at remunerative wage is of more importance and is productive of more benefit and happiness than everything else in the end."

— THE DEPRESSION —

The sales and earnings experience of American Car and Foundry Company during the middle and late 1920s was not much different from that of Pacific Car and Foundry, except on a much larger scale for the parent concern and in a much stronger company. Total assets were around $125 million in 1924, and the earned surplus account stood at $37 million.

American Car's net earnings for the fiscal year ended April 30, 1924, were $6.3 million, and $605,000 was added to surplus, after dividend payments of $2.1 million on the 7 percent preferred and $3.6 million on the common stock. A year later the company reported, "The buying of new equipment by the railroads . . . has been intermittent rather than steady. The rebuilding and repairing of old equipment has been appreciably less in volume than in prior years. Buying for foreign delivery has been in small volume." Net profit, nevertheless, was down only slightly to $6.2 million, leaving $464,000 to be added to surplus after paying the same dividends as in the preceding year.

Earnings slipped again to $6.1 million in the 1926 fiscal year, leaving $400,000 to be added to surplus after the usual dividends. "Railroad buying of new equipment . . . has not been in the volume that reasonably might have been expected," the report noted. There was a sharper drop the following year to a net of $4.6 million, not sufficient to cover the usual common dividend, so the company dipped into its surplus to make the payment. In the fiscal year ended April 30, 1928, earnings slipped further to $3.75 million, requiring the use of almost $2 million from surplus to pay the usual dividends. "The failure of the Company to earn the full amount of its dividend requirements," said the report, "is due to conditions which have impartially affected all concerns engaged in the same general line of industry."

In the 1929 fiscal year earnings again declined, to $2.7 million, requiring almost a $3 million boost from surplus for the dividends. The company reported, however, a pickup in business during the later months of the year, so that "the Management is glad to report that your Company entered upon its fiscal year now current with equipment orders on its books in number appreciably in excess of that which it had at the corresponding period of the preceding year."

Curiously enough, in spite of the 1929 stock market crash, that promise was realized. Earnings for the fiscal year ended April 30, 1930, rose to $5,363,000, and only a little more than $300,000 had to be drawn from surplus to pay the usual common dividend. The report said: "The year just closed has witnessed one of the greatest stock market debacles of recent times— the logical and inevitable ending of a protracted period of speculation. . . . Recovery from such condition is bound to be a slow and painful process—one of alternate advances and recession until the country and its industries once more 'find themselves'. . . . The country and its industries have lived through periods of depression much more severe than that of the present, and there is no reason to believe that we shall not again, and within a reasonably short time, get our soundings and attain a condition of stable equilibrium."

Unhappily, the country and its industries were not to "find themselves" or reach "stable equilibrium" for a long time to come. In the 1931 fiscal year, profits dropped to $1,406,347, not enough to cover the preferred stock dividends. The following year, as the full force of the Depression made itself felt, American Car and Foundry reported a net loss of $2.6 million, in addition to special charges totaling another $2.7 million—the first time in the company's thirty-three years of existence that it had gone into the red side of the ledger. With more than $2 million of the special charges representing losses in its security holdings, the company shifted a large part of its investment portfolio into government securities. The year's only large order was for five hundred cars for New York City's municipal subway, obtained under such keen competitive conditions that there was almost no profit in the business.

It was in this clouded atmosphere that Hardy succeeded to the company's presidency in March 1933, when the former president, William H. Woodin, resigned to take on the duties of Secretary of the Treasury in President Franklin D. Roosevelt's cabinet. Orders received by the company for freight cars in calendar year 1931, *Railway Age* reported, "reached the absurd total of 35, whereas no orders for passenger cars whatever were received."

American Car and Foundry was hardly alone in its expectation that the downturn following the market crash would be short-lived and that the economy would quickly return to its accustomed growth pattern. Indeed, this was a widespread consensus at the time.

Seattle and Pacific Northwest industry declined and followed the nation into the Great Depression in the 1930s. Shown is Seattle's "Hooverville," lean-tos and shacks of the unemployed.

Wrote the *Daily Journal of Commerce* in January 1930, "Is the current slackening the beginning of a depression which will make itself evident during the coming months, or is it a breathing spell to be followed by a resumption of the upward march of expanding commercial activity? . . . Today, the average businessman has recovered from his fright. . . . Analysis of the recent market collapse . . . shows that it was caused by technical conditions within the market itself, quite separate from and independent of the fundamental business situation. . . . Production, consumption and earnings during the coming 12 months should easily equal the prosperity year of 1923."

In the Northwest, *The Argus* was more ebullient: "The statisticians, the statesmen, and the wizards of figures and finance and industry . . . seemed to be agreed that it was a happy old year and that business was good. They prove it by showing that the railroads had the best year of business in a decade, that Christmas shopping was satisfactory beyond all expectations . . . and the reports from key organizations furnished satisfactory totals. . . . Uncle Sam's foreign trade bounded in 1929. . . . Besides, Amos 'n' Andy are on the air every week-day night!"

A year later, in January 1931, Secretary of Commerce Robert P. Lamont issued a more guarded statement about "a period of general business unsettlement." But he was still not willing to concede that the economy had been dealt a crippling body blow. "Many evidences of business improvement appeared in the early months of 1930 . . . ," he observed. "Toward the middle of the year, however, it became clear that production in certain raw material areas had been setting too rapid a pace. . . . Toward the end of the year these cumulative forces were rapidly running their course and the apparent retardation in the rate of downward movement . . . supports the belief that the elements of recession have now spent most of their force."

In Seattle, and in the Northwest generally, the Depression was slower in taking its toll than in much of the rest of the country. For one thing, the region was less industrialized than other areas, in spite of the appearance lent by the belching smokestacks of Seattle's lumber mills. In 1914, a peak year in Northwest industrialization, the average value added by manufacture in Seattle, Tacoma, and Portland was $157, compared with $400 to $500 in such cities as Detroit and Pittsburgh. For another, as *Business Week* noted in 1930, the diversification of Pacific Coast industry and agriculture helped its business to fare better than that of other parts of the nation. And *Argus* columnist Abel K. Yerkes proclaimed, "Regardless of what may happen elsewhere, I am going to say this and mean it: Nothing can stop Seattle!"

Seattle may not have been stopped, but it was slowed considerably. *The Star,* which boasted in 1931 that one "square meal" a day was available to any hungry man, sponsored a soup kitchen where some two thousand fell in line each day. Less attractive were soup lines at the Salvation Army and the Volunteers of America, which made sermons and hymns the price of a meal. In 1932 the Unemployed Citizens' League organized the city into twenty-two districts to run a sort of social experiment in which the unemployed bartered their skills.

Pacific Car and Foundry soon became one of Seattle's most depressed businesses. The slowdown in railroad car orders was general, but even more pronounced for the wooden cars that the company was uniquely situated to build. No new car orders at all came in during 1930,

Pacific Car and Foundry, seeking diversification from the railcar business, began building buses, along with other American car companies, in 1928.

a situation that was to prevail over the next six years. Just before the Depression struck, Pacific Car had acquired the Arrow Pump Company. A few pumps were manufactured, but little more was obtained from that transaction than a new machine shop foreman, Dick Hutsell.

In 1930 net income dropped to $53,000, and preferred stock dividends were cut to $64,000, or half of the annual accrual. No dividends were paid in 1931 or 1932, when operations resulted in net losses of $171,000 and $191,000. The company's total assets dwindled from $2 million at the end of 1930 to less than $1.6 million two years later.

In his 1931 report to stockholders, President Carroll wrote: "The loss shown is the result of the abnormal business conditions which prevailed throughout the country but, more particularly, of the almost total lack of buying by the railroads and the lumber industry. . . . Your Company, seeking to diversify its products, has engaged in the fabrication of structural steel bridges and other steel structures, has added a new department for the manufacture of drop forgings and Arrow rotary pumps, has designed a new Log Yarder and has developed a new cast steel metal. . . . Your Company's experience in these new lines has been sufficiently encouraging to warrant its continuance therein and its belief that, as business conditions improve, its earnings will be materially augmented thereby."

The next year the report was gloomier, and stressed a policy of imposing rigid economies and of reducing "executive and other payrolls." These economies naturally exacted a severe toll in human terms. Seven department heads were laid off in 1932. Members of the engineering department were put on a two-weeks-on, two-weeks-off schedule, unless an order had come in involving their specialties.

For some of the workers the layoffs were not a total disaster. Many had purchased "stump farms" in the hills around Seattle, and used their newfound free time to work their land. And there were frequent human touches. One worker had bought a 1932 Pontiac just before he was laid off, and still owed the bulk of the purchase price. It was clear that he would lose the car, which was his pride. When the plant superintendent, Frank Stewart, heard of it, he went to the man and said, "Here's the money. Don't worry about it. When you get back on your feet, why, we'll talk about it some more."

To safeguard any unused cash, the executive committee put it into government securities, but in dwindling amounts. In January 1931, they decided to buy $150,000 of U.S. Liberty Loan 4.25 percent bonds; the following year their investment dropped to $50,000.

In June 1932 the trustees discussed abandonment of the Portland plant. After hearing the cost of dismantling it and moving the equipment, they decided to leave it as it was. Toward the end of the year the board decided that Carroll and Curd should come to New York to discuss the business and prospects of the company. After full discussion, the board resolved that "no action should be taken at this time with respect to a curtailment of the Company's sales and production activities but that . . . the officers should continue their efforts to make effective further economies, if . . . at all possible."

In 1933 much attention was devoted to the need to file codes of fair competition in Pacific Car's various lines of business under the National Recovery Act. Carroll was authorized to assent to the code for the railway car building industry—which had come to a virtual standstill. At the Pacific Car board's first meeting in 1934 there was a prolonged discussion "of the Company's continuing as a car builder or engaging only in miscellaneous business. . . . It was voted to refer the entire matter to the Executive Committee with power."

Carcometal, because of its strength and weight properties, found immediate acceptance even in the depressed metals market of the early 1930s.

— SCRATCHING FOR BUSINESS —

If any one individual was principally responsible for keeping Pacific Car and Foundry afloat during the dark days of the early 1930s, it was Alex Finlayson, the metallurgist.

Finlayson came to the company in the 1920s, with degrees in law, chemistry, and metallurgy, and with nationally recognized talents. He had taught at Princeton, which wanted him to return, but Curd was aware of his capabilities, and was able to convince him to stay on. At various times Finlayson was foundry manager, manager of the laboratory and of special engineering. He traveled frequently for the company.

While Pacific Car and Foundry rarely interfered with the private lives of its employees, there had always been a strong, even puritanical, feeling about drinking on the job or drinking to such excess that it interfered with work. But Finlayson was an exception to this rule, and his fondness for strong drink was known and quietly tolerated. A diabetic, he made a careful study of the ailment, and managed to keep his diabetes, his chemistry, and his love for Scotch whiskey in exquisite balance.

An engineer, Jarvis Stixrood, recalled that he once had to get a Sharpey specimen—a piece of broken steel kept in the deep freeze—from a refrigerator in the foundry. Finlayson opened the freezer door and picked out the specimen. When Stixrood saw what looked like popsicles inside, he inquired, "What are those?"

"They're popsicles," said Finlayson.

"You've got a refrigerator here. Why don't you keep them in that?"

"These are whiskey popsicles," Finlayson explained.

When he came to Pacific Car, Finlayson had been working on new metal alloys with desirable properties. His research continued after he joined the company, and in 1930 he found what he had been looking for in a steel with low carbon content, but high in manganese, copper, and silicon. With twice the strength of basic steel, it was good for annealed castings, and with a high degree of elastic strength, it was ideal for use in machines, such as tractors, where its light weight was important.

He patented the new material, and named it Carcometal. Chriswell saw an opportunity to sell auxiliary tractor and heavy logging equipment to the same customers who had formerly purchased logging cars, so he had his engineers design a new Carco line of tractor winches, arches, and hoists. The new material not only offered superior service and longer machine life to the customer, but also reduced manufacturing costs for the company.

Carcometal enabled Pacific Car to reduce the weight of equipment to be drawn behind and carried on tractors—a log trailer to take the place of the conventional arch, single drum reversible hoists to be used with the log trailers, double drum hoists with two speeds on each drum for such tasks as clear-cut logging, and combination bulldozers and trailbuilders for various sizes and models of tractors.

A Portland company was then using ordinary carbon steel to build arches—mobile, derrick-like frames used with tractors to lift heavy loads, such as clusters of logs, and transport them from the woods to a loading station. Extremely heavy, the arches would break down frequently. So Chriswell conceived the idea of making arches lighter and stronger by using Carcometal. Pacific Car engineers designed them to be used with steel belts.

The first substantial order came from the Fruit Growers Supply Company, for six tractors with Carcometal arches. Then more were sold up and down the Pacific coast, but mostly in California, where the timbering was on more open ground and tractors could move around more easily than on Washington's rugged forest terrain. In time, tractor logging all but did away with the donkey engine. Using bulldozer blades, it became possible to build a logging road for trucks and trailers in just a few days.

An agent once called Chriswell to say he had sold some Carcometal arches to a lumber company, but that they needed a hoist to fit on their Allis-Chalmers tractor. "We are going to lose the order for the arches," he said, "unless we can change the hoist. Can you furnish one?"

"I don't know," said Chriswell. "How much does the hoist cost?"

The agent looked it up and said, "They are selling them for $1,200."

"All right, I'll call you back."

Chriswell talked it over with Carroll, who was usually cooperative with the engineers and who told him to go ahead and design the hoist. Chriswell then called the agent back and told him, "We'll build an arch, and we'll get a hoist. The price is $1,500. If you can sell it, that's the price."

The agent called back to say he had already made two sales. That was in April of 1932. By the first of July, Chriswell mounted the new hoist on a tractor.

Following the arches and hoists came winches, also made of Carcometal and designed to be attached to a tractor and to couple directly with its power drive. The initial Carco winch was built later in 1932. Designated the HS-101, it was the first tractor winch with a fully housed gear train and anti-friction bearings in an oil bath. It boasted a one-piece, heavily ribbed cast steel case to keep gears, shafts, and bearings aligned, in order to cut maintenance expense and reduce downtime for repairs. Design features like these in time made the Carco winch an industry standard. The company built special winches for Allis-Chalmers, International Harvester, and Oliver-Cletrac tractors, all approved by the engineering departments of their manufacturers, as well as for Caterpillar tractors, to serve buyers who specified the Carco line.

In their efforts to get business wherever it might be available, Curd and Finlayson journeyed to Alaska in June and July of 1932. They made stops wherever they knew that heavy equipment was being used—at Skagway, Dawson, Nenana, Fairbanks, Anchorage, Kennecott, and Juneau.

Their visits were mainly with railroad operators and with mining, dredging, and prospecting operations. On the whole, they were well received, but they found that the business doldrums had spread from the States to Alaska. At the narrow-gauge White Pass and Yukon Railway, for example, they found that no parts purchases other than a few brake shoes had been made for a long time, even though the line had two hundred freight cars. A bank president in Fairbanks advised them to extend credit to only one successful dredge operator and to sell to others only for cash—a commodity of which they had little or none. Other prospective buyers were cordial enough, but said their purchases were all made from Seattle or San Francisco.

Some of those who were already using Pacific Car products appeared to hold them in high regard. In many instances Curd and Finlayson were told that they were the first representatives of any foundry that had ever visited the Alaskan installations. In the conclusion of his report Curd wrote:

> The business we can reasonably expect out of the Yukon Territory and Alaska will be almost entirely alloy castings and . . . forgings. This business is all in connection with the gold mining operations—both dredge and mill. We found no particular use for Carcometal as the grade of castings we are now furnishing filled their requirements very satisfactorily. There is practically no structural work . . .
>
> Summed up, this trip was not directly productive but I feel it was well worth while. I believe we stamped the name of the Pacific Car and Foundry Company indelibly upon the minds of all those worthwhile in the organizations we visited. . . . I am also firmly convinced had we not made this trip we would never have gotten a chance at any of this business.

Page 90: Pacific Car and Foundry first introduced the Carco hoist (winch) to the depressed logging and construction industry in 1932.

Left: Pacific Car and Foundry general manager Harry Curd and chief metallurgist Alex Finlayson made a sales trip through Alaska in 1932, where among other accounts, they called on the White Pass & Yukon Railroad only to find that business there, too, was severely depressed.

Metal technology was the company's major asset when Paul Pigott regained ownership of the company in 1934.

— PIGOTTS TAKE OVER AGAIN —

There were those in Seattle who had always felt that Pacific Car and Foundry Company should be a locally owned and controlled enterprise. None was more so inclined than Paul Pigott, whose unhappiness over the sale to American Car and Foundry Company had never been fully erased from his mind.

In the waning fortunes of the company during the Depression he saw an opportunity to take the company back again. He discussed the matter with other major holders of the preferred stock, and they agreed to have him make the effort.

American Car and Foundry executives readily assented to his proposal. It was clear to them that, in a money-losing enterprise, there was little real value beyond the interests of the preferred stockholders. So, for the nominal sum of $50,000, they sold their interest in Pacific Car and Foundry Company to the two sons of William Pigott and their small group of Seattle associates in February 1934.

At a board meeting late in January, William Hager tendered his resignation as board chairman and member of the executive committee of Pacific Car. The resignation was accepted, and Hardy was elected to succeed him to the two posts. Then, at the annual meeting of shareholders on February 27, the transfer of power became an accomplished fact. None of the representatives of American Car, including Hardy and Carroll, stood for reelection. Elected in their place as a board of directors were the Pigott brothers, James Twohy, T. S. Clingan, Robert A. Hulbert, Curd, and Bassage.

The board then elected Paul Pigott the new president of Pacific Car; Curd, vice president and general manager; William Pigott Jr., vice president and treasurer; and Bassage, secretary and assistant treasurer.

It was Paul Pigott who signed the letter to stockholders that accompanied Pacific Car's annual report, issued in April. The news remained gloomy. The operating loss for the year was $178,000. From this could be deducted almost $15,000 in interest on securities and discounts earned, but there were also non-operating losses: $4,000 in bad debts, a $1,000 drop in value of securities owned, and almost $25,000 in revaluing inventories downward. The net loss for the year was thus $193,000.

Assets shown on the balance sheet totaled just over $1.5 million, while the company's accumulated deficit was more than $500,000. Working capital was in fairly good order, with current assets of $946,000 set against current liabilities of just $215,000.

In his report, however, Paul Pigott struck a mildly hopeful note. "There was an improvement in the volume of business contracts by this company during the last few months of 1933," he wrote, "and this improvement has continued for the first three months of 1934. However, without obtaining any substantial logging car or standard railway car orders it is unlikely that any large sums can be earned, although the company is now operating under a policy of the strictest economy, and every effort to obtain diversified small business, that can be successfully completed with our present plant and equipment, is being made. However, the volume of this business has not been such to date as to completely cover all operating and fixed charges of the Seattle and Portland plants."

Paul Pigott saw a substantial market for Carco tractor equipment, although it would not compensate for the absence of railcar orders.

CHAPTER FIVE

REBUILDING THE COMPANY

It was not much of a company that Paul Pigott and his group of associates repurchased from American Car and Foundry. With no railroad cars manufactured for years, there had been little incentive to maintain the car-building shops. Operations in other parts of the plant had been minimal, and the owners felt no inclination to purchase new equipment or to do anything more than basic upkeep.

Because of the general air of neglect and vacancy, most people were inclined to go along with a local banker's description of the plant as a "run-down pile of rust." The buildings that had once hummed with activity and that gave employment to 1,500 workers in the peak car-building years of 1923 and 1924 had taken on an unaccustomed air of quiet. There were only about 124 employees, and few of those could count on working full time for twelve months a year.

Even worse, perhaps, was the gloomy market outlook in the depressed Northwest. Overall factory employment in 1933 was less than 60 percent of what it had been in 1929, lumber exports were down to less than half of what they had been, and mining output in Idaho dropped from $32 million to $9 million between 1929 and 1932. In some areas wheat prices were as low as 20 cents a bushel, not even enough to pay freight charges; in Oregon and Washington, growers were luckier, getting 37 cents, still hardly enough to cover their costs. In many a fruit orchard, apple and prune trees were pulled up to be burned as fuel.

But despair was not universal. When Thomas Gleed, a Seattle-First National banker, asked, "What are you buying that rust pile for?", Paul Pigott had a ready answer. "Because I think I should furnish employment to the extent that I can."

Like his father before him, Pigott believed in the Northwest, in its people, and in its future. At Wallace Bridge and Structural Steel Company, where he had worked for almost ten years and had risen to the rank of assistant to the president, he spent much of his time selling bridge and steel construction projects. There he got a sense of the sweep and power and potential of the region. But, as he later was to tell his good friend John McCone, he regarded his years with Wallace Bridge as primarily a training period for the real work of his life. By background, personality, and instinct, he felt driven to build, to create work, and more specifically to make Pacific Car and Foundry again one of the Northwest's more active and respected enterprises.

Pacific Car increased its share of the tractor equipment market, including winches and dozer blades, while waiting for the railroads to resume car purchases.

His wealth was enough to provide amply for himself and his family. But wealth, he felt, had a more important purpose—to be used, to be put to work for people. He had a deep personal concern for the welfare and problems of the firm's employees, past and present, many of whom he had known since his childhood.

They shared his sentiments. Whereas Pacific Car and Foundry was "the Car Company" to most of its managers and executives, to the men on the line it was more simply "the car works." In the little town of Renton it was a focus and centerpiece of their lives. If the plant was working on or had been awarded a new contract, the place to hear about it first was in the barber shop or tavern. More than a few homes sported Pacific Car colors, their owners using surplus paint from the car shops. A number of families already had a second generation in the plant's work force, with no thought of children or grandchildren going elsewhere.

But Paul Pigott also had a businessman's sense of the appropriate balance between production and sales, costs and prices, and of the paramount need for investment to yield a return. Otherwise, he was aware, wealth and jobs might all fade away. From his work at Wallace Bridge, as well as what he had heard in family councils, he had a good grasp of Pacific Car affairs—who on the staff was weak and who was strong, where there was deadwood and where there were oak timbers.

To make Pacific Car a vital and viable enterprise he set up a three-point program: (1) diversify the product line; (2) rehabilitate the plant; and (3) build a top-caliber engineering and production team.

Everyone knew there was small hope of any railroad car business developing soon. The nation's railroads already had more cars than they could use, and those they had were repaired in their own shops. Any orders that might come through probably would be for steel cars, not for the wooden ones in which the Northwest specialized, and go to Eastern shops. "We have to come on line with some new products," Pigott said. "In reacquiring this company, we've got to invent some things to do."

The inventing was done from spartan offices in Seattle's White-Henry-Stuart Building— a space two windows wide, divided into offices for president Pigott and corporate secretary Bassage, with room for two secretaries at the corridor end. It was anything but impressive to a visitor, but Pigott knew that the way to impress his customers was with product quality and reliability, not office decor.

The first moves were made in those lines in which the company had been most successful in the past, such as logging equipment—particularly the heavy-work accessories that could take full advantage of the crawler tractors coming into use in the logging industry. To complement such earlier Pacific Car innovations as the logging sulky, winch and arch, the company created a new line of hoists, bulldozer blades, and power winches to increase the versatility and utility of the tractors. Pacific Car engineers developed a line of extra-heavy pulling winches, some of them with double or triple drums, to help drag and yard huge logs, up to 10 or 15 feet in diameter, out of the western woods.

In other areas, the company scraped and scratched to get what work it could, and to turn out whatever products its equipment could fashion. At various times Pacific Car was making, along with its more traditional lines, such items as fish salters, pineapple pickers, and light poles.

Gradually the company began to take on more and more work in some of its old familiar lines—building steel members for railroad and highway bridges, or for the rare building construction project that might come along. One summer a part of the plant was kept busy making

MANUFACTURED
BY
PACIFIC CAR AND FOUNDRY COMPANY

a huge dredge for the U.S. Refining and Mining Company, in Alaska. Affectionately known as a "doodle bug," the dredge consisted mainly of a string of conveyors and heavy equipment, perhaps two-thirds of a city block long, to be used to haul gravel out of Alaskan rivers.

These efforts soon began to be reflected in operating results. Before the end of 1934 employment doubled, to 250 workers, as more jobs came into the plant. Gross sales for the year climbed to $724,000, and in 1935 they mounted even more rapidly, to $1,247,000. The company was still operating in the red, but the net loss was sharply reduced, from $193,000 in 1933 to $75,000 in 1934, and most of that represented depreciation charges and a $25,000 write-off of inventory values, losses that had been accumulating over the years.

During 1934 the company built an 84-foot crane runway, its first capital improvement in many years, to enable it to take on business that it previously could not handle. A single bridge fabrication job booked that year was enough to justify the expenditure.

Of the tractor auxiliary equipment, the annual report said it "is now firmly established throughout the Pacific Coast and we enjoyed a substantial business last year, with very favorable prospects for this year. This business in itself is profitable, but the volume is not sufficient to carry the burden of the non-operating car building facilities."

In 1935 the company's net loss was trimmed back even further, to a bare $1,200. The expected increase took place in logging equipment sales. "Our inventory of used logging equipment has been reduced," Pigott reported to the stockholders, "collections of past due accounts have been good and the plant has been well maintained." While there were some orders for railroad car parts to be used in repair work, there were still no car orders. "Until the railroads again place orders for heavy equipment . . . ," said the report, "our principal business will be the fabrication of steel structures, the building of logging equipment and the sale of steel and alloy castings."

— ACQUIRING HOFIUS STEEL —

The business that was started by William Hofius back in 1895, which became the Hofius Steel & Equipment Company, fell on hard times early in the Depression, just as did many a similar enterprise. In mid-1933 the business became insolvent and was closed down. Clarence Styer, who had retired from Pacific Car and Foundry, leased the building and its equipment, calling his new business Steel Fabricators, Incorporated.

In 1936 Styer's company was up for sale. Pacific Car and Foundry bought Steel Fabricators, Incorporated, which then became the company's Structural Steel Division. Styer and his principal aide, Paul Jacobsen, continued to run the plant for Pacific Car. Paul Pigott, meanwhile, purchased at a bank foreclosure sale the old Hofius plant that Styer had leased, and became Pacific Car's landlord for that property.

It was a business with which Pacific Car was thoroughly familiar, but generally conducted on a larger scale. It was devoted almost entirely to the fabrication and erection of steel for dams, bridges, and industrial buildings. To a large extent, the orders came mainly from city, state, and federal authorities, which sponsored the lion's share of such major construction activities during the Depression years, both to create jobs and to channel energies toward useful projects.

The company's engineering staff was divided into mechanical and structural departments. Chriswell was put in charge of the mechanical engineers, supervising work on logging products and on the development of new uses for Carcometal. Alex Thompson took over the structural department, and in short order this came to include the estimating function.

At first the structural jobs that came to the company were small, run-of-the-mill projects. Then the state saw fit to give Pacific Car the steel fabrication work for bridges planned for the western terminus of the Sunset highway (I-90) over Lake Washington to Seattle.

A growing number of steel fabrication orders then began to come from the federal government for work on major projects, including the Grand Coulee, Bonneville, La Grande, and Ross dams, buildings for the Bremerton Navy Yard on Puget Sound, and private contracts such as the Boeing plants in Seattle and Renton. The Structural Steel Division became a two-hundred-man shop that was responsible for some fairly sophisticated machine shop fabrication. For the dams they built such elements as the penstocks, the water control gates, and the huge, curved retainer gates at the top.

Bridge work involved working from line drawings supplied by the sponsoring authorities —county, state, or Army Engineers—and then doing the detailed engineering drawings. The standard elements used would be the I-beams, H-beams, or channels rolled by the major mills, most often U.S. Steel or Bethlehem. Then Pacific Car's detail draftsmen would plan the placement of holes, clips, angles, down to a sixteenth of an inch, so that all the pieces would fit together in the finished bridge, with an overall assembly drawing as the construction road map. A major project undertaken in 1939 was for a floating bridge across Lake Washington.

While Pacific Car was able to provide an increasing number of jobs for workers in the mid-1930s, the executive ranks were filled more slowly. One who joined the company early in

The Lake Washington
Floating Bridge,
using structural steel
components supplied
by Pacific Car and
Foundry, was completed
in 1940.

1937 was Ferdinand Schmitz, who had been working as a paper mill superintendent, and who let a friend know that he was anxious to return to Seattle and be rid of the brand of office politics that prevailed in big companies. Before long, Paul Pigott wrote to him to ask for a meeting.

Pigott outlined the company's work to Schmitz, showed him the plant, and took him to the Rainier Club for lunch. Asked what he thought about working there, Schmitz said, "It certainly looks interesting. Of course, there is always that matter of compensation."

"I've got nothing to do with that," Pigott told him. "You have to see Harry Curd about that."

Schmitz went to see Curd, whom he had known and who said to him, "Well, Ferdie, we would sure like to have you with us." But when Schmitz told him his salary was then $600 a month, Curd was slowed down. "Our top salary out there is $275 a month. I just can't pay you more than that." And Schmitz replied, "Okay, I'll take it."

He then went to see Pigott, and to tell him, "Well, I guess you've hired yourself somebody." And Pigott told him, "You're the only person that I have hired since I've had the company."

"What do I do?" Schmitz asked him. "You learn the business," was the reply.

Schmitz was given an office and set about on his assigned task—which he also deemed to be selling himself to the plant foremen. He toured the plants, noted such things as a flock of sheep in the yard to keep the grass down, and heard of the load of railroad car wheels that had dropped into the mud flats and sunk out of sight, never to be found. When, after a suitable interval for becoming acquainted with the plant, Pigott asked him what he thought of it, Schmitz replied, "I guess the sheriff hasn't taken over, so I think we are lucky."

Schmitz was made the assistant general manager, under Curd. When he suggested an incentive bonus system, such as there had been at his previous position, Pigott replied, "Why don't you put it in? If we could pay it we could all make more money." Schmitz installed it, and all management personnel, himself included, were soon making 15 to 20 percent more.

One irritant for Schmitz was the annual rent of $5,500 that the company paid to Pigott. One day, Pigott, feeling that the company's cash position was improving, asked Schmitz: "How would you and Curd like to buy the structural plant for the car company?" "We would sure like to get rid of the rent that we have to pay every month," Schmitz answered. "What is your price?" Replied Pigott, "Just what I paid for it—$50,000." So, on June 30, 1938, Pacific Car bought the plant from Mr. and Mrs. Paul Pigott for $50,000.

— BUSES AND TROLLEYS —

In April 1936, Pacific Car and Foundry Company purchased Heiser's Incorporated, a financially troubled manufacturer of bus and truck cabs, for $23,000. When Heiser's had become insolvent, it executed an assignment of its assets for the benefit of creditors to the Seattle Association of Credit Men. Pacific Car's purchase was from the credit association. The contract provided that the association was to realize 50 percent of the profits from Pacific Car's new motor coach division until the end of 1939.

To enter this new field of activity, Pacific Car decided to utilize facilities at the Renton plant that had been largely unused, and established a Motor Coach Division. "The field for the manufacture and sale of motor coaches seems to be enlarging," said the company's 1936 report to shareholders.

The new division began to build bus bodies, some for city and intercity transit, but mainly for schools. At the start, this activity was anything but profitable. Periodically the North Coast Transportation Company, which was owned by the Puget Sound Power and Light Company,

Buses, infrequently manufactured by Pacific Car since the late 1920s, became more important after the 1936 purchase of Heiser and Tricoach and the association with the Newell brothers.

would order six buses that they used on regular trips to Portland—three of them from Pacific Car and three from the Tricoach Corporation, of Seattle. For Pacific Car there was no profit in filling these orders, but Tricoach somehow managed to make a profit on them.

Tricoach, it turned out, had a problem that dovetailed with Pacific Car's. The Tricoach Corporation had been started in 1934 by the Newell brothers—Richard, a designer and engineer who had worked for Heiser, and Robert, a bus salesman who worked for a Portland firm. They were financed by George Yost, the aging operator of bus lines around Seattle. Both brothers excelled at their specialties, but when they heard that Seattle was planning to convert from streetcars to buses and trolley coaches, they knew that they were in a good position to get the business, but that their small shop could not handle it.

When the interstate Washington Motor Coach Company ran a special demonstration bus trip on some brand-new vehicles, both Pigott and the Newell brothers were aboard. They talked, and Pigott asked if they were interested in a joint venture. They replied that they were indeed. More talks, with lawyers included, followed.

On August 3, 1938, they entered into a contract, to run until the end of 1945. Pigott was less interested in acquiring Tricoach than in securing the talents of its two chief executives. Basically it was a management agreement, rather than a sale or joint venture. Pacific Car leased Tricoach's small supply of machinery and equipment, and provided manufacturing space and financing. The Newell brothers were to manage the Motor Coach Division. The arrangement could be terminated at any time by either party. The Newells received nominal salary guarantees that started at $250 a month, and that eventually reached $500, plus a share in the profits of the division. Richard Newell later recalled that every new accountant who came to Pacific Car would try to reinterpret the contract in Pacific Car's favor. But Pigott would have none of it, and would say, "No, that was not the deal we made."

Pacific Car's engineers went to work designing a new model highway and city type of coach for which it was felt there would be a good market. And the Newell brothers set to their task, Bob as the go-getting salesman, Dick as the driving production man.

Dick Newell would not stand for what he regarded as nonsense from any quarter. In his second month, when he received the bill for heating his plant, he came to ask about the amount. "That's what we have been allocating to that building all the time," Schmitz told him. "Well," Newell replied, "with no meter on it I'm not going to pay it." A meter was put on the steam line.

At another time, Paul Pigott grew tired of looking out his office window at a pile of uncollected rubbish outside the Motor Coach Division's area. He had some people clean it up, and the bill—for $30—was sent to the division. Soon Dick Newell stomped into Pigott's office, and he demanded, "Where the hell did you get this figure?" "Well, that's for cleaning up out there," Pigott told him. "I'm running that plant," raged Newell, "and when it's time to clean up, I'll clean it up! I can clean it up for half of what you're charging here."

In spite of such economies, the Motor Coach Division failed to show a profit for three years. But in 1939 the division finally got into the black, and moved into a position to earn much more. In November of 1939 they received an order from the city of Seattle for the construction of one hundred trackless trolleys and thirty gasoline-driven passenger buses. To fill the order, Pacific Car entered into a joint venture with the J. E. Brill Company, of Philadelphia. Pacific Car was to assemble the trolley coaches under license from Brill, which was a subsidiary of American Car and Foundry Company.

— CHANGING THE CAPITAL STRUCTURE —

When the new owners took control of Pacific Car from American Car and Foundry, one circumstance may have been every bit as discouraging as the run-down condition of the plant. That was the albatross of an accumulated deficit, resulting from years of showing net losses, and the law's strictness against paying any dividends to investors until that deficit was wiped out.

One way to eliminate the deficit was to accumulate earnings, but the prospects for that were dim indeed in the mid-1930s. Another way was to recapitalize, and Paul Pigott had immediate plans to do this. In his first letter to shareholders, early in 1934, he wrote:

> No dividends can be paid to stockholders under the present capital structure, until the present . . . deficit of $538,679.88 has been eliminated, either by earnings or by some action on the part of the stockholders which would result in a reduced capital structure. In view of the large capitalization, it would appear advisable for the stockholders to consider some plan whereby the par value of the Preferred stock can be reduced to such an extent as to create a Capital Surplus account. If this is done, any earnings resulting in a profit can be distributed to the stockholders according to their respective interests.
>
> A plan is being formulated by the officers of the company, together with its attorneys, and will be mailed to the stockholders for their consideration in the near future.

At the time the company was repurchased, the outstanding capitalization consisted of 3,700 shares of Class A preferred, $100 par value; 14,995 shares of Class B preferred, $100 par value; and 36,000 shares of common, no par value but carried on the books at a nominal value of $3,600, or 10 cents a share. There were substantial arrearages owing on both classes

In 1939 Pacific Car, in conjunction with Brill, a division of American Car and Foundry, produced the Pacific Car and Foundry Brill flyer for the city of Seattle and other bus systems.

of preferred, since no dividends had been paid on these shares since June 1930. Pigott's initial proposal was to cancel all the common stock—most of which he and his family owned—and to convert the two classes of preferred into a new common stock, giving to the holders of Class A preferred two shares of the common for each preferred share they owned, and to holders of Class B preferred one share of common for each preferred share they owned.

After drafting such a proposal with the help of the company's lawyers, Paul Pigott wrote to his uncle, T. S. Clingan, then with Bethlehem Steel in San Francisco, to seek his advice on the move. Apparently "Uncle Scotty" was unimpressed, because the proposal never went to stockholders in that form. Instead, there was a much less radical change in capital structure, but one that nonetheless opened the way toward payment of dividends. An amendment to Pacific Car's articles of incorporation was filed in August 1934, providing for 3,700 shares of $100 par Class A preferred stock, 17,000 shares of no par Class B preferred, and 36,000 shares of no par common stock.

Changing the Class B preferred from $100 par to no par permitted a write-down in the stated value of the stock, resulting in a capital surplus that was larger than the accumulated earnings deficit. Also written down was the value of the common, from $3,600 to $1,800. The overall result was a surplus of almost $211,000 shown on the balance sheet at the end of 1934, in spite of the fact that there was an additional loss reported for the year.

By 1936, however, business had improved sufficiently for the company to show a net profit of $194,000, its first since 1930. And toward the end of 1936 the company wiped out all the arrears on the Class A preferred with a dividend payout of $144,000. The decision to do so was influenced as much by tax considerations as by a desire to clear the record. Pacific Car would actually have preferred to retain the earnings to build up its depleted capital, but this would have made the company subject to a depression-time "undistributed profits tax" of some $35,000.

With the dividend accruals paid off, the company was again in a position to retire any of the Class A stock it might be able to acquire at an appropriate price, out of surplus funds available. The 1936 year-end balance sheet showed a capital surplus of $873,000 and an earned surplus deficit of just $258,000, which had been reduced by some $50,000 in profits after dividend payments. The 1936 annual report said:

> If some suitable plan can be agreed upon which would retire all of the Class A stock it will be possible for the company to retain a large portion of its current earnings and at the same time escape the heavy undistributed profits tax by distributing its earnings partly in cash and the remainder in other ways. With this object in mind the officers of the company . . . are working upon a plan to be submitted to the stockholders which, if approved . . . , will bring about the desired objective.

A proposal to simplify the company's capital structure was approved by a large majority of stockholders during 1937, but because of protests by minority shareholders it was not put into effect. The company's attorneys and tax consultants also turned thumbs down on a plan to pay dividends on the Class B stock partly in cash and partly in dividend scrip or notes. After this, any basic change in the capital structure was to wait several more years.

In 1937 the company's sales rose dramatically, from $2,770,000 the previous year to $4,514,000. Earnings, however, dropped to $154,000 in the year's roller-coaster economy. Business

With an again empty rail yard at Renton in 1936, Pacific Car continued to update and further develop its plant.

rose sharply during the first eight months of the year, when the nation felt it was on the way to complete recovery from the Depression, then dropped precipitately with the onset of what was called the "Roosevelt recession" during the final four months. This time the company decided to retain all of its earnings but the $22,000 in current Class A preferred dividends, which it paid. There had been a substantial investment of capital funds during the year for a new machine shop building and a number of shop tools, to keep pace with the growth in sales of the logging equipment line.

The wisdom of retaining capital was underscored when sales dropped to $1,598,000 in 1938 and a net loss of $112,000 was shown, in good part because of development and advertising costs for new lines of logging equipment and motor coaches. The outlook for 1939 was much more promising, however, since substantial orders were received late in 1938 for structural steel and motor coaches. Even so, the report said, "dividend possibilities are quite remote for the near future."

The next year lived up to its promise, as 1939 sales rose to $2,776,000, resulting in a profit of $108,000 after taxes. Earnings had been buoyed by work on the Lake Washington bridge, by a high level of logging equipment sales, and by the first profits of the Motor Coach Division.

— PAUL PIGOTT IN CHARGE —

Those who worked closely with Paul Pigott soon learned to know him as a strong-minded, persistent, highly intelligent individual. He demanded a great deal of himself; from others he expected all of which they were capable, along with complete candor. Otherwise, they would feel the sting of his sarcasm. He strove to excel in everything that he did; he was an outstanding low-handicap golfer, and he and his brother, William, were bowling champions.

A longtime friend, Charles Lindeman, of the *Seattle Post-Intelligencer,* characterized him as:

. . . a sharp tongue and a sharp wit. He's a hard man to keep up with on repartee.

He's a restless, impatient man. Fishing and hunting, he'll run the legs off his companions —except that they have learned to let him take his own pace, and they stay back. When he casts, he expects a strike or he pushes on down the stream. Companions stay behind to work the waters more thoroughly; similarly they stay back to cover a cornfield better in pheasant hunting. At end of day, Paul may not have as much to show as his companions, but he wants to be on the move . . .

Pigott is headstrong, a man who assumes leadership of the party, instinctively . . . , without any prior arrangement. . . . Pigott is impatient with people who cannot keep up with him—mentally or physically.

He was nevertheless able to maintain excellent rapport with the workers in the plant. He would frequently wander around, speak to everyone on a personal level, find out what was going on, even work with tools to see how a job was handled. A general manager once dreaded to see Pigott's car pull into the parking lot, never knowing what to expect. So he developed a series of calling stations, with informants telling him where Pigott was and what he was doing, in order to be fully prepared for the ultimate visit in his office.

On another occasion, Pigott was in the steel shop, talking to a worker who was relating all his personal troubles. Touched, Pigott told him to take a couple of weeks off, promising, "We will pay you." That was in the days before paid vacations. Then the steel shop superintendent, Clarence Handlen, came into Pigott's office, his trademark steel rule glistening in his back pocket. He took out the rule, slapped it on his hand, and declared, "Pigott, if you want to run this goddam shop you go ahead and run it, but you are not going to run it when I'm around. Now, you either stay out of there or don't tell my employees what they can do." Pigott stayed away from the steel shop for the next eight months.

There was no written directive, but it was clearly understood that Paul Pigott, like his father before him, wanted the requests of any recognized church to be met by the shops. Churches planning new buildings or additions would usually have members of their congregations obtain the various bits and pieces needed and then contract the work. When members of any church, regardless of denomination, came to Pacific Car, it was clearly understood that they were to get what they wanted, with no profit or markup.

The first union in the plant under Paul Pigott was local 1368, which later became the Carbuilders Union. Started in the late 1930s, it was purely and simply a company union, initiated by the company, and largely controlled by the company through a president the company named. But in labor-conscious Seattle, other more legitimate unions soon came into the plant.

Pacific Car's resumption of railroad car building began in 1936, after a six-year drought, with an order of 500 refrigerator cars from the Pacific Fruit Express Company, aggregating about $1 million. The order was also chiefly responsible for the company's first profit in six years, and it buoyed hopes for a general resumption of car building.

The company then completed about a dozen mine cars and a caboose for the Alaska Railroad. More sizable orders arrived early in 1937. Pacific Fruit Express ordered 500 refrigerator cars, Northern Pacific 520 boxcars, and Western Pacific 50 flatcars. But orders dried up in the late months of 1937, and the company built no railroad cars at all during 1938. In 1939 some flatcars were ordered by local railroads.

In the company's annual report for 1939, Pigott made a general assessment of the company's car building operations, and the conclusion was inescapable that he no longer regarded this as the company's major or potentially major source of business. From 1920 to 1929, he pointed out, approximately 88 percent of Pacific Car's business was in building new or rebuilding old railroad cars. From 1930 to 1939, however, railroad car orders accounted for only 41 percent of the company's aggregate of $15 million in orders. Wrote Pigott:

> It has been evident to your management for a number of years that it would be increasingly difficult to maintain a profitable operation if we had to depend principally upon the railroads for our orders and as a consequence considerable moneys have been spent to equip our plant to engage in other lines of manufacturing. It is significant that in 1939 we have reported a profit although car orders accounted for only 4% of our sales.
>
> During the last ten-year period . . . approximately $600,000 has been put into the plant to acquire new machinery and equipment. A much improved plant equipped to actively seek other types of business on a competitive basis has resulted, even though our working capital has been materially reduced.

Even as this was written, Pacific Car and Foundry had begun to move in its next major direction. War had broken out in Europe, and the company was beginning to look into and quote on a number of contract proposals for the awakening defense efforts of the U.S. government and for the British Purchasing Mission in the United States.

The 1936 Pacific Fruit Express purchase of refrigerator cars was the first order for rolling stock received by Pacific Car since 1929.

■

CHAPTER SIX

■

THE WAR YEARS

Although the United States was not yet a direct participant in the war, 1940 was a year of rapidly mounting activity in virtually all of its industrial plants. As Americans went back to work, war and the uneasy prospect that the United States might be drawn into the hostilities replaced economic depression as the nation's primary concern.

At the Pacific Car and Foundry Company, business increased for all of the major departments. The Motor Coach Division completed its production and delivery of the gasoline coaches and trackless trolleys for the city of Seattle at a profit. Orders for logging equipment rose with the increased demand for the lumber and by-products of the Northwest forests. And the fabricated structural steel department was busy filling the steel needs of aircraft plants, the Navy Yard, and airport construction, along with the normal structural steel requirements for highways and bridges. Even the railway car business joined the new swell of activity early in 1941, when the Pacific Fruit Express Company ordered one thousand refrigerator cars, enough to keep the car-building facilities busy for six or seven months, after three years of sharply curtailed operation and idleness.

Total sales for 1940 were up almost 50 percent to more than $4 million. Net profit rose to $163,000, after provision for depreciation and for $73,000 in income and excess profits taxes.

Pacific Car also got its first orders for the nation's defense program during 1940. A joint venture with the Lake Washington Shipyard was awarded one contract from the U.S. Navy to build flotation devices to hold anti-submarine nets, and another for six small seaplane tenders. The role of Pacific Car in executing the contract was minimal, consisting of no more than fabricating some of the materials, but its part in providing the lion's share of the financing was indispensable. Pacific Car also got a Navy Department contract to build fifteen steel barges.

When the Newell brothers observed the pronounced shift from civilian to defense activity in industrial plants, they felt there was little future in their contract, which was restricted to bus bodies. So they asked Pigott to release them from it. Instead, he suggested that they revise the contract to incorporate certain areas of defense work. At the time, Paul Pigott was a director of Boeing Airplane Company, Pacific Car's Renton neighbor, and a friend of Philip Johnson, Boeing's president. Boeing had received its biggest contract to date for building something over five hundred B-17 bombers, and was looking for others to take over part of the work. Pacific Car

Mrs. Eleanor Roosevelt addressed Pacific Car and Foundry employees, as Paul Pigott looked on, speaking of the war and asking them to "buy bonds."

was thus in a good position to get in on the ground floor as a Boeing subcontractor, and it was asked to fabricate aluminum wing spars for the aircraft, a job that was largely turned over to the Newells.

All of this industrial activity was soon reflected in Pacific Car's 1940 balance sheet. Current assets rose to $1,832,000, and current liabilities to $1,060,000. While this provided a comfortable margin in terms of financial strength, bank borrowings were still needed to keep the plants humming. It was therefore deemed prudent to increase the company's working capital further, so no dividend action was taken during 1940.

The wing spar work continued through most of 1941. The first B-17s were on their way to Hawaii when the Japanese hit Pearl Harbor on December 7, 1941.

— BUILDING SHERMAN TANKS —

While Pacific Car was able to get subcontracts from its neighbor and Navy contracts in the Seattle area, Washington, D.C., was the place to look for Army work. Ferdinand Schmitz was one of those who made frequent trips to the East, and he encountered Ray Middleton, who had been a major in Army Ordnance during World War I, and who used his connections to help industrial firms find their way through the Army Department maze and land production contracts. Middleton was one of Washington's "5 percenters," who did their work for 5 percent of the profits on contracts they helped obtain.

Pigott sent Alex Finlayson to interview Middleton. Then Pigott, Alex Thompson, and the machine shop foreman went to Washington to confer with Finlayson. At the airport, Finlayson delivered an unflattering report. But Pigott wanted to press on further, and ultimately he and Schmitz saw Middleton about getting some contracts for castings. He asked them what kind of facilities they had, and they told him it was a car-building plant. "Why don't you build tanks?" he suggested.

Middleton did the negotiating, and secured an order for Pacific Car to build General Sherman M4-A1 tanks. Another Middleton client was the Continental Steel Company, of Chicago, which was casting hulls for turrets for the tanks. From them Thompson obtained a huge bundle of blueprints for the complete tank. He turned that over to his estimator, who came up with a figure of $200,000 per tank.

Pacific Car, with a variety of related skills but no experience in building armor products, and with a foundry that was too small, began building army tanks. Dick Newell, who had gained much experience in line production on the trolley and gasoline coaches, was put in charge of the tank-assembly line. The men on the line did not have much difficulty in switching from the manufacture of heavy railway cars to the tanks. The equipment used for railcar manufacturing simplified the job of handling heavy parts, and the assembly line had plenty of know-how in welding a number of component parts. Indeed, the transition was so smooth that the company was shipping tanks manufactured in June on flatcars it had completed in May.

The first Sherman tank was delivered to an Army Ordnance Proving Ground in May 1942. The official letter of acceptance pronounced it "the very best that had been at the Proving Center."

Almost all of the castings required for the manufacture of the tanks—seventy-three steel and twenty-one armor—were cast by the company in its own foundry, more than any other manufacturer of similar tanks. The only castings that had to be shipped in were the largest— the bulky hull and the smaller turret, cast from armor plate.

The geometry of the casting work was anything but simple. There were a great many curved sections, rather than the squared corners that lend themselves to casting, and there were differing thicknesses of metal in various parts of the tank. The castings were machined to exacting tolerances by machine tools provided by the government, and the company's machine shop produced the gun mounts in their entirety. The sheet metal work, estimated at almost a sixth of the entire tank operation, along with the small amount of upholstery used for the seats, was done by the Motor Coach Division. The main gear for revolving the turret was not made by Pacific Car, but subcontracted outside.

In 1940 the company's metallurgists had modified Carcometal to produce some of the highest-quality cast armor then available. Further research turned up ways of cutting down the scarce metals used in alloys for cast armor, without impairing the quality. This work also increased machinability of the metal, achieved greater uniformity, and cut back sharply the time for its production. The time saving was accomplished mainly through new methods of heat-treating, which consisted of heating the metal to a certain point in ovens, maintaining the

Over nine hundred Sherman tanks were manufactured by Pacific Car and Foundry during World War II.

temperature for a certain period, depending on the thickness of the metal, then quenching it to draw it down to the proper level of hardness. Experiments helped cut the heat-treating time cycle from seventy-two to less than nine hours.

In June 1942 the Ordnance Department commended Pacific Car both for producing larger quantities of cast armor without sacrifice of quality and for the alloy metal savings. The company was one of five in the United States accredited for casting armor plate. The company turned over the results of this research to the government for use by others. The other foundries supplying cast armor used many strategically scarce materials, such as nickel, boron, rare earths, and chromium. Pacific Car was always able to dispense with the first three, and ended its use of the fourth in 1943.

A new, modern foundry at Pacific Car had long been one of Finlayson's dreams. With the tank contract, the government promised to build such a plant, with the capability of casting tank hulls and turrets. Pacific Car, which was to lease the building, helped draw up the plans. Included in the foundry design were a number of heat-treating ovens for the cast armor.

Almost simultaneously with the start of the tank-building program, the Defense Plant Corporation began to put up the foundry. The Atherton Construction Company erected the new building on Pacific Car's lake bottom land. To support the building's weight, they drove a forest of two thousand piles into the ground, held in place by their own skin friction and cut off below the permanent water level to eliminate rotting. Waterproofing was required for all the foundry pits in the plant.

When finished in early 1943, the new installation was the largest and most modern electric steel furnace foundry in the country. An eighth of a mile long and covering some 167,000 square feet, it contained approximately 1,400 tons of structural steel. Although it was equipped for daylight operation, it was to be totally blacked out, so that operations would not be interrupted in the event of the air raid alarms still expected on the Pacific Coast. The electric furnaces were powered by a transformer substation that furnished twice the electrical energy used by the nearby Boeing plant. Temperatures were automatically controlled, and castings were mechanically charged, discharged, and quenched. Underground storage tanks could hold 12,000 gallons of diesel oil for the heat-treating and annealing furnaces and core ovens.

The tank work required other facilities, as well. A proving ground was set up, with a firing range for the big tank guns. The Army plant inspectors also insisted on the installation of a sprinkling system. Pacific Car said they could not afford it, but the Army insisted that work on the contract could not go on without it. An agreement was finally worked out under which the Army would have the system installed, and Pacific Car would repay the costs when the tanks were all delivered.

War work, treated by many concerns as a bonanza, had little or no effect on Paul Pigott's moral scruples. Don Douglas, a childhood friend and neighbor of the Pigott family, was first hired by Pacific Car in September 1942. He soon became aware of the delays caused by the difficulty in securing some critical parts. Once, when Douglas was planning a trip east, he said to Pigott, "I'd like to take a few boxes of our Washington apples back there. I think they might help us get some of those parts." Pigott's reply was: "Absolutely not! We just don't participate in that sort of thing."

While the basic tank concept was that of the government, there was occasional updating to meet new specifications, and this was done by Pacific Car's own engineers. Long before the war, Pacific Car had demonstrated the ability to engineer quality products, and wartime pressures

A new foundry was built by the U.S. government at Renton and leased to Pacific Car for casting tank turrets and other related parts too big for forming at the smaller Renton foundry.

did not weaken their resolve to maintain those standards. Their aim was to build a better tank at a better price than any other manufacturer, and the company felt that it achieved that objective. The tank prices kept dropping along with manufacturing costs. Those who encountered the tanks in service usually described them as a superior product, with better machining and finishing, smoother shifting of gears, more durable paint, and general absence of defects.

In time, however, the armored services had all the tanks they needed. With ten different manufacturers producing Sherman tanks, and all of them moving up on the production learning curve, producers were, in the words of one observer, "stamping them out like cookies." Pacific Car, as one of the smaller manufacturers, was among the first to have its tank contract canceled, on November 15, 1942. For eighteen months the company had been building 30 or more a month, and had gotten up to 94 in one month. Their total output was 926 tanks. Army Ordnance compared their prices with those of a number of other producers, and declared Pacific Car's the lowest.

The high pitch of war work was readily reflected in the company's overall level of activity. Sales in 1942 reached $18 million, almost double the record $9.7 million of the previous year. Profits also went up, but not as much, from $31,000 in 1941 to $515,000 in 1942. Wartime income and excess profits taxes rose much more sharply, from $492,000 in 1941 to $1,354,000, and the company retired $142,000 of its debt in 1942. In 1941 the company paid off a four-year accumulation of dividends on its Class A preferred stock, amounting to almost $90,000. That year Pacific Car also sold off its Portland property, idle for more than a decade.

The 1942 annual report, issued quite late in the year, was already able to foreshadow the end of the tank contract. It said, in part: "The company's operations have been converted entirely to needs of the Government in its war effort, and a large portion of our production has been taken up with the manufacture of the Medium Tank. . . . The U.S. Army Ordnance procurement program for medium tanks . . . has been materially curtailed in recent months and . . . it may be that future reductions in the Army's needs . . . will materially reduce our activity along this line."

Sales in 1943 rose sharply again, to $49 million, or almost triple the 1942 level. Profits increased moderately, to $789,000. The tank contract accounted for about 72 percent of the company's total 1943 sales during the ten months or so it continued.

— THE TANK RETRIEVER CONTRACT —

The end of the tank program was far from the end of Pacific Car's total emphasis on production of war materials. Early in 1943 the company was awarded a contract to produce a tank recovery vehicle, known as the M-26 truck tractor, for the Army.

At the time of the World War II fighting against German General Erwin Rommel in the North African campaign, it was found that there was no adequate way to recover tanks that had become disabled or bogged down in the desert. Many of the tanks were simply abandoned or left behind. The Army started work with the Reo Motors Corporation to design a vehicle for recovering the tanks. Reo built prototypes of trucks for pulling large trailers, supposedly capable of picking up two medium tanks. The trucks had five wheels on each side, but their turning was dominated by the front wheels. These trucks would turn on pavement, but had great difficulty manipulating in mud or sand. The Army canceled the contract and tried to turn it over to a subcontractor, which turned it down. The contract was then given to a San Francisco inventor, who had developed a type of heavy-duty axle for a six-wheeled vehicle. But with a plant hardly bigger than a blacksmith's shop, he simply did not have the capability to build the huge recovery vehicles in quantity.

The San Francisco Ordnance District then called on Pacific Car to send its representatives down. The Newell brothers went, along with Paul Fetterman, a company attorney. When Fetterman asked Pigott how long he might have to stay in San Francisco, he was told, "You can probably catch a plane back tonight." He left with a briefcase and some blank pads. Two weeks later, he was still there, having purchased shirts, socks, underwear, and toothbrush.

The Army wanted Pacific Car to take on an assignment of the contract, and to somehow bury in it the costs of the previous contractors and subcontractors. After long dickering, a contract was worked out that the Army officers felt would not reflect their earlier profligacy in committing funds for no results, and that Pacific Car believed would protect its own interests. The company then became the sole contractor for the M-26 tank recovery vehicles. At first there was some difficulty in settling with the San Francisco inventor, but then it was decided that the axles were not patentable, and the Army instructed Pacific Car to ignore him.

The original plan was for Pacific Car to completely redesign the truck and to subcontract out a good deal of the work on the M-26. But as the medium tank contract began to wind down, the company decided to do all the work itself, and to involve all of the company's divisions.

That worked fine until the government classified Seattle as a critical labor area in 1943. In order to release more workers to the airplane plants and shipyards, the government ordered

Pacific Car assembled the M-26 tank retriever in Billings, Montana.

other major war contractors to move their operations out of Seattle to inland sites. Pacific Car first balked at the idea, having already set up its Seattle production line for efficient operations. But the government announced that they had just ninety days to come up with a plan for moving production of the tank recovery vehicles out of Seattle.

So the company set out looking for alternate sites, and found one at the Midland Empire Fairgrounds in Billings, Montana, where there was an ample labor supply. Thompson was delegated to go to Billings, make the appropriate building modifications, arrange to obtain equipment, and transfer the vehicle assembly line from Seattle. He spent several months at this task, and gradually more and more production people were transferred to the leased buildings at the fairgrounds. A total of 1,372 of the tank recovery vehicles were turned out by the company, which also used the Billings site to rehabilitate hundreds of trucks that had been built by other manufacturers.

Pacific Car and Foundry had not subcontracted for the Boeing Company since it fabricated B-17 wing spars during the early part of World War II. It chose instead to concentrate on projects where it could serve as a prime contractor. In 1943, the company's Renton plant got back into the business of building wing spars for the B-17 and for the new wartime giant of the skies, the Boeing B-29.

Everett Pacific
Shipbuilding and
Dry Dock Company,
begun in 1942 by
Paul Pigott and his
brother, William Jr.,
was purchased in
1944 by Pacific Car
and Foundry.

— MARINE WORK AND LABOR PROBLEMS —

The first taste of marine work in the joint venture with the Lake Washington Shipyard whetted Paul Pigott's appetite for more of the same. There was important work to be done that he could handle and that could produce a reasonable profit.

In the original arrangement with the Lake Washington people, Pacific Car's principal role was to produce a bond for $1 million as evidence of the financial ability to complete the contract. Pigott made arrangements with a bank to issue it in the form of a blank check for $1 million, since Pigott did not know whether it was to be made out to the Bureau of Ships or some other payee. Ferdinand Schmitz took the check to a meeting in attorney William Allen's office. The head of the Lake Washington Shipyard tried to get the check, and a virtual wrestling match ensued, with Schmitz managing to hold on to the $1 million prize. It turned out that the check was not needed, and Pigott returned it to the bank after paying interest on it for a few days.

After the initial contracts were fulfilled, the Lake Washington firm earned enough profit to handle the financial responsibility requirement, and their people went to Washington to get contracts on their own, saying nothing to Pigott.

Pigott never fully indicated the distress he felt over this turn of events, and was even skeptical when Pacific Car got a Navy contract to build barges. He asked Schmitz, "What are you going to do building scows?" He was told the craft would be built in the company's paint shed, and then a house mover could haul them to the nearby Cedar River, from which they would be floated down to Lake Washington. "I hope it comes out okay," said Pigott.

When it did, Pacific Car showed renewed interest in seeking Navy work. It had its engineering department and an architect make up a plan for a shipyard to be built on a flatland on Lake Washington, where Boeing was eventually to build an airport. The Navy people admired the drawings, but said, "We are not going to allow any more shipyards on the lake. If the locks are blown up, none of the ships can come out."

Paul and his brother, William Jr., then decided to get into the shipyard business on their own. They incorporated the Everett Pacific Company, capitalized at $50,000, in February 1942. Capitalization was raised the following month to $250,000, with all of the stock purchased by the Pigott family and a small group of associates, including Schmitz and the Structural Steel Division's Styer and Jacobsen. Their intent was to lease from the government the Navy shipyard facilities then under construction on a 62-acre site at Port Gardner Bay in Everett, Washington, some 30 miles north of Seattle on the east shore of Puget Sound.

Ground was broken for the new shipyard on February 13, 1942, and the work swiftly transformed a stretch of tidal wasteland into a major West Coast shipbuilding facility. The lease was consummated as planned. Although construction was far from completed, the company began the keel-laying for an 18,000-ton floating dry dock, to be known as *Rebuilder,* barely three months later. In November they started building ten net layers for the Bureau of Ships, the first of what was to be fifty-one auxiliary vessels—barrack ships, cargo barges, and steel harbor tugs.

With the award of the earliest contracts, Paul Pigott began looking in earnest for qualified people to supervise construction work at the shipyards. He wrote, among others, to his uncle Scott Clingan, a vice president at Bethlehem Steel. "I know that the many ship yards have been a serious drain on the personnel of the existing organizations throughout the country," he said, "and Bethlehem probably is in the market for competent men also. However, on the chance there might be someone in the Bethlehem San Francisco shipbuilding organization that would fit into our group, I am writing this letter. There may be one or two assistant superintendents that Bethlehem may not be able to promote as quickly as they would like who might like to be given the opportunity to earn more money for the next couple of years . . . provided, of course, your organization would see fit to loan them to us."

Pigott pointed out that Everett Pacific had received numerous applications, but that they were looking for the very best people they could get. Apparently it was a successful quest. Everett Pacific turned out to be an extremely valuable training ground, supplying Pacific Car and Foundry with some of its ablest executives.

William Pigott Jr., was elected president of Everett Pacific. Paul's older brother had never been able to develop much interest in running an industrial plant. Yet with the addition of Paul's skills, the yard had completed nearly $50 million in U.S. Navy contracts by the beginning of 1944, and its employment had reached fifty-five hundred, with a monthly payroll exceeding $1.5 million.

Building the shipyard at Everett helped to some extent with the problem of getting labor, since wartime gasoline rationing precluded long trips for many workers. In Seattle itself, labor shortages were ameliorated by a substantial in-migration from other regions and by training large numbers of women for war plant work. It was estimated that the 1940 census population of some 380,000 for Seattle and nearby Bremerton had swelled 20 percent by mid-1942, when war industry employment reached 100,000, with Boeing taking the lion's share.

By 1942 women accounted for a fourth of Pacific Car's total employment, as trainees in the machine shop, driving jitneys, inspecting tanks, cleaning, and taking over clerical work that men had handled before. The new foundry had facilities for women when it was built. Women attended classes in the machinist's trade from 2:30 A.M. to 7 A.M., and a special school was opened nearby to train women for work in war industries. Those with chemical education or experience were welcomed in the Pacific Car laboratories. Skeptics about the abilities of women were soon converted. Said Dick Hutsell, manager of the machine shop, "I didn't want them in my shop at first, but they have proved their ability in every instance. They are especially good at small, repetitious operations." When Seattle's big Bon Marché department store sent its phalanx of buyers to New York in 1943, they went not to look at sportswear for the weekend skier, but work clothing for women welders and riveters. Their purchase of three-month stocks of low-heeled shoes would in other times have been enough to last for several years.

Many of the latecoming workers at Everett Pacific were new to their trade and were trained on the job. There was a single closed-shop labor contract, encompassing all trades—engineers, hoisting engineers, machinists, boilermakers, welders, electricians, pipefitters, carpenters, joiners—and wages under it varied little between journeymen and helpers.

Labor problems were mainly jurisdictional, and various unions insisted on doing what they deemed to be their work. Even in wartime, their favorite remedy was to walk off the job if others poached on their territory. The yard, for example, had some vehicles called Carry Cranes —small trucks with booms attached. Seeing a potential problem, industrial relations director Ray Moran called in the heads of the Teamsters and the Hoisting Engineers unions. "Which of you has jurisdiction over this Carry Crane?" he asked. Both claimed it, and Moran eventually decided to give the work to the Teamsters. Minutes after a Teamster stepped into a Carry Crane, the Hoisting Engineers walked off the job. Moran appealed to the headquarters of both unions in Washington, but got nowhere. Finally he discontinued the use of Carry Cranes, loaded them on a flatcar, and shipped them out. The Hoisting Engineers then returned to work.

Starting in August 1943, Everett Pacific began to dredge and clear out additional land for a ship repair division, intended primarily for postwar work by the company. In March 1944, just before the shipyard's twentieth launching, Everett Pacific announced that all of its outstanding stock had been purchased by Pacific Car and Foundry. Schmitz was elected president of the firm, renamed Everett Pacific Shipbuilding and Dry Dock Company, and Paul Pigott vice president and treasurer. The purchase price was the amount that had been paid in for the capital stock plus earnings retained by the shipbuilding company.

The new repair facility, built at a cost of more than $8 million, was dedicated on July 4, 1944. It was capable of handling vessels of up to 50,000 tons. Its principal drawback was the cost of running ships there from Seattle for repairs.

During the course of the war, Everett Pacific turned out great numbers of small and large seagoing craft, ranging from tank landing vehicles to subassembly work on aircraft carriers and destroyer tenders. It built three huge floating dry docks, each capable of lifting a vessel of 18,000 tons. The dry docks, with their own power and operating as independent units, each contained 7,500 tons of steel, more than 200 tons of welding rod, and 153 miles of welded steel.

The Navy developed great respect for the company's engineering capabilities. In 1944 Pacific Car received a Navy contract for research and development in ship propulsion with what was known as the Kirsten cycloidal, or vertical axis, propeller. Two were built from a set of blueprints and specifications and installed on a harbor tug and a Navy LSM craft. Tests tended to prove the claims of the inventor for the revolutionary propeller's greater efficiency and maneuverability.

In another development, the Navy sought designs from a number of companies for a new

A Navy LSM equipped with a Kirsten cycloidal propeller demonstrated its maneuverability in Puget Sound during the 1940s.

type of device to transmit power at different gear ratios without interruption for its amphibious tanks. The model devised by Pacific Car and Foundry won out, subject to test, over those submitted by Ford and Food Machinery Corporation. The company saw an important postwar market for such a device, to be used under conditions where changing gears in the conventional manner could result in serious loss of headway in the machinery. The applications, they believed, might include tractors operating farm equipment or other heavy loads and running heavy trucks on adverse grades.

— ACQUIRING KENWORTH —

Since the late 1930s, Paul Pigott had shown an interest in the Kenworth Motor Truck Corporation, a custom truck builder controlled by P. G. Johnson with several small shops near Seattle's Lake Union. In late 1944 there was an opportunity to purchase the controlling stock interest from the widows of Kenworth's three principal figures, two of whom had died within a short period.

It was a costly purchase, and Pigott was hesitant about committing a substantial part of Pacific Car's assets to such an acquisition. But he believed that the motor truck industry was in its infancy. The future of the industry in the transportation field looked far more promising to him than that of building railroad cars, which had reached an advanced stage of maturity. So Pacific Car and Foundry Company bought all of Kenworth's outstanding common stock— 3,000 shares—at a price of $1,222,500.

Kenworth's own history had many parallels to that of Pacific Car and Foundry. Its beginnings traced back to 1910, when the Gerlinger family, founders of railroads and a logging and construction firm, opened an agency to sell the Stoddard-Dayton automobile in Portland. The family's successful ventures had been engineered by Louis Gerlinger and two of his sons, George and Louis, Jr. A third son, Edward, had no such record of achievement, so they put the new business in his care.

The company dropped its Stoddard-Dayton line and took on the Pathfinder and Holley automobiles, the Federal Truck, and a small delivery truck called the Vim. The name was changed in 1912 to the Gerlinger Motor Car Company, and not long afterward a second agency was opened in Seattle, selling Oldsmobiles and Standard, Federal, and Menominee trucks.

The Portland agency decided late in 1914 to build its own truck, patterned after the Federal but improved for western conditions. The shop foreman designed the vehicle, using a Continental six-cylinder engine and a chassis fashioned from structural steel, since dies and stampings for a pressed steel frame proved too costly. The result was a stronger truck, completed late in 1915 and sold, with neither cab nor body, to a local brick hauler. It was named a Gersix, for the size of its engine.

Two more trucks were built in 1916, mainly for hauling wood and coal fuel on runs of up to ten miles. The Northwest trucking industry was improving, but not the Gerlinger business. Edward's lavish promotional parties did not do much to boost sales, and the company went bankrupt early in 1917. Its assets were taken over by two Seattle businessmen, Edgar K. Worthington and Captain Frederick S. Keen, both of them involved in marine financing ventures and both more interested in a new source of business for their finance companies than in manufacturing.

In 1916 Congress passed the Federal Highways Act, which gave a further boost to trucking, but not much was done about it before America's entry into World War I, which postponed road building. The newly named Gersix Manufacturing Company was then troubled by its inability to get the parts it needed. When six-cylinder engines were no longer available, it switched to the four-cylinder Buda engine, which was to power their trucks for many years. Few trucks were built during the war, and the industry remained in a confused state afterward. But as highway construction increased and the company solved problems of load, power, starting, steering, vision, lights, brakes, comfort, and appearance, its business improved. It kept pace with the industry's increases in truck size, improved engines and axles, and the introduction of five-speed transmissions.

When Captain Keen retired near the end of the decade, Worthington brought in a new partner, Harry W. Kent, a younger man who had joined him in other business ventures. Kent complemented Worthington's financial talents by bringing in those of the manager—meeting schedules and payrolls, cutting costs, and installing a system that he had used in shipbuilding to show the cost of each manufactured item.

Sales increased to fifty-three trucks in 1922, and the company began showing a profit. In December 1923 Worthington, Kent, Theodore Jenner, and Adolph Engstrom reincorporated as the Kenworth Motor Truck Corporation—derived from the Kent and Worthington names— with capital of $60,000.

Production mounted to eighty trucks in 1924, when the company began to pay dividends, and to ninety-four in 1925. By then, Kenworth's supersalesman, Vernon Smith, had set up a distribution system around the state, with dealers located in Tacoma, Bellingham, Yakima, and Mt. Vernon. The trucks had become larger and more powerful. Buda engines were retained, but there were now pressed-steel frames, seven-speed transmissions, doors, pneumatic tires, and more comfortable cabs. The company's trucks were custom-built to fit the needs of each customer.

Smith used the promotional technique of writing to customers for their comments, and then using the endorsements for further sales. "They are truly built for carriers as witness the loads they generally convey," wrote W. A. Steigleder, superintendent of the Bolcom-Canal Lumber Company, in 1925. "In response to your question as to the satisfaction Kenworth trucks are giving us," wrote August Kristofferson, head of his own dairy business, "would call your attention to the fact that we now have twelve trucks of this make. The first was bought nearly three years ago and watched very carefully." And C. A. Niven, president of the Acme Cartage Company, wrote in 1928, "It is the finest piece of equipment that we have . . . owned in the fifteen years that we have been operating trucks. . . . The service that your plant gives from the time the order is taken until the truck is delivered is amazing."

Sales kept climbing to 159 in 1927, 163 in 1928, and to 223 in 1929, the year Kent succeeded Worthington as president. The trucks cost a little more than standardized vehicles, but buyers felt that customized quality made them worth the difference. The chief designer was John C. Holmstrom, who was hired in 1923 as a floor sweeper by his brother, Charlie, the plant superintendent. Working while he finished high school and attended the University of Washington, John Holmstrom advanced to mechanic's helper, mechanic, and then truck designer in 1926. Smith's selling of customization forced Holmstrom to advance from simple assemblies of standard parts to more and more sophisticated combinations. And Holmstrom himself, having worked in the repair shop, emphasized easier accessibility to parts that might have to be repaired. His trucks also reflected the needs of western haulers, who had

Kenworth sand- and gravel-hauling trucks at Pioneer Sand and Gravel, Seattle, Washington.

Harry W. Kent, Edgar K. Worthington, Theodore Jenner, and Adolph Engstrom incorporated the Kenworth Motor Truck Corporation in December of 1923 and later moved their plant to Mercer Street in Seattle.

to contend with steeper grades, longer hauls, and, frequently, more primitive roads than those in the East.

With the start of the Depression, Kenworth made every effort to keep production and wages up. But sales slipped to 161 vehicles in 1931, and then virtually collapsed in 1932, when only 85 were built. The company tried to keep up sales in every way that it could. It built custom chassis for fire trucks for the Sumner Volunteer Fire Department in 1932, and some of these vehicles were still in standby service in 1980. It created special hybridized vehicles for freight haulers and oil companies, and began manufacturing trailers—everything from single-axle semis to three-axle, six-wheel trailers—and started selling trucks and trailers as matched rigs.

More innovations followed. In 1933 Kenworth became the first U.S. truck builder to install a diesel engine as original equipment. Murray Aitken, who drew layouts for the truck and eventually became Kenworth's general manager, recalled, "It had a small Cummins engine—100 horsepower, if that. Cummins at that time was the leader in the diesel field. It was a race between Kenworth and the Indiana Co. Cummins recognized Kenworth as the first to put a factory-installed diesel engine into a new truck, but I guess it was nip and tuck."

The exhaust on the truck went straight up. John Holmstrom had driven a Kenworth that had been repowered with a diesel, and a misadjustment in fuel injectors caused black smoke to pour out. When he had difficulty seeing well enough to change lanes he directed that diesel exhausts be installed to rise vertically. Inexpensive diesel fuel was used as a selling point to counterbalance the higher initial cost of the trucks.

Kenworth sold its first sleeper cab on a three-axle diesel near the end of 1933. Seeking new business sources, the company went into a full line of school buses, city buses, and intercity coaches, purchasing bodies from Heiser and Tricoach. A streamlined deck-and-a-half bus with an all-steel body, built for North Coast Lines, proved the most popular. And a city bus was built with a rear-mounted engine in 1934.

Vernon Smith went to Hawaii in 1936 on a sales trip, and found the sugar harvesters using railroad cars with temporary tracks to haul the cane out. They would have preferred trucks, but those had difficulty getting traction on the volcanic loam of the fields. So Smith had the company turn out a six-wheel-drive gasoline model, followed by diesel models, and these were in use on most of the Hawaiian sugar plantations within a few years.

Some innovations were developed in response to various state trucking limitations. Length restrictions helped lead to the cab-over-engine truck, first built for the C. M. Martin Company, of Phoenix, Arizona. Robert Norrie, Kenworth's assistant chief engineer, related, "The state of New Mexico allowed you only a 45-foot overall length. So we put the diesel engine in the cab-over, we built a three-axle trailer and, as I recall, it was 44 feet, 11 inches, when the State Patrol measured it in Demming, New Mexico."

Kenworth fortunes experienced a turnaround in 1936. At the start of the year production was off from the level of 119 trucks sold in 1935, the company had a machinists strike on its hands, and a group of directors were seeking to take control of the company away from Kent. He turned for help to his friend and neighbor Philip Johnson, who several years earlier had become, at the age of thirty-seven, president of both Boeing and its offshoot, United Air Lines. Johnson saw enough potential in Kenworth to purchase about 25 percent of the company's stock, and he was made second to Kent in the management hierarchy.

Johnson helped settle the strike quickly, and got the company back into production. Then he made a much-needed loan of several hundred thousand dollars to Kenworth. He helped the company get a contract to design and manufacture beaching gear for Boeing's new "Flying Boat," the Model 314 Clipper—Kenworth's first move outside of the motor vehicle industry. And he was largely instrumental in putting new emphasis on engineering and manufacturing, which had been subordinated to sales and finance.

Kenworth trucks were assembled in stalls during the 1920s.

In October 1937, Kent died suddenly of a heart attack, at the age of fifty-five. He was succeeded as president by Johnson, who had not long before been forced out of Boeing and United, mainly as a consequence of the government's cancellation of airmail delivery contracts and an antitrust suit against United Aircraft & Transport Corporation, the parent firm of the two companies. In August 1937, he had an opportunity to organize Trans-Canada Airline, and moved to Canada, but made frequent trips back to Seattle to keep track of Kenworth. Johnson had conceived the idea of having Kenworth take over Tricoach and the Newell brothers. Talks were well along when Pigott contracted with the Newells to build buses for Pacific Car and Foundry.

Kenworth engineers continued to improve their product, in good measure by saving weight. They introduced aluminum cabs, aluminum hubs, hydraulic brakes, four-spring (bogie) suspensions that were hundreds of pounds lighter than those of competitors, and a rear-axle torsion-bar suspension that was to become a virtual trademark on Kenworth trucks. The company's principal engineers had gone out for a sandwich and beer one evening in 1938, with Holmstrom paying for the light repast, when Aitken made a blackboard sketch of a primitive torsion-bar suspension, replacing heavy leaf springs with two simple slim bars. Later, on a plane trip, Holmstrom made some key engineering improvements on the idea, and the company built its first torsion bar and installed it on a truck. The pressure of war production put a temporary halt on its development, but the one suspension held up all through the war. Before the war had ended, a second version was made, and there was more evolution in the suspension thereafter.

The company's business improved through 1936 and 1937, then dropped back to a production of only 131 trucks in 1938 before climbing back to 160 in 1939. That year Johnson returned to Seattle, and was again elected president of Boeing, serving simultaneously in that capacity and as president of Kenworth.

By 1941 Kenworth was prospering, with more than 250 workers spread among seven different leased locations, in addition to the main plant. The company was turning out a number of small parts for Boeing's B-17 "Flying Fortress" bombers, and it held an A-3 defense priority, which was the highest rating for an automotive manufacturer not directly involved in defense contracts. Trucks, too, were vital to the nation's defense effort, and Kenworth turned out 286 of them that year.

Immediately after Pearl Harbor, Holmstrom went to Washington and came back with a contract to build 430 four-ton M-1 wreckers. Equipped with six-wheel drive, winches, a powerful crane, floodlights, and cutting and welding equipment, the six-by-six trucks were prepared for all sorts of service and maintenance work on trucks or tanks. Before the end of the year, Kenworth had orders for about 1,500 more of the heavy-duty vehicles. Holmstrom changed the production from the company's method of using separate stalls for each operation to a moving production line going through the various assembly, paint, and inspection stations.

When the War Department declared Seattle a critical labor area, Kenworth was asked to move its M-1 wrecker program elsewhere. General manager Adolph Engstrom balked. "We feel that the cost of providing new facilities is too great to warrant moving out of the state under the present contract, which is in excess of $10 million. If further contracts were provided, we would attempt to secure facilities elsewhere."

He was soon assured there would be more contracts to keep his workforce busy. In September, Kenworth leased facilities in the Yakima, Washington, fairgrounds and moved their

truck assembly operation there. Truck production dropped rapidly because of material shortages, and total output for 1943 was 709 military and 87 commercial vehicles. The War Production Board removed Kenworth's entire allocation of commercial vehicles for 1944, but later relented somewhat.

Kenworth's main Seattle plant was quickly converted to production of B-17 parts—nose sections, bomb bay doors, and bulkheads. For a time Kenworth was still permitted to build fifteen trucks a month, and Kenworth's production manager, John Czarniecki, placed a fence down the middle of the plant to maintain the desired secrecy of the Boeing work.

By 1944 Kenworth's workforce had grown to 800 employees, including 507 in Seattle, of which 415 were women. "These girls came out of kitchen sinks and didn't know how to hold a screwdriver," said Czarniecki. "We had a training program in the basement of the old plant. As soon as the girls could use that screwdriver, we brought them upstairs and put them on production work. Those girls won the war for us. You teach a girl how to do something and she does it exactly the way you told her. If you tell a man, he'll try to improvise and screw it up for you."

Kenworth production of parts for Boeing's B-29 "Superior Fortress" began in August 1944. The experience in working with aluminum parts was eventually transferred to their postwar truck production, where Kenworth fabricated aluminum frames, cross members, gussets, cabs, fuel tanks, and hoods. All told, Kenworth built more than 3,000 assemblies and subassemblies for the B-17 and B-29 aircraft during the war years. Its 1944 vehicle output amounted to 716 for the military and 217 for commercial use.

In September 1944, Philip Johnson suffered an apoplectic stroke on a business trip, and died the following day at the age of forty-nine. Kenworth continued to conduct its day-to-day affairs under Engstrom, Smith, and Holmstrom. Johnson's widow was named to fill the vacancy on the board caused by his death. But she, along with the widows of Kent and Frederick Fisher, a director who had died a few months earlier, all decided to sell their stock, which controlled the company. The widows offered it first to a group of employees headed by Engstrom, but they were unable to secure the needed financing. Paul Pigott's name turned up next, and Pacific Car made the acquisition.

Pigott was named president of Kenworth, Schmitz became a vice president, and Holmstrom was moved up to vice president and general manager to replace Engstrom, who resigned. Robert Norrie succeeded Holmstrom as chief engineer. Vernon Smith was kept as vice president in charge of sales, and John Cannon, then on military leave, was kept as secretary-treasurer.

Paul Pigott not only recognized Kenworth's potential, but he was aware that Johnson had been the moving force behind the company, and took on the responsibility of filling that void himself. Like Johnson, he was completely in accord with the Kenworth ideas of custom truck building and engineering innovation, which he encouraged. For the immediate future, however, both Pacific Car and Kenworth were fully absorbed with the requirements of war production.

In March, Kenworth's three production lines on B-17 parts came to a halt, and with the end of the conflict in the European theater, the government canceled all of Kenworth's military truck production. In anticipation of Japan's surrender, Norrie and a team of engineers began working on plans for the company's postwar line of commercial trucks.

Eight of the prewar models were retained and brought up to date. Kenworth then produced an oil hauler with a supercharged engine, the first on the West Coast, using mainly leftover war materials. Several new models were added, the most significant of which were the Model 825, with torsion-bar suspension; the Model 584, a heavy-duty dump and logging vehicle, rated at 95,000 pounds gross vehicle weight; the Model 848, an all-round truck rated at 65,000 pounds; and the Model 888, a chain-drive giant rated at 110,000 pounds.

John Holmstrom, left, and Philip Johnson were frequent business travelers to the Hawaiian Islands in search of cane truck orders for Kenworth.

The capital reorganization of Pacific Car and Foundry that Paul Pigott had first tried to bring about in 1934, then again in 1936, was substantially accomplished in March 1943. Stockholders approved a plan under which the old 6 percent Class A preferred stock was exchanged, share for share, with a single new issue of 6 percent preferred, and the old Class B preferred was exchanged, share for share, with a new issue of common stock. The old common stock was canceled.

A certificate of amendment to the articles of incorporation was filed March 31, 1943, providing for 2,700 shares of new preferred, $100 par value, and 25,000 authorized shares of common, no par value. Class B preferred shares held in the treasury and those purchased from shareholders who did not wish to exchange their stock were canceled, and a total of 13,477 shares were exchanged for a like number of shares of new common. The stated value of the new common on the balance sheet was $50 per share.

On December 11, 1945, shareholders approved another change in capitalization, splitting the common stock ten for one. The stated value on the balance sheet was reduced to $5 per share, and there were then 250,000 shares of common authorized and 134,770 issued and outstanding. The authorization of preferred stock was reduced from 2,700 to 2,250 shares, which was the number then outstanding.

At the time of the 1943 recapitalization, a dividend of $1.50 was declared on the preferred stock as of January 1, and a dividend of $1 on the new common. Both dividends were made payable upon the surrender of the old shares for the new.

Pacific Car's sales and earnings for 1944 dropped by about a third from the record high levels of 1943, sales declining to $33 million and net earnings to $534,000. The company's 1945 sales and earnings returned to approximately the 1943 level, as sales set a new record of $49.4 million, and net profit was $722,000, after payment of more than $2.1 million in federal income and excess profits taxes. Regular dividends were paid on preferred stock, totaling $6 per share, while quarterly dividends of $1, plus a year-end disbursement of $2, were paid on the common stock, or a total of $6 on each share outstanding prior to the stock split.

Paul Pigott had a personal distaste for trading the stock of his own company on the open market, and he expressed disapproval of any broker trying to push Pacific Car stock in efforts to sell it to the public or boost its price. He deemed such behavior immoral. Earnings, he believed, should go back into the company as long as they could be used there, although he was aware that stockholders looked for—and deserved—a decent return on their investment. Even though he was aware that the plowed-back earnings increased the intrinsic value of the stock, he refused to buy shares when they were selling at a low price, as he was once advised to do by Tom Gleed, president of Seattle-First National Bank and a director of Pacific Car. "I'm not trying to make money for myself," Pigott told him. "If any of my associates want to pick up the stock, that's their affair."

Similarly, he did not want Pacific Car to make a profit from any transaction that might be in any way off-color. At the end of the war there were tons of steel in the Everett shipyard that could have been purchased from the Navy for $5 a ton. Two of his managers working on termination of wartime activities came to Pigott and suggested that Pacific Car buy it and store it for a time. "It will be worth $40 a ton in no time at all," one of them said.

"I'll think about it," Pigott told them.

They returned about a week later. His mind was clearly made up. "If you want to buy it

Kenworth employees produced B-17 and later B-29 subassemblies for the Boeing Company during World War II.

yourselves, go ahead," he told them, "but we are not buying it. No one is going to say that this company or Paul Pigott got rich off the war."

They did not buy the steel. In short order, it did go up to $40 a ton.

But there was one person who could powerfully influence Pigott. At one time he was in Washington with Schmitz, just before a planned vacation with his wife, Theiline. "Ferdie," he said, "you're going back to Renton, and you and Curd are on the executive committee. Do you suppose that you could put me on the payroll?"

"I think that can be arranged," Schmitz told him. "What do you have in mind?"

"Well, Theiline has been giving me the devil for not coming home with a salary check. Make it $12,000."

Curd and Schmitz held a meeting and put Pigott on the payroll at a salary of $12,000 a year.

But Pigott could be adamant on the subject of profits that he believed had been earned. All contracts for war work were subject to renegotiation, depending on the profits ultimately realized from them. This encompassed about 95 percent of Pacific Car's 1944 and 1945 sales, and more than two-thirds of Kenworth's sales for 1944. Pacific Car had begun its war work on the basis of charging their costs plus a fixed fee. The company's major war work contracts were converted to a basis of charging fixed prices during 1944, since this permitted the realization of increased profit margins for greater efficiency. All work at Everett Pacific was on a cost-plus-fixed-fee basis, with some of their contracts subject to profit limitations, so that a refund had to be made for 1945, when the shipbuilding firm was wholly owned by Pacific Car.

After conferences with Pacific Car representatives, the Price Adjustment Board in San Francisco ruled that the company had made excess profits of $2,285,000 for 1944, an amount that was more than four times as high as its total profits after taxes. Pacific Car set up a reserve in that amount, but appealed the decision to higher authorities in Washington, eventually winning the appeal.

One special renegotiating problem involved Pacific Car's contract with the Newell brothers. Their share of the profits on war work was considerably beyond the amounts that the armed services would allow, leaving Paul Pigott with the sticky problem of getting the Newells to agree to a revision of those contracts to reflect the government requirements.

The consequences of contract renegotiation sometimes came as a shock to the production executives. At Kenworth the Boeing subcontract work had been obtained on a bid basis, so Czarniecki made special efforts to keep the costs down after submitting the winning bid. He recalled, "I kept track of the man-hours per unit. I tried to produce the successive units on a Bradley curve—in other words, as you gain experience you can reduce your man hours. So as we went along on this Bradley curve, it worked out real well."

Then he was told that Kenworth would have to return $330,000 in profits to Boeing. Said Czarniecki: "I thought that all of this profit we were generating would be for Kenworth. It turned out that we couldn't keep more than 10 percent. We could have just as well taken this work at cost plus 10 percent. Here I was sweating blood and working long hours to get our man-hours productive, and we did. But I felt real good about it, anyway, because it was all in the war effort."

M-266
TARCO S.D. HOIST &
YARDER ON CAT "75"

CHAPTER SEVEN

RETURN TO PEACETIME

Although the end of hostilities brought sharp cutbacks in producing the weapons of war, the nation was still mindful of its lack of preparedness in the late 1930s. Upon the conclusion of World War II, the United States continued to maintain a substantial defense program, concentrated especially in the areas of research, development, and testing.

For the industries and the companies that had dedicated the great bulk of their resources to the war program, however, the 1945–46 reconversion to peacetime production was a difficult and often trying experience. There was a great reluctance to let go of the experienced workers, so assiduously recruited and trained a short time earlier, but labor was restless under wartime wage controls. There was impatience to begin satisfying the needs and demands of traditional customers, in the face of frustrating shortages of materials and supplies. And there were many calls on the nation's supply of capital for retooling and renovating industrial plants that had forsworn needed improvements and replacement for too long.

Pacific Car and Foundry Company experienced most of these problems, but was able to solve some of them readily. Its principal plant at Renton was in relatively good condition, and the company looked forward to getting it into full-volume production. Early in 1946 negotiations were completed for the purchase of government-owned machinery and equipment at the plant for a total of $375,000.

The company began to receive some orders for the repair and rebuilding of refrigerator cars, which put the car-building shops back to work, and bids were submitted to railroads for both new car construction and car rehabilitation. Soon there were orders in quantities of 250 to 1,000 cars at a time, from Pacific Fruit Express Company, Fruit Growers Express Company, Merchants Dispatch Transportation Corporation, Western Fruit Express Company, and the Northern Pacific Railroad. The bulk of these were for refrigerator cars, a field in which Pacific Car led the nation from 1946 on.

The car-building program created an unusual inventory problem in the extraordinary postwar environment. As various materials became available from suppliers, they were accumulated in the plant until an adequate stock of all the items needed for production could be obtained. It took months, for example, to get the necessary wheels and axles to fill orders. Iron wheels were available, but the railroads would not accept them because of their excessive tendency to wear out, and insisted on steel wheels. At the end of 1946 the company's inventory

Tractor equipment production was given top priority in Pacific Car and Foundry's postwar production.

reached the uncommonly high valuation of $8.3 million, while unfilled orders totaled more than $35 million.

Disposing of excess materials left over from war production was less of a problem. After making very inadequate provisions at the start, the federal government later passed an excellent termination act, which greatly simplified the rapid disposition of excess inventories. This was especially helpful at the Billings, Montana, facility, which had been loaded down with large orders for tank retrievers. Heavy supplies of materials were flowing into the plant at the time the Battle of the Bulge took a successful turn, signaling a relatively quick end to the war in Europe. These supplies were then easily sold or otherwise transferred under government direction.

Since winch sales had been made exclusively to the government during the war, Pacific Car set about afterward in an aggressive campaign to recapture its prewar position in supplying tractor auxiliary equipment—arches, winches, hoists, bulldozers, and transmissions—to the logging industry. The campaign was successful, and the Carco Division's sales in 1946 were about the same as they had been during the war, which was substantially above the prewar level. Not long thereafter production was reaching five or six times the prewar figure. A sales office and warehouse service were set up in Chicago to take care of the swelling demand for Carco products in the East, the South, and in Canada. The Chicago warehouse served a dual function, offering both service to Pacific Car's customers and savings in freight costs for the company. It provided a central distribution point, giving Pacific Car the ability to service nearby tractor manufacturers, such as Allis-Chalmers, Case, International Harvester, John Deere, and other Carco customers. Moreover, the warehouse received, consolidated, and transshipped parts to Seattle for use in Pacific Car, and later Kenworth, products.

In many fields it was feared—without foundation, it turned out—that there would be a decided lag in postwar demand. The company therefore sought out all the new forging, casting, and job order work it could find. It also went after everything available in structural steel orders, ranging from little one-story commercial buildings and service stations to major structures and hydroelectric plants for the government. These efforts were successful enough so that the steel plant had to be enlarged to accommodate its business, and full employment was maintained.

Paul Jacobsen, a civil and structural engineer with a solid background in his field both in this country and abroad, and a longtime friend of Paul Pigott, was made the division's general manager. Its superintendent was Clarence Styer, who continued to run his plant like the small shop it had been when Pacific Car acquired it. Just after the war, one of his younger sales engineers, Emmett Miller, was building a home, largely with his own hands, but ran out of money when it was less than half done. He went to banks, but they were wary of such a homegrown building plan. Styer heard of this, and asked him, "How much money do you need, Emmett?" Miller told him, and Styer said, "Come on in to my office after lunch." When Miller got there, a check for the full amount was waiting for him. He signed a note, and repaid the debt not long afterward, when the house was completed and it could be financed more traditionally.

With a postwar acceleration in the industrial growth of the Pacific Northwest and Alaska, the Structural Steel Division experienced an unprecedented demand for its products. They participated in the fabrication and erection of steel for bridges, factories, public buildings, airplane hangars, and virtually every other type of construction. The division modernized and expanded its facilities in 1949, and in 1950 it built a new 85-by-420-foot structure, complete with new craneways and modern machinery.

The company's Motor Coach Division moved up to capacity operation in 1946, turning out both sport trailers and school coach bodies. Its Pacific School Coach returned to its position of dominance in the school bus business of the Northwest states. In 1950, however, the Motor Coach Division was transferred to the Kenworth plant.

Pacific Car's executives were neither surprised nor dismayed by the postwar drop-off in sales from close to the $50 million level in 1945 to just $19.4 million in 1946, nor by the small decline in net profits from $722,000 to $696,000. From these earnings the company was able to pay $111,000 in dividends, including 60 cents per share on common stock and all current requirements of its own and Kenworth Motor's preferred; retire $45,000 of its preferred shares; and invest nearly $500,000 in buildings, machinery, and equipment for the Renton and structural steel plants. Total capital reinvestment, including Kenworth, amounted to $972,000.

In 1947 the company's consolidated sales rose to a healthy $30.5 million, and net profit passed the million-dollar mark for the first time, at $1,223,000. The usual dividends were paid, and $70,000 in Pacific Car preferred stock was retired. Investment in new manufacturing facilities dropped to $287,000. New peacetime records were again set in 1948, when sales climbed to $35 million and net profit to $1,379,000. The remaining 1,100 shares of Pacific Car preferred stock were called and redeemed. The common stock dividend was unchanged, in spite of higher earnings, and the annual report explained, "Your Board of Directors has continued the policy of paying a modest dividend until our bank loans can be further reduced or until we obtain needed working capital through long-term financing. . . . Expanding sales have created a capital requirement for plant replacement and new equipment in excess of our depreciation reserves."

An added reason for such fiscal conservation was the fact that the first postwar dip in the economy was already in sight. The company's backlog of unfilled orders, which stood at

Upon completion of defense contracts, Kenworth began producing a variety of trucks, including the Model 588 logging truck.

$7.1 million a year earlier, was down to $6.4 million at the end of 1948. The unhappy promise was borne out in the following year. Weakening demand for timber and wood products hurt the logging equipment business. Construction activity in the Northwest held up surprisingly well, but the railroad car business was hit hardest of all. The car-building facilities in the Renton plant were kept busy only about half of the time.

By the end of the year, however, the beginnings of a business pickup were evident. The company's consolidated sales were up somewhat in 1950 to $28 million, while profits rose sharply to $1,258,000. Common stock dividends, which had been increased during 1949 to 25 cents a share in each quarter, were again raised, to 40 cents, in the second quarter of 1950. A total of $438,000 was spent on additional plant facilities, and $324,000 went to pay current dividends and to retire all of Kenworth's outstanding preferred stock. The remaining $446,000 in profits was retained in the business as working capital. "It is a pleasure to report that the company properties are in better condition than at any time in its history as a result of continued improvements that were carried on . . . to modernize and expand our plant," the annual report said.

During this immediate postwar period Pacific Car received a number of defense contracts, from the Army Ordnance Department and from the Navy Bureau of Ships, and indeed, at no time since 1940 had the company been without major government contracts. Most of that work involved research, design, and development, rather than large production orders that might result in substantial profits. Not long after the war ended, Pacific Car entered the government's Mobilization Planning Program, which meant that it committed its facilities and capabilities to all-out military production if a national emergency were to arise.

The first postwar contract was for research and development on the T-95, a motor carriage for a 155-millimeter gun. This was one of the first self-propelled guns conceived by Army Ordnance. The company manufactured two prototype vehicles.

The company then undertook the design and development, on a limited scale, of improved types of armored vehicles. Pacific Car assigned its best engineers and technicians and most

Pacific Car and Foundry military contracts continued into the 1950s with the development of the T-95 motor carriage for a 155-millimeter self-propelled cannon.

experienced shop hands to these programs. Kenworth also kept in touch with the Army Ordnance Department after the end of the war, and built several experimental vehicles for them. In each case, only one or two prototypes would be produced, so that little was realized in the way of profits. But the company nevertheless considered such work its duty, and it helped keep skills sharpened, should they be needed.

— A NEW HOME FOR KENWORTH —

After acquiring the Kenworth Motor Truck Corporation, Pacific Car did not take long to make its presence known. On one of the first tours that Paul Pigott made through the main Kenworth plant on Mercer Street, he was escorted by John Holmstrom, then vice president and chief engineer for the truck company. Holmstrom, eager to get some of his own ideas across to the new owners, pushed the idea that Kenworth should move strongly toward equipping heavy trucks with diesel engines, and eventually dominate that field. Pigott was impressed, and upon the resignation of Adolph Engstrom, Holmstrom was made vice president and general manager, and his ideas were given fuller sway.

Pacific Car clearly impressed itself on Kenworth's salaried employees during the 1945 Christmas season. A bonus of a month's salary was distributed, compared to the customary year-end distribution of about 2 percent of annual salary. Robert Waggoner, office manager of Kenworth's special wartime operation in Yakima, Washington, phoned Seattle to see whether there had been some mistake. He was told there had not. "That," said Waggoner, "really got our attention."

But Kenworth's most pressing problem at the time of the Pacific Car takeover was that of its cramped and scattered quarters. "We expect our present and past volume of business for heavy-duty trucks and buses to increase considerably in post-war years," Pigott said, promising, "We are going to be ready with manufacturing facilities far in advance of any others west of the Mississippi."

At first the plan was to build a new plant in Renton for Kenworth. But in October 1945 Pacific Car announced that it had purchased what had once been a Fisher Body plant on East Marginal Way in South Seattle for something over $500,000. Boeing, which had used the plant during the war years, vacated it by December. Holmstrom pronounced it "ideal," with its main building well suited to the manufacture of highway vehicles in a series of long production lines.

Kenworth took possession of the new plant at the start of 1946, and Murray Aitken was put in charge of converting it to Kenworth's use. Even though the work of conversion continued all around, the first truck came off the line in the new plant on March 3, 1946. Observed Aitken, "Everything's confusion, but it's organized."

Each operation was moved to the new plant as soon as it could start there, but moving day for most of the company was April 15, 1946. A new office building was put up at the site, and was completed on July 5. The new plant's open house reception was held on August 11. While the conversion was going on, trucks continued to be produced at Yakima, where fifteen hundred had been built since the facility opened. The shops there began closing down, and by the end of April the move to Seattle was completed.

Both Pacific Car and Kenworth had built buses and different types of truck bodies before the war, and on occasion Pacific Car had built bodies for Kenworth trucks. With the acquisition, Pacific Car's foundry and machine shops were equipped to furnish various parts to Kenworth that the truck manufacturer had previously purchased on the outside.

Seattle, Washington, March 3, 1946. John Holmstrom, Murray Aitken, and Vernon Smith celebrate production of the first truck in Kenworth's new facilities at East Marginal Way.

Kenworth's new tie to Pacific Car meant that funds would be more readily available for any desired capital improvements. The truck company's fixed assets were increased by $250,000 with the construction of the new office building, pavement, the purchase of new machinery, and the installation of a moving assembly line chain. The new plant was capable of producing vehicles and parts at a rate of more than $1 million a month, which was about four times Kenworth's prewar capacity.

The postwar demand for its products was such that Kenworth could have sold all the trucks it was able to build. Mass production was no longer a secret to the truck builder, which had turned out 2,141 military and 897 commercial vehicles during the war. Now there were three production lines, beginning with assembled frames, which then went up the line to have more parts added. The truck next moved into a paint shed, was tuned up by mechanics, then had a final check before rolling out into the delivery yard.

Kenworth could easily have produced more than one hundred trucks a month, in addition to a substantial number of buses for which orders were already on hand. The principal stumbling block, however, was the continuing scarcity of materials and component parts during the first nine months of 1946. Diesel engines had become almost standard equipment for the big over-the-road haulers, but they were hard to come by. The Cummins Engine Company, for example, was allocating its output to Kenworth and other old customers. Then, by the time supplies began to arrive with some degree of predictability, a strike started in September, holding up production for five weeks.

Kenworth nevertheless turned out 705 trucks in 1946 to set a new peacetime record, selling all it could make and turning down almost two thousand orders. The company had had dealers, Tom and Les Jenkins, in Los Angeles and San Francisco before the war, and they added a branch in Fresno, California. By the end of the war there were dealers in Spokane, Billings, Denver, Portland, and Salt Lake City. Sales chief Vernon Smith went to work to expand the distributor system further, and in July 1946 he had representatives in Texas and Puerto Rico. Then he made an extended tour of Central and South America, which included visits to Cuba, Jamaica, Haiti, Trinidad, and the Dominican Republic. Before the end of the year there was active representation in Mexico, various South American countries, the Hawaiian Islands, and Canada. Inquiries began to come from customers and dealers throughout the country, as well as from abroad, and Kenworth began 1947 with a $12 million backlog of unfilled orders. Not all of the orders were filled. John Cannon, the company's treasurer, became suspicious of some buyers' ability to pay for the vehicles. Banks would not finance many trucks, and the company itself had no financing program worked out. The dealers, Cannon knew, were in no position to underwrite the many purchases. Cannon finally went to Paul Pigott and said, "It doesn't make sense to me. Everybody says these orders are good, but I just can't see who's going to pay for them."

"Why don't you go out and find out?" Pigott suggested.

Said Cannon, "Okay. I'll leave in ten days."

"No," said Pigott, "you're going to leave tomorrow morning."

The following morning Cannon was on his way, visiting dealers, checking out duplicate orders, looking into ability to pay and financial responsibility. "I went down to Mexico," he recalled, "where we had a bunch of bus orders that weren't worth anything. By the time I got a week into my trip, one thousand orders had been canceled at Kenworth."

But the company still had all the good orders it could handle. A steady stream came from the Hawaiian cane plantations, where the war had interrupted the conversion from rail to truck hauling for the sugar harvest. Others drifted in from South America, where Smith had signed agreements with eighteen agencies to represent the company. The largest of these was an order

Pacific Car and Foundry, seeking new facilities for Kenworth production, purchased the Fisher Body plant in January 1946.

Kenworth began building fire trucks, such as this 1936 truck for Spokane, Washington, during the Depression, and continued to supply this market for the next three decades.

for fifty bus chassis from Montevideo, Uruguay. Many other bus orders began to come in when Kenworth announced its first four postwar models in October 1946.

The seller's market of the early postwar years neither halted nor slowed Kenworth's determination to be preeminent in engineering research and innovation. Kenworth first began in 1936 using aluminum components for truck cabs, an aluminum chain drive, and all-aluminum castings in suspensions. Kenworth gained additional experience in the use of aluminum during World War II as a subcontractor for Boeing, building sections for the B-17. After the war Kenworth developed the first aluminum frame when machines were made big enough to extrude an aluminum frame rail.

H. E. Simi, nationally known for bus designs, joined Kenworth to head bus engineering and production, and he drew up plans for a new line of streamlined light metal buses. The company exhibited its pilot model of a new intercity bus in January 1947. An order soon came from Portland for fifty trackless trolleys.

A total of twenty-seven new truck models were introduced between 1945 and 1950. One group kept especially busy was the publications department, turning out parts books for the company's growing postwar service and parts departments.

Kenworth continued to take special pride in its ability to produce trucks to meet the special needs of customers, and sometimes expended extra efforts to fill unusual requests. One rush order came in to prepare, within six weeks, two huge snowplows—the biggest ever built, some 40 feet wide—to keep open the Alaskan road from Valdez to Fairbanks. For motive power, two heavy Kenworth trucks were sent, with instructions that they be filled with rocks, then have water poured over them. When the water froze, the full weight of the rigs would be more than 100,000 pounds. It was an outlandish idea, but it worked.

Much more financially interesting, and ultimately rewarding, was an order from the Arabian American Oil Company for a special kind of truck that could maneuver easily with heavy loads on the hot desert sands of the Middle East. With no railroads or highways, with extreme daytime temperatures of 125 to 135 degrees Fahrenheit, and with constantly shifting sands, transportation was one of Aramco's most difficult problems. Most truck makers, when they saw the customer's specifications, decided that the engineering problems were hardly worth tackling at a time when they could easily sell every truck they made elsewhere. But Paul Pigott was a member of the board of Standard Oil Company of California, which was not only a one-third owner of Aramco, but also the member of the consortium charged with handling transportation and oil field problems. Looking ahead, he decided it would be well worth Kenworth's time and energy to tackle the tough engineering and design problems.

Kenworth contracted early in 1947 to build trucks to meet Aramco's requirements. The engineering department went to work to design a desert vehicle, known as the Model 853. It had twin, side-by-side radiators, a 300-gallon fuel tank, a powerful 318-horsepower gasoline engine, six-wheel drive, and large flotation tires. To decide on the tire size, Aramco engineer Richard Kerr measured a camel's hoof print, balanced it against the weight of the camel, and specified a similar relationship between tire size and truck weight.

The Model 853 was first tested on sand dunes near Yuma, Arizona, in May 1947. The first shipment of sixteen trucks was made three months later. The trucks performed satisfactorily in the Arabian desert. Their rated capacity of 65,000 pounds gross vehicle weight was often exceeded, with no detrimental effects.

The initial contract called for a total of twenty-six trucks, and the required extra parts made up 15 percent of its dollar value. Specifications would vary for different users, such as the Trans Arabian Pipeline Company (Tapline), building the line from Beirut, and Bechtel Corporation, starting at the Saudi Arabian end. Kenworth representatives serviced the trucks in Saudi Arabia until 1950, although orders for the trucks continued to come in from Aramco, Trans Arabian Pipeline, and other oil companies abroad for many years after that.

Kenworth truck production rose to another peacetime record of 891 units in 1947, slipped back to 870 in 1948, and dropped to 693 in the recession year of 1949, before turning upward

Kenworth trucks with 318-horsepower gas engines, side-by-side radiators, and low-pressure balloon tires traverse the Saudi desert carrying supplies for the Qatif Abqaiq Pipeline.

again to 842 in 1950. But the engineering department was kept busy throughout. In 1949, when the Northern Pacific Transport Company asked for a combination truck and bus, the Motor Power Equipment Company, Kenworth's distributor in Billings, developed the concept. Then Kenworth engineers went to work to design the "Bruck," which could carry seventeen passengers and had more than 1,000 cubic feet of cargo space. A few were built for Northern Pacific, but the idea did not catch on elsewhere.

While this work was going on, Kenworth was also engineering and building a special crash truck for the Air Force. The body and pumping gear were built by other suppliers, as was common in fire engine manufacture. An effort was made also to apply a Boeing gas turbine engine, originally developed to power naval vessels, to the truck industry. The completed turbine unit weighed only 200 pounds, less than a tenth the weight of the traditional power plant, but it turned out to have decided disadvantages: slower pickup, a need for more gear shifting, noise, and extremely poor fuel efficiency. The turbine-powered truck never got into production, but Kenworth received favorable national publicity.

Kenworth's growing business increased the need for spare parts for its trucks in service. By the end of 1950 construction had begun on a new 30,000-square-foot parts warehouse.

— PRODUCING FOR WAR AGAIN —

When, in 1950, the United Nations Security Council voted to resist the incursion of North Korean Communist forces into South Korea, the United States assumed the brunt of the military responsibility. Pacific Car and Foundry was selected almost immediately as a West Coast prime contractor, and was awarded large-scale research and development contracts.

The biggest of the contracts called on the company to proceed simultaneously on the development of a prototype mobile gun carriage for the Army and on the tooling, procurement, and component manufacture for the production run of the same vehicle. In the "guns and butter" mood of the Korean War days, production for the military was expected to be accomplished alongside the job of meeting the record commercial demands of that period.

The Army Ordnance order was for 388 of the vehicles designated as the T-97 and T-108, at a total cost of just over $80 million. Resembling tanks, the two vehicles were self-propelling, track-laying gun carriages of advanced design. They were basically alike, except that the T-97 mounted a 155-millimeter rifled gun and the T-108 carried an 8-inch howitzer.

An initial study of component parts showed that approximately 570 castings would be needed for each vehicle. Pacific Car decided to produce the hull, turret, and gun cradle assemblies, and to subcontract out other parts, with special emphasis placed on furthering the government's own program to help small business.

One building at the Structural Steel Division was enclosed and a heating system installed to maintain the desired temperature for armor welding. A second building was rearranged to machine the hulls and turrets. T. B. Monson, Pacific Car's general manager, initiated negotiations with the Navy to lease and reopen the Everett shipbuilding plant—not, this time, to build seagoing vessels, but to fabricate ordnance parts for assembly at Renton. The lease was signed in October 1951, when plans were drawn to employ four to five hundred people to fashion the components and also to build and assemble Navy LVTs. Pacific Car's engineers designed all the needed tools, many of which were produced in the company's own shops.

The T-97 hull was divided into five subassemblies, their component parts welded and X-rayed before being brought together for the final assembly. A Renton plant building that had been used for school bus manufacture before that operation was turned over to Kenworth, was rearranged for the production of some of the major subassemblies and for the final assembly of the T-97 and T-108 vehicles.

Design of the mobile gun carriage called for engineering of a high order, in good part because of the exacting functional requirements. Conventionally, fixed field artillery pieces at the time were towed or trucked to their positions, and the work of emplacement was difficult and often slow. Accompanying vehicles were needed to transport ammunition, artillery crew, and sighting devices. The T-97 had to be built to contain all of these, including the big guns, to move easily at speeds up to 31 miles per hour, to bridge a deep ditch 8 feet wide, to cross streams 4 feet deep, and to pivot in place, despite its great bulk.

The Army Ordnance Arsenal had designed somewhat similar vehicles about a year earlier, but Pacific Car's engineers were almost solely responsible for the T-97 and T-108 design. They created a vehicle that could be brought to a stop, readied for fire, and started firing in a minute and a half; firing could then be stopped, hatches closed, and the vehicle got under way in another minute. To correct earlier deficiencies, a number of design corrections had to be made in the road wheel and track support wheel spacing; in disposition of shock absorbers; in the trailing wheel; and in engine cooling. To provide for stability while firing through an elevation radius of fully 70 degrees, the big gun's recoil distance had to be engineered down to a short 18 inches. For the equilibrator, the device that was to keep the gun in approximate balance in order to minimize

Paul Pigott took an active role in the development and production of the T-97 and T-108 self-propelled guns manufactured by Pacific Car for the Army in the late 1950s.

Development and
production of the T-108
self-propelled gun was
carried out at the Renton
plant.

the power needed to swing or raise it, a system of compressed gas was devised as a counterbalance. As a result, only a small motor or hand crank was required to maneuver the gun,
even though the vehicle itself might be unbalanced or poised on a hillside.

Pacific Car found there were a number of advantages to dealing with local small business
subcontractors, in addition to furthering the government program. These firms had greater
flexibility in adapting to changes, and their proximity made it easier to work out engineering
questions and problems. Moreover, savings were achieved when Pacific Car passed along the
price advantages of its greater purchasing power on many standard parts. And the prime
contractor was more self-sufficient when supported by nearby subcontractors that were not
weighted down with other war work.

On one occasion, it was necessary to develop a chain rammer motor for the gun carriages,
and Pacific Car sought bids from twenty companies, all of which turned the job down, citing
overloads in their engineering departments. One said it would take eighteen to twenty-four
months to develop such a motor, and that the cost would be $30,000. But one firm, Fassett-
McKenney, of Port Blakely, Washington, which had experience developing electrical devices
for Westinghouse, undertook the assignment and agreed to come up with a prototype within
sixteen days. When they did, they were given a contract to turn out the production units,
and they made no charge for the engineering.

In all, Pacific Car issued seven thousand purchase orders under the major contract, with
half the dollar volume going to firms in the West, half in the East. The dollar value of armor
plate alone, all procured in the East, was about equal to the dollar value of the cast armor
poured by Pacific Car. There were 101 suppliers in the Seattle area, another 16 elsewhere in

the state of Washington, and 31 others on the West Coast, for a total of 148, against 114 in the eastern states.

The company continued its research work on the heat treatment of carbon and low alloy steel. At the start of the Korean War the metallurgical department began a study, under Alex Finlayson, of traditional practices in heating and cooling rates, temperature ranges, soaking times, and quenching procedures, in the light of new knowledge and theory of metallurgy. As a consequence they found that some steps being taken were unnecessary, and that others employed excessive time or temperatures. After hundreds of laboratory tests, procedures were modified for all steels cast in the foundry, at measurable savings of $8.68 a ton. The low percentage of alloying metals made for further savings in Pacific Car's cast armor, although the quality regularly exceeded the specified requirements.

Recruitment and training of personnel to man the additional assembly lines posed new problems. Exactly six journeyman mechanics were offered to Pacific Car by the unions when the production line was started in January 1951, since most preferred work in automobile dealers' shops, where they could earn 25 cents more per hour. Five foremen who were trained in ordnance work during World War II were called in from other parts of the company, along with an assembly line superintendent. The supervisors trained 180 workers on the job, many of whom later received journeyman cards. In spite of the introduction of many new design features and changes, only one week's production time was lost. And with negligible labor turnover, the efficiency of the assembly line continued to increase.

These savings were reflected in the cost of the vehicles to the government. The original estimate was for a price of $199,000 per gun carriage. For the first seventy vehicles turned out, the price was lowered retroactively to $177,000 each. For the next ninety-one units a price of $150,000 was established, against which Pacific Car voluntarily refunded $6,000 per vehicle. For the next ninety-one a price of $129,000 was set, and the price then dropped to $126,500 per vehicle for the balance of the contract.

Kenworth also had its share of military work during the Korean War. In 1950 it was given a contract to construct T-10 transporters for the Army's new 280-millimeter gun. Kenworth engineers worked from specifications without knowing the vehicle's intended use. The design and testing were carried on in great secrecy while production began behind special curtains, since the vehicle was to mount the "Atomic Cannon"—the first artillery weapon capable of firing an atomic shell.

The T-10 consisted of two tractors independently powered and steered and each equipped with four-wheel drive and special hoisting equipment for the gun, gun mounts, carriage, and secondary recoil mechanism. More than 80 feet in length and with a gross vehicle weight of 85 tons, this was the largest vehicle Kenworth had ever built. For tests, Kenworth installed an intercom system between the two drivers, an idea the Army liked so well that it was specified as standard for the production units. The secrecy was lifted late in 1952, when the huge vehicles were demonstrated publicly, first at the Army's Aberdeen, Maryland, proving grounds and then at Kenworth.

Kenworth produced a total of sixty-seven of the T-10s. It also built for the Army military versions of a number of its truck models, including the desert-conquering 853s.

The company was almost continuously engaged in various research and development programs for the military, along with possible civilian applications. The new type of mechanical transmission, capable of transferring power at varying gear ratios without interruption, first designed for the Navy, was further developed and patented in 1946 under the trade name of Carcomatic transmission. A Navy amphibian vehicle was equipped with one of the seven-speed transmissions and an automatic clutch in 1947.

The Kirsten cycloidal propeller, built for the Navy late in World War II, was guardedly tested on a 900-ton Navy craft in Puget Sound in mid-1946. It performed a number of feats deemed incredible: it could come to a dead stop in a few seconds from a speed of almost 15 knots; complete a "merry-go-round" turn of the ship on its own axis; and stop several feet off a wharf, then move the craft with a sideways "crab walk" into its berth. All this was in addition to the high degree of efficiency of the cycloidal propellers.

Invented in 1921 by Professor Frederick K. Kirsten, of the University of Washington, the propellers were first applied to marine vessel propulsion by an Austrian firm in 1928. The U.S. government's interest was not sparked until late in 1944. Pacific Car, with exclusive rights to make the propellers in the United States, received additional contracts for their manufacture in 1947 from both the Army and Navy. To exploit the Kirsten propellers, Pacific Car in 1955 organized a subsidiary, Vertical Axis Propellers, which used the Renton facilities and personnel. The corporation was dissolved early in 1960, but its activities were continued by the Renton division.

Production under military contracts began to wind down during the 1950s, and the contract to produce the T-97 and T-108 self-propelled guns finally came to an end in April 1955, although some employees were kept working on modifications to the vehicles for the remainder of that year. This did not bring military development work to an end. In 1957 Pacific Car was awarded two research and development contracts to build and test prototypes of new vehicles for the Army Ordnance Department.

Produced in secrecy by Kenworth in 1950, the T-10 "Atomic Cannon" transporter was deployed as a strategic weapon by the U.S. Army.

The Kirsten cycloidal propeller was tested on a variety of hulls until its development was discontinued in 1962 because of its high cost and limited market.

— MARINE WORK —

Although shipbuilding activity virtually ceased with the end of World War II, there was plenty of work to keep the Everett Pacific Shipbuilding yards busy. During the first half of 1946 the U.S. Navy was the principal customer, bringing in a number of ships in their decommissioning and inactivation program. There was also a substantial volume of work connected with dry-docking and repairing ships of all classes for the Maritime Commission, the Army, and private contractors. Everett Pacific Shipbuilding and Dry Dock Company was dissolved as a separate entity during 1946, and the yard's assets and functions were made into a division of Pacific Car.

Departments and personnel were trimmed back in the conversion from a wartime to a peacetime operation. Gradually this became mostly repair work and the conversion of naval transports to commercial use, along with ship scrapping for commercial customers whose vessels had been pressed into emergency use during the war but could not compete efficiently in postwar commerce. As shipyards in Seattle were able to offer better service at a savings of both time and money, it became clear that the Everett yard was too big and too poorly located to be run economically in peacetime. In October 1949, Pacific Car informed the Navy that it was terminating the lease on the Everett facilities, and the yard was closed down at the end of that month.

The yard was reactivated to help with the Korean War buildup on November 1, 1951. The intention originally had been to use the facilities only to help with the Army Ordnance contract for mobile weapons carriers, but as orders arrived from the Navy for amphibious craft, including ninety-one tank landing vehicles, the Everett yards were pressed into service for more familiar activities. Some work continued at the shipyards until early in 1955, when Everett was finally deactivated, not to be used again.

But Paul Pigott did not stay away from marine work very long. Partly because he knew how profitable the business could be, partly because of the urging of O. A. Tucker, Pacific Car's vice president in charge of shipbuilding operations, and partly, perhaps, because of his spirited rivalry with Horace McCurdy, operator of Puget Sound Bridge and Drydock Company, another Seattle firm, Pigott got back into shipbuilding. The entry was through the purchase of the business and assets of the Commercial Ship Repair Company on June 1, 1953. Pacific Car acquired Commercial Ship's offices and dockside repair shops at Pier 66, Seattle, and leased its marine railway and yard shops at Winslow, on Bainbridge Island, across Puget Sound from Seattle.

Having got wind that Commercial Ship might be up for sale, Tucker had sent an assistant, Joe Gerber, out to evaluate the plant. Gerber came back to Tucker with what he felt was an honest figure, but also rendered his judgment that Commercial Ship Repair's equipment, labor, and dockside facilities were inadequate, and that the entire operation was too small for Pacific Car to deal with. But Tucker favored the purchase, and Pigott not only had great faith in Tucker's judgment, but also was always interested in diversifying Pacific Car's operations.

Commercial Ship Repair had been started late in 1945 as Commercial Steel & Boiler, a co-partnership between Eddie A. Black and his father-in-law, James J. Featherstone. Black was a 1937 graduate of the University of Washington who first went into advertising and automobile sales before signing on as a shipfitter's helper at the Winslow Marine Railway in 1941. By the end of the war he had been promoted to assistant general superintendent under Featherstone, whose long career in boiler and shipyard work had earned him the honorary title of "Dean of Ship Repair."

The two joined forces after the war to open their small shop on Seattle's Duwamish Waterway. In July 1946 they moved to more adequate space on Pier 66 and changed their firm's name to Commercial Ship Repair. Toward the end of 1947 they scored a major coup by acquiring the Winslow Marine Railway and Shipyard, promoting themselves from a small dockside ship repair organization to a substantial factor in Seattle's ship construction and repair industry. Winslow's history traced back to 1907, and it had grown to be an important part of the Northwest's wooden shipbuilding industry, when the shipyard owned by the Hall Brothers boasted some of the best workmanship of that craft. During World War II Winslow built seventeen all-steel minesweepers, at a cost of $25 million, in addition to completing $5 million in repair work.

Black had worked very hard at the job of building up the enterprise, investing all possible earnings back into the business. But in the postwar shipbuilding slump, Commercial Ship Repair had gradually fallen on harder and harder times. It had a considerable amount of assets, but very little capital, by the time Pacific Car appeared on the scene, so that its acquisition was a providential stroke for Black, who had bought out his father-in-law's interest earlier in the year. A good part of the purchase price went to pay off a long list of creditors.

The deal was to be consummated on a Monday, with Tucker to take charge of Commercial Ship immediately. During the preceding night, however, Tucker died of a heart attack. Black was then made a vice president of Pacific Car and Foundry and general manager of its Marine Division. He continued to be the owner of the Winslow shipyard, with its 8 acres of land, railway, buildings, docks, and other facilities. In 1955, however, he sold the entire establishment to Pacific Car, while remaining a vice president of the company.

Work at Commercial Ship Repair's yard and docks consisted mainly of ship repair and conversion service for all classes of vessels, up to and including carrier size. Under Black's management, it earned a reputation for fast, round-the-clock repair services. It was common for crews and equipment to be sent to ships needing repairs at loading docks, in the stream, or at neighboring ports, in order to complete work so that the ships could hold to sailing schedules. But as ship repair work dwindled, the division was discontinued on August 31, 1959, and its equipment and facilities were liquidated. Pacific Car was not to return to marine work again.

Pacific Car reentered the maritime industry with the purchase of Commercial Ship Repair on June 1, 1953.

CHAPTER EIGHT

■

A LITTLE BIG COMPANY

In the first half of the decade of the 1950s, a period of substantial growth in the U.S. economy, a number of the nation's corporations expanded rapidly enough to wonder whether they might still be classified as small businesses or had already emerged into the realm of big business. Pacific Car and Foundry, after some postwar backing and filling, had clearly moved up from the stage of large small business to that of a little segment of big business.

The company's sales levels quickly equaled and then surpassed the World War II peak of about $50 million. In 1951 sales totaled $45 million; in 1952 they reached $52 million; and in 1953 they climbed to $81 million. Profits did not increase proportionately, mainly because of the reimposition of wartime excess profits taxes, but they rose nevertheless, from $1,167,000 in 1951 to $1,229,185 in 1952 and then to $1,681,000 in 1953. Pacific Car's backlog of unfilled orders reached a record level of $109 million at the end of 1951, almost double that of the year before. Then as major military orders were filled, it declined to $32 million at the end of 1953.

A continuing concern of the management was a need for sizable bank loans to maintain the required inventory and working capital levels. The 1951 annual report pointed out that the company had to have at its disposal approximately $16 million at all times to carry on its business. More than half, or about $8.5 million, was available from the shareholders' equity in the corporation—while bank loans maintained a level of around $7.5 million—most of this representing earnings retained over the years.

The cash pressure did not discourage further investment, and plant additions and modernization were made as their need became evident. And, with higher profits, the company adopted a slightly more generous dividend policy, paying the customary 40 cents in the first quarter of 1951, then raising the common dividend to 50 cents per quarter, or $2 a year per share.

By the end of 1953 Pacific Car, with five plants in and around Seattle, was engaged in almost every industrial activity in which it had ever participated. In addition to the work on military contracts, it was the leading builder of refrigerated and insulated railroad cars; it manufactured tractor winches, arches, and cranes, and fabricated bulldozer equipment, rigging for wire rope, and steel light poles; it produced forgings, castings, weldments, steel fabrications, and machined items on a commercial job order basis; it operated a marine repair and construction facility; and its Structural Steel Division was engaged in steel fabrication and

Pacific Car and Foundry mechanical refrigerator cars represented a significant part of the company's 1950s railcar production.

erection of everything from a small retail store to bridges, hangars, dams, complete factories, and a five-story addition to a department store.

There were a number of special business risks involved in many of these projects, particularly those undertaken for the federal government. Some contracts were to be executed over periods as long as three years, with no provision for price escalation. This meant that the company took on the hazards of increases in material and labor costs. Inspection on government work was often not standardized, meaning that special provisions sometimes had to be made to satisfy an individual inspector. Insufficient detail in preliminary drawings, plan changes, and cancellations on government work were all usually costly to the contractor.

Pacific Car and Foundry also had the many special problems arising from the fact that it was not located in a predominantly industrial area. The development of its great variety of metalworking shops grew out of necessity, since there was no nearby supporting industrial complex. The company was all but forced into setting up its own metallurgical research and development facilities, and into performing its own analyses for many phases of its manufacture. It extended these functions even further because of its special emphasis on engineering skills and inventiveness. As a consequence, Pacific Car and Foundry had grown into the largest and most versatile manufacturer of industrial products in the Pacific Northwest.

Total sales of the company continued around the $80 million level for the next several years, ranging from a low of $76 million in 1954 to a high of $86 million in 1955. Earnings ranged much more widely as the production mix changed, with profit margins being very narrow in more competitive areas, such as railroad cars, and wider for auxiliary tractor equipment and structural steel. With the removal of the federal excess profits tax in 1954, the profit level surged upward to $2,360,000. It then rose to $3,606,000 in 1955, dropped back to $2,818,000 in 1956, and fell sharply to $1,757,000 in 1957.

The company's dividend policy became decidedly more generous in this period. Dividends continued at the rate of $2 a share in 1954, but they were in fact higher than in the preceding years, since a 10 percent stock dividend had been voted at the end of 1953. Another 10 percent stock dividend was voted at the end of 1954, increasing the number of common shares outstanding from 134,770 before these actions to 163,071 afterward. The dividend was raised in 1955 to 75 cents a quarter, or $3 a year.

In December 1955 the directors recommended an increase in authorized capital stock from 250,000 shares of no par value to 750,000 shares of $20 par value, the resolution also calling for a three-for-one stock split. Stockholders adopted the recommended changes at their annual meeting in February 1956, and for the remaining three quarters of the year dividends of 30 cents per share were paid on the new stock, which was equivalent to 90 cents a share per quarter on the old stock. Dividends remained at the 30 cents per quarter level through 1957, even though profits dropped sharply that year to equal just $3.60 per common share.

Pacific Car in 1955 kept up with the new trend toward the use of mechanically refrigerated railroad cars to transport fresh and frozen foods. First developed by the Pacific Fruit Express Company, this car offered many significant advantages over the previously ice-refrigerated car. The old car had to be packed with up to ten thousand pounds of ice. In addition, salt was used to enhance the cooling properties of the ice, and as it melted the salt water rapidly rusted the frame of the railcar. Mechanically refrigerated cars could maintain a constant temperature varying no more than two degrees regardless of the car's external environment, thus making longer hauls practical and reducing spoilage. Other design modifications included the use of roller bearings rather than flat block bearings, and the age-old problem of the "hot box" was eliminated. The

The company performed its own analysis on many of its products, both for research and development purposes and for quality assurance.

railroads were quick to understand all of the advantages of the new cars, and they systematically placed orders for mechanically refrigerated cars to replace the icebox car. Pacific Car soon began producing large quantities of these cars for a variety of customers, later including the Pacific Fruit Express Company.

In addition to car lines working at capacity, the company had record deliveries of winches, with sales to the government and to government prime contractors, for installation on heavy ordnance recovery vehicles, exceeding sales to commercial customers.

Capital requirements and capital expenditures of the company were also significantly higher in the mid-1950s than they had ever been before. The level of outstanding short-term bank loans climbed to around $12 million in 1957, and that year arrangements were made for a twelve-year term loan of $6 million from The Prudential Life Insurance Company, with interest of 5.5 percent.

Capital spending approached $2 million per year for both 1955 and 1956, then dropped off to a still robust $498,000 in 1957. The 1955 investment included $742,000 to modernize plants and install new machinery, all aimed at improving product quality and cutting costs. The remainder went to purchase the Winslow ship repair yard and to acquire land and, in some cases, start building construction of Kenworth sales outlets in Denver, Colorado, and Dallas, Texas; a new warehouse in Chicago, Illinois; and a Kenworth factory in Burnaby, British Columbia.

The Chicago purchase was for a new building to consolidate separate warehouses there for tractor equipment and for truck parts. Most of the other real estate purchases, as well as a sizable part of the 1956 capital spending, went for additional manufacturing and distribution facilities for the growing Kenworth operation.

— KENWORTH GOES INTERNATIONAL —

Kenworth had indeed become the single most important element in the growth of Pacific Car. In the early 1950s Kenworth was moving to become a major factor in the production and sale of heavy-duty highway trucks. Output jumped from 842 units in 1950 to 985 in 1951, then went into four figures for the first time in 1952, reaching 1,079.

The truck manufacturer had never been very comfortable or successful with smaller road vehicles. In 1950 Pacific Car transferred limited production of the Carcovan, a small, stand-up vehicle designed to compete in the pickup and delivery market, to Kenworth. But this operation did not last long in the trucking plant, when Kenworth found that it was using space and resources that might better be applied to other purposes.

But heavy-duty trucks were another matter. Along with the expanded development of the nation's highway system, begun in the early 1950s, the entire trucking industry was growing rapidly. By 1952 trucks were hauling an estimated 170 million ton-miles of freight per year, or some 16 percent of all goods moved overland. Extra heavy-duty units accounted for no more than 1 to 2 percent of overall truck output, but they hauled a disproportionate share of the freight. In this field Kenworth had become, by 1953, a substantial producer and the largest in the West, with an unmatched reputation for the quality of its products.

Research and engineering was more than just a matter of increasing the size of engines, springs, tires, and axles, but rather one of creating total new designs from such components, or sometimes even redesigning the components themselves.

Many models continued to be engineered for special-purpose work. One of the more outlandish in appearance was the Clipper, a chassis built for Franks Manufacturing Company, of Tulsa, Oklahoma, to carry a portable oil well servicing unit. A number were sold to different oil well service firms.

In a major development, Kenworth began production of the first of its earthmovers in 1952. With a payload capacity of almost 12 cubic yards, these end-dump vehicles were first tested in 1950 at the site of the Chief Joseph Dam, demonstrating a good potential in such fields as excavating, open-pit mining, and even logging.

Kenworth started to develop a new cab-beside-engine (CBE) line of trucks in 1953, offering both weight savings and improved visibility. These soon proved popular among fleet operators in the Midwest, and before long orders were coming in for 300 trucks from Yellow Transit Freight Lines, of Kansas City, 60 from Denver-Chicago Trucking Company, and 117 from Merchants Motor Freight, of Minneapolis and St. Paul. But the idea never caught on with drivers, who steadfastly preferred the two-man cab-over-engine models.

As Kenworth truck sales began to spread through the Midwest and East, the company not only outgrew its parts department behind the main plant, but also encountered logistical problems in supplying parts and service for dealers and customers. John Holmstrom sent John Czarniecki to locate and open a more central parts and service operation. In 1953 a lease was signed on 6,000 square feet of warehouse space in the Chicago suburb of Berwyn, Illinois, and Czarniecki started hiring people to run it. Holmstrom called him one day and asked, "John, how is it that the only people you employed are Polish?" And Czarniecki replied, "Well, John, you know that if you want to get a job done right, you've got to get either a Pole or a Swede—and there aren't any Swedes in Chicago."

In 1955 Pacific Car built a new 25,000-square-foot warehouse in Chicago to replace existing freight consolidating and customer service facilities. Later this was replaced by a 50,000-square-foot warehouse, and still later it was expanded to 100,000 square feet of storage and freight handling space.

For its growing network of dealers, Kenworth had to prepare improved service and parts manuals, and to hold annual meetings in Seattle for the service managers, which in the early days were often attended by the owners themselves. As Kenworth and the number and size of its dealers grew, the need for expanded field service and training became obvious.

In the early 1950s Kenworth developed off-road earthmovers for mining and construction use.

The difficulties in supplying standard parts and service manuals for custom-built trucks soon made it clear that something better was needed. So Kenworth put all the requirements on microfilm, so that every one of its dealers could have a complete parts record of every truck built. This moved them a giant step ahead of their competition in efficient parts replacement and servicing.

In 1953 Kenworth acquired the assets of a former distributor in Denver and organized Colorado Kenworth Corporation, which became an important facility for truck service and repair, as well as a truck sales outlet. When the dealership went up for sale, a group of Kenworth executives went to Pigott and told him they were interested in buying it themselves. "Wait a minute," he said. "You can't work here and own that, too. I could just picture some customer needing a truck in Los Angeles and the reaction when you sent him to Denver for it, even if that were the best place to buy it." Pigott, however, offered to lend them the money if they decided to leave the company and take over the dealership on their own. They declined.

Kenworth had long had a substantial market for its products in Canada, and since 1945 business there had been handled through its distributor, Ferguson Truck and Equipment Company, Limited, in Vancouver, British Columbia. In 1954, when the Canadian government increased tariff rates on trucks manufactured in the United States, it became necessary to manufacture trucks in Canada. So on February 22, 1954 Pacific Car formed a wholly owned subsidiary, Canadian Kenworth Limited, and Kenworth began to look into the costs of a plant to turn out sixty to one hundred trucks a year.

They decided the venture would have a reasonable chance of success. At the end of 1954 Kenworth signed an agreement with W. J. Ferguson, president of Ferguson Truck and Equipment Company, Limited, provided the Canadian government would approve lower import duties for

Kenworth first began producing trucks in Canada for the Canadian market during 1955 at the newly erected facilities in Burnaby, near Vancouver, British Columbia.

the new firm. In February 1955, government approval was obtained, on the assumption that at least 40 percent of the product would have Empire content. Kenworth paid $400,000 to the Fergusons for their assets and for a 12-acre building site in Burnaby, an industrial area of greater Vancouver. Not long afterward a contract was signed to build a plant and office structure, totaling 44,000 square feet.

Donald F. Pennell, assistant sales manager at Kenworth, was named general manager of Canadian Kenworth Limited, and he moved to Vancouver to direct operations there on September 30, 1955. Some Ferguson Truck employees were soon transferred to the Kenworth payroll. Canadian Kenworth officially started in business on January 3, 1956, when the remaining Ferguson employees were transferred, although they remained on the Ferguson premises until later that month. There was a total of eighty-eight employees, only fifteen of them involved with production, on the payroll.

"We started off with shop people who were basically repair oriented, and with no factory experience at all," Pennell later recalled, "but they learned fast. We outsold the other manufacturer in Vancouver, Hayes Manufacturing Company, every year from the first year we opened the factory." Canadian Kenworth eventually bought out the Hayes firm.

The first engineering chassis released at Canadian Kenworth was dated February 1, 1956, and the customer accepted the truck on April 18. Another truck, however, constructed from a partially assembled unit from Seattle, was completed two days earlier. The employee count climbed to around 180 (including a young industrial engineer named Charles M. Pigott, Paul Pigott's second son) before the end of 1956, when it leveled off. The new company showed a small loss for its first full year of operations, a result that remained unique in its records.

The need to establish financing for the sale of Kenworth trucks in Mexico required frequent exploratory journeys to that country in 1954 by Pacific Car attorney George Lhamon and treasurer Don Douglas. Their early missions were an attempt to secure enough pesos for financing Kenworth truck sales in Mexico. "It was just not possible," recalled Douglas. "There were simply not enough pesos available to finance our truck sales." Against the advice of Pacific Car bankers it was decided that the company would make dollars available in Mexico for financing Kenworth sales. The fears of continued devaluation of the peso and the possibility of Mexican government restrictions on the free exchange of pesos for dollars were outweighed by the company's desire to build a market for Kenworth trucks.

On September 12, 1955, the Pacific Car board adopted a resolution authorizing the dissolution of Kenworth Motor Truck Corporation as a corporate entity, and the formation of the Kenworth Motor Truck Company, to be operated as a division of Pacific Car and Foundry. Except for some superficial administrative changes, the motor truck maker continued to operate as it had before. In 1956 Kenworth was enabled to concentrate even more fully on its principal product lines, when the bus department was transferred back to the parent company. Buses had remained a limited and extremely regional business, while the market for Kenworth's other products was expanding throughout the United States and beyond the nation's borders.

Kenworth sales, which had dropped below the 1,000 level to 861 units in 1954, rocketed to a record 1,507 in 1955, rose again to 1,577 in 1956, and then fell off slightly to 1,410 in 1957. In its second year of operation, Canadian Kenworth was operating at a profit, producing and selling more trucks than the company had ever sold in Canada before.

Kenworth transferred the manufacture of buses back to Pacific Car in 1956 in order to concentrate on the development and production of trucks.

— EMPLOYEE RELATIONS —

In Pacific Car's earliest days of heavy dependency on railroad car building, work was often a feast-or-famine situation. When there were plenty of orders in the shop, there was also plenty of work for everyone. When orders slacked off, people were laid off.

It was a situation that most of the workers could live and deal with in the early 1900s. A great many of the shop personnel had small farms nearby, and they tried to program their activities around those of the plant. There were fences to build and cattle to care for and crops to bring in. They were never surprised when work ran out at the plant, but were sometimes taken aback when work was plentiful for long periods and they had no time to take care of their farms.

Over the years, however, as employment increased at Pacific Car and more of the shop hands tended to be city dwellers, both the workers and the company were increasingly concerned with greater work regularity. On the company's part, this was promoted by seeking product diversification, more aggressive selling, and sometimes holding on to the workforce in leaner times. From the workers' viewpoint, unionization seemed to offer greater control over their employment destinies.

Unions at the Pacific Car plant at first were completely voluntary—some workers joined readily, while others resisted them. Little by little, however, union shops were made a key bargaining issue by the unions, and compulsory membership for all production workers became common. But workers recognized that the owners, and Paul Pigott in particular, were interested in them and their welfare. Their attitude was never very militant toward the company, and there was no sharp dividing line between the labor philosophy of the company and that of the unions.

At the end of World War II, labor relations for Pacific Car were on a satisfactory basis. There were agreements with the Machinists Union, the Molders, the Blacksmiths, the Boilermakers, the Sheet Metal Workers, the Auto Mechanics, the Teamsters, the Warehousemen, and The Federal Union (Car Builders). Ray Moran, who had been handling the much stickier union problems of the Everett shipyards, was put in charge of labor relations for Pacific Car and, later, for Kenworth as well.

There were a number of strikes during the postwar period, and Moran developed expertise in strike negotiation. One union, the Machinists and Automotive Machinists, was responsible for most of the stoppages, almost always in their efforts to get more money than the other unions appeared to be willing to accept for comparable work. This was an issue on which Pigott refused to budge, and which helped give Pacific Car the reputation of being "tough as nails" in labor negotiations. The company could see only chaos if the different unions were paid varying rates for the same or comparable skills, and was willing to take a strike on that issue.

One technique the Machinists sometimes used was to attempt to unsettle the entire area by striking one plant one month, another plant the next, and still another the third, keeping the employers guessing as to which would be next. As a countermove the employers formed a council known as Washington Metal Trades, Incorporated, established primarily to sit down and negotiate with all the unions on an area-wide basis. As a leading industrial employer in the Northwest, Pacific Car was instrumental in founding the council, and remained active in its affairs, contributing to much of its leadership over the years. Pacific Car's own firmness in following negotiating principles was adopted by the organization, which became perhaps the most effective association of its kind on the Pacific Coast.

A number of Pacific Car's labor contracts expired on April 1, 1952, and the workers went out on strike at that time, staying out for the full month of April. Operations at the Everett plant were also closed down for the same period, because of prolonged labor negotiations there. In its annual report for 1951, which was issued about midway through this period, the company included what might be deemed an editorial on the fallacy of trying to conduct labor negotiations under an umbrella of government controls. It said, in part:

> Total wages and salaries paid by the Company last year amounted to $10,123,000. A 10% increase in our wage costs, together with the attendant increase in overhead, would exceed the Company's profit in 1951. It is imperative that prices for the Company's products be increased to offset any wage increase which may be approved by the Wage Stabilization Board.
>
> Management of an industrial concern is restricted in dealing with labor, and in the setting of prices by regulations of the . . . Board and the Office of Price Administration. The usual prerogatives of Management in establishing wages through collective bargaining and posting prices for its products have been more and more usurped by Government, with the result that Management is less in control and can assume less responsibility for the Company's operations under our present laws.
>
> In our opinion price and wage controls as administered by our Government are detrimental to mass low-cost production and should be abolished.

The following spring the Metal Trades Craft Union in Seattle struck some sixty plants, including four of Pacific Car's, idling the company's forty-one hundred workers and shutting down all production. In 1954 the company sent its message directly to employees through an article in its house organ, *Carco News,* telling about shutdowns in some railroad car-building plants and imminent closings of others. Pigott referred to the article in a letter to all Renton employees, which then said: "We in management have had splendid cooperation from every department throughout the plant in our efforts to cut costs and maintain quality. Without employees who are willing to do a full day's work every day and think of ways to cut hours from car building schedules, we might well have been listed as one of the plants that have closed due to the scarcity of . . . orders. . . . I want to let you know we appreciate your efforts and are proud of the way you do your work."

The labor climate in Seattle was set in good part by the powerful Teamsters Union, led by Dave Beck. Regardless of what other criticism might have been leveled at the Teamsters, Pacific Car found that they were rigorous in living up to their contracts. If the agreement said they could cross picket lines in strikes not authorized by the Central Labor Council, the Teamsters would cross the lines. The word of other unions at Pacific Car was usually just as good, and they did not walk off the job over petty grievances, as had been the case at Everett.

Most strikes at Pacific Car were over the gut issues of money—"pork chops," as labor leaders called them. But as income taxes ate deeper and deeper into wage increases, the unions turned their attention toward such untaxed gains as health and welfare benefits and pension plans. Pigott was at first opposed to a worker pension plan. He became convinced finally when Moran demonstrated that the payments to the plan were in lieu of a similar hourly wage increase.

Pacific Car, rather than seek outside suppliers, continued to develop their machined-part production capabilities.

Pigott might earlier have been influenced by the feeling that pension and similar benefits should more appropriately be a matter of management initiative. In the spring of 1948 the company had launched a group medical-hospital-surgical plan for employees and dependents of all divisions except Everett Pacific, which already had a satisfactory plan. At Renton, participation rocketed within a few days from 30 percent to 90 percent of total personnel.

The company had also established a pension plan for salaried employees back in 1947, funded by annual company contributions that started out at $95,000, then dropped down to $70,000 after past service deposits had been made, and thereafter climbed gradually to almost $190,000 in 1956. At the beginning of 1955 the company also put into effect a profit sharing plan for salaried employees. Contributions made from the company's net profit were $167,000 in 1955 and $130,000 in 1956.

At the request of several members of the supervisory group, Pacific Car in 1956 inaugurated a plan for purchases of stock, difficult to acquire on the open market, because shares were so thinly held. Stock purchases by employees were financed under the plan by payroll deductions. In the first year of the plan, approximately 95 employees took advantage of it. By the following year, there were 270 employee-stockholders out of an overall shareholder roll of just 660.

— MANAGEMENT NOTES —

The first effort by an outsider to work his way into the controlling echelon of Pacific Car and Foundry Company was made in 1946. That year a lawyer-stockbroker from San Jose, California, Hugh S. Center, became a candidate for the board of directors. The Washington State legislature had adopted an act providing for cumulative voting for corporate directors. Center's group, made up principally of people to whom he had sold Pacific Car stock, marshaled enough shares to put him onto the board. Of the five directors nominated by management, only four—Pigott, Schmitz, William G. Reed, and E. H. Stuart—were elected. The board then reelected Pigott, president; Schmitz, executive vice president; Tucker and Holmstrom, vice presidents; and J. E. LeBlanc, secretary-treasurer. H. N. Curd, who came to the company in 1919 and had been a director, vice president, and general manager, died in June 1946.

The following year Stuart moved to Los Angeles, and asked to be relieved of his duties as a director. He was replaced by Thomas Gleed. Douglas was named to replace LeBlanc as secretary-treasurer, and Lester Leeman was elected controller. The courts then ruled that, at the time of incorporation, a corporation's articles created a vested interest that could not be changed by subsequent legislation. With the requirement for cumulative voting thus removed, Center was voted off the board and John Holmstrom took his seat.

Schmitz resigned from the company to start his own business in 1949, and left the board the following year. T. B. Monson took his place as a vice president, and Tucker was elected to replace him as a director. The board was expanded to six members in 1953, and Monson was added as a director. By 1956 the list of vice presidents had lengthened to six—J. Holmstrom, T. B. Monson, Paul Jacobsen, E. A. Black, R. D. O'Brien, and D. E. Douglas, who was also treasurer. W. H. Scudder was secretary and assistant treasurer, and M. E. O'Byrne was controller. O'Brien was named to the board in 1957, and labor specialist Moran became a vice president.

Through all these management changes, Paul Pigott clearly remained the guiding spirit of Pacific Car and Foundry Company and of its basic operating philosophy. This was a composite of his sound business sense, ethical principles, regional loyalties, and patriotism.

Once, when Kenworth was awarded an important military contract, he called a staff meeting. While the executives had not been conscripted as individuals, he said, they had been as a company. "I expect and want each of you to do a very, very efficient job, as far as quality and cost are concerned. We must make a profit, but it must be a reasonable profit." Consistently, during negotiations for military contracts, he would insist on avoiding unusual risks and on seeking no more than a reasonable profit—pointing out, incidentally, that the Renegotiations Board might take away a larger profit in any event.

A financial executive once discovered a five-figure discrepancy in Pacific Car's favor, after the Army audit had been completed and everything appeared to be in order. He took the matter up with Douglas.

"Are you sure?" Douglas asked.

"Yes, I'm sure," he responded, "but I'll review it once more if you wish."

"Please do so."

The figures were gone over again, reaffirming the first finding. Douglas took the matter up with Pigott, and a check for the amount was forthwith sent to the government.

Even with the growth of the company and the addition of Kenworth, Pigott tried to maintain a personal relationship with as many people in the plant as he possibly could. Lou Gerlach, later to become Kenworth's sales manager, who "figured Pigott wouldn't know me from a bale of hay," was startled one day when he chanced to run into Pigott, who asked, "Lou, how are things going?"

Pigott's inquisitive mind was almost impossible to satisfy with information about the plant and its workers. A young employee who once drove him from Renton to Seattle was confronted with a nonstop barrage of questions during the entire trip.

An employee once wormed his way into a closet to wire a hot water heater when his outside light became blocked off. "Get the hell out of my light!" he shouted. The shadow obligingly moved aside. Its owner asked, "What are you doing?"

"I'm wiring in a hot water heater," said the employee. "Oh," said the outside voice. When the employee emerged, there stood Pigott, apologizing for cutting out the light.

Pigott never used profanity, and his expletives rarely went beyond an exasperated, "My gracious!" And he never lost his penchant for good housekeeping and neatness around the plant. A mass of coils was once taken out of a government tanker undergoing conversion, and they were piled out in the Everett salvage yard. Pigott came into Joe Gerber's office and said, "Joe, look at that. Isn't that terrible!"

"No, not particularly, Mr. Pigott," Gerber replied. "We just took those off the tanker yesterday, and I haven't had time to sort them out yet, but we will."

"What are you going to do with it?" Pigott asked.

"I'm going to sell it all for $10,000," said Gerber, picking the figure out of the air.

A week or so later Pigott was back to ask, "What happened to all of the coils?"

"I sold them to Lewis for an installation for $10,000," Gerber told him.

"Oh," said Pigott, and never asked Gerber another question about what he did in the salvage yard.

Deeply involved as he was in business matters, Pigott found time for his family as well. He and his wife, Theiline, reared six children. Paul Jr. (Pat) was the firstborn, followed by Ann T., Charles M., Theiline A., Mary Ellen, and James C. Pigott. Paul and Mrs. Pigott reserved nights each week exclusively for family activities, including tennis, golf, and swimming. Like Paul, his family loved and excelled at outdoor sports.

Much of Pigott's time and energy went into the business, but he also fervently pursued his love of outdoor activities. A natural athlete, he participated in a variety of outdoor sports. He and two friends each owned a third interest in a small plane, which they took on frequent fishing trips into British Columbia or to a ranch owned by one of the friends east of the Cascade Mountains.

He retained outside affiliations that he believed in strongly or that he thought would be helpful to the business or that needed his help. He was for many years a director of the Seattle Chamber of Commerce, of the Stanford University board of trustees, of the Seattle University board of regents, of the Boeing Airplane Company, and of the Washington Mutual Savings Bank. In addition he sat on the boards of General Insurance Company (later Safeco Corporation), Seattle-First National Bank, Metropolitan Building Company (later Unico), and some others. He accepted a directorship of Standard Oil of California because he felt it important that the company have a board representative from the Pacific Northwest, and he traveled extensively to acquaint himself with Standard's installations.

He would contribute time and money to causes he believed in strongly. He quietly gave $5,000 as one of a group of businessmen who helped launch the Seattle Blood Bank. And in 1946 he worked hard with a group backing Homer Jones, a Republican candidate for Congress. Born into a family that had long been stalwarts of the Democratic Party, Pigott registered as a Republican himself.

But Pigott knew he would not be around to lead Pacific Car indefinitely, and he was concerned about the succession of leadership. Among those who were marked for better things was Robert D. O'Brien, who had joined Kenworth in 1943, after having been superintendent of

From left: Ray Medler, Robert O'Brien, John Holmstrom, Paul Pigott, Don Douglas, Charlie Holmstrom, and Bob Norrie reviewed Kenworth activities during the mid-1950s.

In 1959 Canadian Kenworth developed an all-wheel-drive truck for skidding logs from British Columbia forests.

Standard Oil stations in the Seattle area. Hired by John Holmstrom, O'Brien before long became chief assistant to Vernon Smith, Kenworth's hard-hitting and resourceful sales manager. When Smith retired in 1952, O'Brien was named to succeed him, while Don Pennell and Donald Grimes were promoted to assist him, respectively, as heads of wholesale sales and fleet sales.

O'Brien in 1956 succeeded John Holmstrom as vice president and manager of the Kenworth Truck Division, and Holmstrom was moved into the new position of company vice president in charge of engineering and research and development. O'Brien was elected to the Pacific Car board early in 1957, and in 1958 he was appointed sales vice president for all of Pacific Car and Foundry Company, and Robert Norrie was named general manager of the Kenworth Truck Division.

Paul Pigott's oldest son, Paul Jr. (Pat), was interested in the family's lumber business, and his passion for automobile racing influenced him to develop a Volkswagen dealership in Bellingham, Washington. Pigott's second son, Charles M., like his father, took an early and undying interest in Pacific Car and Foundry. He spent his summers working at various jobs including the forge, foundry, and steel shops. He also worked at the Kenworth Division. His bosses were instructed to treat him as they would any other worker, and, like them, he carried his lunch in a brown bag.

As soon as he had finished college and his military service as a U.S. Navy aviator in 1956, Charles Pigott came to work in the plant. Paul Pigott asked Renton plant general manager Ted Monson to take the youngster under his wing and teach him the business, but after further consideration Charles was assigned to Don Pennell and sent to the smaller Canadian Kenworth so that he might develop a better overview of how a division was run. He served there in a number of capacities of increasing responsibility until 1959 when, at the age of thirty, he was transferred to the Renton plant, and there continued his education under Monson.

CHAPTER NINE

GROWTH AND DIVERSIFICATION

In the late 1950s Pacific Car and Foundry stood proud of past accomplishments and ready for new challenges.

The company's product line was as diverse as it had ever been, particularly in Renton, Washington. Still heading the list, as they had since the earliest days, were railroad cars. Virtually every type of car was being produced, from cabooses to baggage cars, but the heaviest volume had become insulated and mechanically refrigerated cars, thousands of which had been built for twenty-two railroads and companies that shipped perishables.

Still a major part of Renton's production was industrial tractor equipment—Carco arches and hoists for the logging industry, and winches ranging from 3,000 to 110,000 pounds, the largest used principally in western forests to pull up to 50 tons of logs. Some fifteen hundred tractor dealers sold Carco products.

Castings fabricated from carbon steel and steel alloys, as well as forgings, were sold to more than five hundred customers, among them Bethlehem Steel, Todd Shipyards, Puget Sound Bridge & Dry Dock, and Kaiser Steel. Forged anode "stubs" were produced for the aluminum reduction plants of the Aluminum Company of America, Reynolds Metals, and the Aluminum Company of Canada. Pacific Car also manufactured street lighting poles for a large number of customers.

Military work, except for government research and development contracts, was at a low ebb, accounting for less than 5 percent of the company's sales.

On almost seventy acres of ground, the Renton Division had more than 600,000 square feet under roof, including the railcar and vehicle assembly shops, a steel foundry, a machine shop, a forge shop, a steel fabrication shop, a light sheet metal and aluminum fabrication shop, warehouses, offices, and some smaller production facilities. The foundry, leased since its construction during World War II, was purchased from the U.S. government in 1958, for $100,000 down and a $600,000 note, payable over ten years. A complete metallurgical, chemical, and physical testing laboratory kept busy with quality control and research of new products and industrial processes. The company also leased a 140-acre test track near the Renton plant as a proving ground for developing and refining products.

Peterbilt Motors Company was purchased by Pacific Car and Foundry on June 24, 1958.

The Commercial Ship Repair yard and marine railway at Winslow, Washington, were leased by Pacific Car in 1953 and later, in 1957, purchased as part of the Commercial Ship Division of the company.

Then there were the other divisions, principally the Kenworth Motor Truck Company, turning out to the customers' order heavy-duty trucks and related equipment for highway and off-highway use. At the Kenworth plant one might encounter a Hawaiian sugar plantation manager, a California logging operator, or a turbaned Arab discussing axles, wheels, motors, or weight-to-load ratios. The Structural Steel Division continued to work on a multiplicity of orders, mainly involving heavy steel construction members machined to fine precision tolerances. And finally there was the Commercial Ship Division, working on repair and maintenance of U.S. government and privately owned vessels of all kinds and sizes.

In 1958 Pacific Car had on its payrolls between three thousand and thirty-five hundred employees, about 10 percent of whom were engineers. The Military Division employed about eighty engineers and concentrated on research and development to carry out "Vehicular Engineering Agency" contracts for the Army Ordnance Tank and Automotive Center, in Detroit. To house its Army Ordnance engineers, the company began construction in 1958 of a new $300,000 engineering building, completing it in 1960.

The company's total sales in 1958 were $76 million, about the same as they had been in the four preceding years, while profits were up somewhat to $2,280,000. Earnings were decreased by a change in inventory accounting procedures from the first-in-first-out (FIFO) to the last-in-first-out (LIFO) method. LIFO was first suggested to Pacific Car's controller, Mike O'Byrne, by John Larson of Ernst and Ernst. Together they demonstrated the tax benefits of LIFO to Don Douglas, who along with O'Byrne presented Pacific Car's arguments to the Internal Revenue Service, which was only then establishing guidelines for the use of LIFO, for its approval. In addition, the company decided that provisions for possible contract losses appeared to be unnecessary. An aggressive effort by the company to establish itself as a source of ground handling and transportation equipment for the nation's missile effort resulted in some orders for vehicles for the Army's "Pershing" missile program.

In 1959 sales moved up sharply to a record $107 million, while net profit rose moderately to $2,583,000. There were some disappointments that year. After Pacific Car had designed, developed, and tested to the Army's satisfaction families of self-propelled guns and lightweight amphibious vehicles, no procurement orders were appropriated. And a strike severely restricted operations at the Renton and Kenworth plants for four months during the year. In a more than usually conservative dividend policy, the company cut back its distributions of dividends paid on the common stock.

With one exception, the company's relationships with its unions remained good. Pacific Car insisted on strict adherence to provisions of collective bargaining agreements, once they were negotiated. Ray Moran noted that there were "remarkably few grievances, and where they arise, settlements are reached promptly." The exception was the Machinists local, which struck Pacific Car and fifty-two other Seattle-area machine shops in May 1959; they were later joined by their associated Automotive Machinists local. All the other unions at the plants had reached settlements and ratified terms of their contracts, but the Machinists held out for more. About three weeks after the strike began, a back-to-work movement was started by members of other unions, and in nine days almost one thousand production employees were back on the job at the Renton and Kenworth plants.

Clearly the company's weakest division was Commercial Ship Repair, in an industry that continued to falter in the Seattle and Puget Sound area. Pacific Car decided that the division's future prospects were no better. Paul Pigott announced that the company would close down its facilities at Winslow and at Pier 66 at the end of August 1959. The inventory, equipment, and real property of Commercial Ship Repair were disposed of later in the year.

Although the company continued to do some business in cycloidal propellers, this marked the end of Pacific Car's efforts in the ship repair field. Eddie Black, head of the company's Marine Division, resigned from the company in mid-1960 to pursue his personal and new business commitments.

There was always a great deal of thought given to entering into new, or withdrawing from marginal, products. "The company and its divisions undertook new ventures from time to time," recalled Don Pennell. "They were not all successful. . . . The good thing is that the company never devoted more resources to these ventures than they justified and hence was able to drop projects quickly. . . ."

Holding forth much brighter hopes was the Truck Building Division. When Kenworth was acquired in 1945 its truck sales for that year amounted to $9.4 million. The company's annual report for 1959 announced that sales of motor trucks in 1960 were expected to reach $85 million. This was the outgrowth not only of Kenworth's sharply increased sales and production, but also of two 1958 acquisitions by Pacific Car and Foundry—the Dart Truck Company, of Kansas City, Missouri, and the Peterbilt Motors Company, of Oakland, California.

— THE 1958 ACQUISITIONS —

Pacific Car's board of directors voted on February 25, 1958, to authorize the purchase of the bulk of the assets of the Dart Truck Company. Within two weeks the KW-Dart Truck Company was incorporated as a wholly owned subsidiary of Pacific Car, and KW-Dart acquired substantially all of Dart Truck's assets. Dart had for many years concentrated on building large off-highway dump trucks and specialized vehicles for the oil, mining, and heavy construction industries; Pacific Car felt these units would not only complement its own line of earthmovers, but also strengthen its position in that market. Another potential gain was seen in the distribution economies that could be effected by the Midwest location.

Established in 1903 as the Dart Carriage Works, in Anderson, Indiana, Dart was a motor vehicle pioneer. It began building half-ton trucks, built like wagons, with solid tires and high wheels, primarily for the local market. Their two-cylinder, 25-horsepower engines were water-cooled, and gave the trucks a top speed of 27 miles per hour, where roads were available. The company did well, and in 1907 moved into a new 50,000-square-foot plant, equipped with electrically powered tooling, in Waterloo, Iowa. That year the company introduced a new four-cylinder engine truck, with a sliding-gear transmission, but with roller chains to transfer power to the rear axle. These trucks were used as fire vehicles, for deliveries, and in road and street construction. The chain drive was replaced two years later with a new drive train, which used propeller shafts and Timken worm drive axles.

William F. Barber, who had been foreman of the truck assembly department, was given the job of organizing and managing a parts and service department. W. H. Johnson joined the company as factory manager in charge of engineering and production in 1912. Dart was then building four different trucks ranging in size from a half ton to three and a half tons, and in price from $675 to $3,400.

Selected as one of several truck companies to serve the Quartermaster Corps during World War I, Dart proposed the use of its Model CC two-ton truck. Six were built and tested in Mexico, using U.S. Quartermaster Corps bodies. They served their purpose so well that the Army ordered them into production, and 326 were built during 1917 and 1918.

During the 1920s, Dart capitalized on this experience to direct its efforts toward supplying specialized vehicles for the burgeoning oil and mining industries, and to enter the tractor field as well. A star salesman in this period was Max W. Cline, who sold trucks and more than half of the farm tractors the company produced.

The company's principal stockholder, who owned more than 75 percent of the company, died in the early 1920s. When his estate had to be liquidated, Dart's operations came under the jurisdiction of the court, which decided in 1924 to sell Dart and its assets at public auction.

The buyer was A. H. Coward, a prosperous oil company executive who had used Dart trucks in his oil field operations. Coward changed the company name to Hawkeye-Dart, and made plans to expand operations in the heavy-duty truck market. But he, too, died before the year was over. Cline, sensing the strong sales potential for Dart trucks, acquired the production facilities and the service parts inventories needed to continue the manufacture and support of the trucks. He moved the plant to Kansas City, Missouri, persuaded Barber to come and join him, and recruited George House, a top-notch mechanic from the Waterloo plant.

Dart trucks became a more and more common sight in the Midwest and in the oil fields, where there was relative prosperity in the 1930s. An innovator in design and engineering for specialized truck applications, Dart was successful in selling its vehicles for large mining and quarry applications. Two men responsible for many of the technical advances were engineer Johnson, who rejoined the company in 1937, and Clifford Barber, son of the early assembly foreman, who signed on as an engineer. During World War II the firm supplied tank retrievers, truck crane carriers, and some 450 pontoon trailers and dollies to the military.

Dart Carriage Works
moved in 1907 to
Waterloo, Iowa, where
it produced a wide
variety of trucks before
the plant was moved
to Kansas City in 1925.

Oilfield service trucks were first developed by Dart in the 1920s, and later Dart trucks equipped with Braden winches were a common sight in Midwestern oil fields.

Page 171: Dart developed trucks and loaders for the off-road hauling and handling needs of the mining and construction industries.

Dart Truck Company was purchased from Cline by the George Ohrstrom Company, of New York, in 1947. Ohrstrom turned over control and management of Dart to its subsidiary, the Carlisle Corporation, of Carlisle, Pennsylvania, in 1950. Carlisle then sold the principal assets of Dart to Pacific Car early in 1958.

Pacific Car almost immediately announced plans to build a new $1 million plant on a 15-acre site at the North Chouteau Trafficway, in Kansas City. The 110,500-square-foot manufacturing and office facility was completed in December 1958. There KW-Dart continued to build its traditional off-highway vehicles, and took on full responsibility for producing Kenworth's 800 series of earthmovers.

When Pacific Car's Kenworth Truck Division was unable to meet the growing demand for its trucks in 1959, arrangements were made for KW-Dart to turn out a number of traditional Kenworth highway trucks at the Kansas City plant. At first the Dart plant merely assembled parts shipped from Seattle, but it was soon building Kenworths from the ground up. The development, it turned out, came at a very fortunate time, because Kenworth was shut down during a 113-day strike in Seattle.

In 1959 KW-Dart also authorized the manufacture and sale of some of its own vehicles in Canada by Sicard, Incorporated, of Montreal, under a license agreement. As a result, the KW-Dart mining vehicles quickly achieved growing acceptance in Canada. At the end of 1959 the KW-Dart subsidiary was dissolved, and the company was made a new division of Pacific Car. When Pacific Car's military production dwindled in 1960, the KW-Dart Division proved an exception, with a government contract for crane carriers accounting for about 25 percent of its total sales volume.

Under the Pacific Car banner the KW-Dart Division continued its record of innovation in engineering design and development. Because almost all of its manufactured units were specifically built for the jobs they were to perform, KW-Dart maintained a large engineering and service staff, which often oversaw the assembly of vehicles right at the job site.

The engineers were largely responsible for an impressive number of Dart "firsts" in equipping off-highway trucks—fluid-drive couplings, power steering, triple-reduction axles, torque converters, power down hoists, power shift transmissions, bottom-dumping tractor-trailer coal haulers, and end-dumping tractor-trailer earthmovers. They developed a line of specialized trucks with gross weight ratings from 40,000 to 700,000 pounds; jet aircraft refuelers with up to 10,000-gallon capacities; 280-ton "truck train" salt haulers; and a range of oil field equipment that included the world's largest "dune buggy." Its products were sold around the world, mainly to coal and ore mines and major construction and hydroelectric projects.

In 1967 KW-Dart's plant facilities were more than doubled, with 120,000 square feet of plant space and new equipment added to improve product quality. Because the "KW" was misleading it was dropped from the name in 1970, and the division reverted to its old designation of Dart Truck Company.

— PETERBILT ACQUISITION —

Pacific Car's second major acquisition in 1958 was the Peterbilt Motors Company, with the purchase of all the outstanding stock in June of that year. Unlike Dart, Peterbilt was directly competitive with Kenworth, selling Class Eight (33,000 pounds and up gross vehicle weight) highway trucks. Peterbilt possessed an enviable reputation for sound design, service, and follow-up after the sale.

The Fageol brothers started what became Peterbilt in Oakland in 1915 as the Fageol Motor Car Company, building luxury motor coaches and trucks. American Car and Foundry Company in 1924 offered a high annual payment for the rights to build Fageols in the East. The Fageol company proceeded to go heavily into debt to expand its Oakland plant and to build a new plant in Kent, Ohio, on the strength of this offer, but the arrangement was never consummated. The Fageol firm went into bankruptcy in 1929 and, as the Depression deepened, into receivership in 1932. The receivers, the Waukesha Motor Company and the Central Bank of Oakland, operated the company until 1938. That year they sold it to T. A. Peterman, a logger and a plywood and door manufacturer in Tacoma.

The purchase came as a surprise to those who knew Peterman in the lumber business; one of these was William Reed, who was later to become a director of Pacific Car and Foundry Company. Reed's Simpson Timber Company (Simpson Logging Company until 1960) sold him quantities of fir logs and considered him a good sawmill operator, if an indifferent logger. Peterman turned out to be a good enough businessman to manage a truck building company. He changed the name from Fageol to Peterman Manufacturing Company, under which he incorporated the business in 1940. Peterman purchased Fageol with the intention of developing a chain drive logging truck and, though he produced two, neither was successful. The company's eventual success stemmed from solid conventional truck designs. Peterman was actively involved with the company until his death in 1945.

The plant was left in the sole possession of his widow, Ida C. Peterman. She sold the company's assets, but not the underlying land, to a group of management employees of Peterbilt who were about to borrow $800,000 in 1947 to finance the venture. They adopted the corporate

T. A. Peterman took a lumberman's interest in producing high-quality Peterbilt trucks for the demanding West Coast logging industry. At left, a 1940s Peterbilt logging truck that dwarfed its highway-truck competition.

title of Peterbilt Motors Company, and ran the business under that name. Mrs. Peterman announced that she intended to develop the plant's site into a shopping center, and Peterbilt's owners were faced with the problem of raising $2 million for a new plant. The owners, headed by Peterbilt's president, Lloyd A. Lundstrom, were approaching the age of retirement and, rather than incur a large long-term obligation, chose to put the company on the block. One of those who showed an immediate interest was Paul Pigott.

Having decided he wanted Pacific Car to acquire Peterbilt, Pigott moved toward his objective without delay. He called company lawyer Paul Fetterman one afternoon and said, "Can you go to San Francisco with me? I'm talking about buying Peterbilt. I'll tell you about it on the plane."

On board the plane Pigott met a friend and began talking with him, waving Fetterman off when he tried to ask about the proposed purchase. Finally Pigott said, "I'll tell you more about it when we get down to the hotel." When they reached their hotel, the two went out to dinner. Pigott spoke in generalities about the deal he had in mind, and named a dollar figure that he felt he was willing to pay. "I think it will probably have to be a stock purchase," he told Fetterman.

The following morning Robert O'Brien came down to join Pigott and Fetterman, and met with them after breakfast. After a brief discussion, Pigott suggested to Fetterman, "Why don't you just prepare some form of a letter agreement?"

Fetterman said he would, although he was still not certain what the agreement was. He drafted a letter in general terms and had it typed, so that it would be ready to give to Lundstrom when he arrived. At ten o'clock that morning they met with Lundstrom and his financial man at the Palace Hotel. The group talked for a few minutes. Then with his usual directness, Pigott took Lundstrom to another room, returning a short time later to announce that they had reached an agreement. Pigott described the arrangement in general terms to O'Brien and Fetterman, looked at his watch, and declared, "My goodness, I'm due at another meeting. You can finish it up."

The others then went to a lawyer's office in Oakland, prepared a letter of agreement, had it signed by all the necessary people, opened a new bank account, and Fetterman and O'Brien flew back to Seattle that night. Pigott signed the agreement the following morning. Said Fetterman some years afterward, somewhat wistfully, "They just don't do it that easily any more . . . Paul was impatient about details. He knew where he was going, and he pointed in that direction and went there."

Peterbilt Motors was operated as a wholly owned subsidiary by Pacific Car from the date of its acquisition, June 24, 1958, until it was dissolved as a corporation at the end of 1960 and made a division of the parent firm. A year after the purchase, Pacific Car acquired a 31-acre site in a new industrial area in Newark, California. There Pacific Car built a new plant of 176,000 square feet, with ample land area for further expansion, and Peterbilt moved into the new quarters in August 1960.

At the time of acquisition, Donald Pennell, the Pacific Car executive who had headed Canadian Kenworth, Limited, was moved in as general manager of Peterbilt, to help the firm conform to Pacific Car operating practices. But Peterbilt continued its own tradition of high-grade customer service, and remained one of Kenworth's stiffest competitors, even though both were under the same ownership. Peterbilt's sales were made principally through sixteen western distributors. Later in the 1960s Peterbilt trucks were exported to the Philippines and Australia.

Pacific Car in 1967 purchased a 50-acre tract in Nashville, Tennessee. Construction soon began there on a 200,000-square-foot plant accepted from the builders by Peterbilt on July 1, 1969. The Newark plant was working at full capacity, and the new facilities would not only increase the production capabilities of Peterbilt, but also provide better service to eastern and southern heavy-duty truck markets.

— KENWORTH IN MEXICO —

Pacific Car next established a manufacturing relationship in Mexico. As George Lhamon and Don Douglas had predicted some years before, the Mexican government imposed import restrictions on vehicles manufactured in the United States and laid quotas on the assembly of vehicles in Mexico from parts manufactured elsewhere. Since World War II, Kenworth had developed a sizable business south of the border through its distributor in Mexico City, Distribuidora Quintana. So they decided, as they had in Canada, to initiate local production.

R. D. O'Brien learned of the Vildosola family and he requested a meeting with Gustavo Vildosola, who assured O'Brien that the Mexicali facilities were available and the Vildosolas could "easily get into the truck business."

O'Brien made an inspection trip to Mexicali and he described the plant as "an open-sided affair. There were no walls down one side. It was all open toward the middle, no roof, no nothing, and a dirt floor. . . . It was a disaster!" O'Brien observed that the plant was not impressive, but the Vildosola family was. Gustavo was honest, eager, and cooperative, and his

In 1958 Mexico's Kenworth truck production was accomplished out of doors with abundant manpower and pride.

father, a senator in the Mexican congress, from Baja, California, was highly regarded in Mexico. O'Brien worked out an agreement with the Vildosolas whereby subassemblies would be shipped to their plant in Mexicali on a consignment basis. Payment would be received after the trucks were assembled and sold in Mexico City. In the beginning they produced five trucks a month.

Paul Pigott made his first trip to Mexicali after O'Brien suggested that the company take a financial interest in the Mexican operation. After a quick tour Pigott cornered O'Brien with an unbelieving, "You have got to be kidding!" Nevertheless, for six months the Vildosolas purchased Kenworth trucks under the royalty agreement negotiated by O'Brien. The Vildosolas added a roof to the center section of their plant and a cement floor was poured.

Mexico clarified its import provisions, and it was necessary to take a financial interest in producing Kenworth trucks in Mexico or no longer be competitive in that market. In 1960 Pigott agreed to form a new company in Mexico to be capitalized at $100,000. Pacific Car put up all the money, and took a minority (49 percent) interest. The remaining 51 percent, constituting control, was retained by the company's managing director, Gustavo Vildosola Castro, and members of his family, all citizens of Mexico. The company was in compliance with the new Mexican ownership law, and Kenworth Mexicana Limited was ready to get on with the business of building trucks.

Edwin Sundstrom, a twenty-year Kenworth veteran, moved to the Mexican facility to help guide its manufacturing operations. By the time production began late in 1959, Kenworth Mexicana had accumulated a six-month backlog of orders for heavy-duty, over-the-highway, bulk and liquid commodity transporters for the Mexican market, and occasional orders were soon coming from other Latin American countries. At the start, a number of components and parts assemblies were furnished from Kenworth stateside plants, but these shipments diminished quickly as the Mexican plant expanded its operations and concluded agreements with local suppliers.

Kenworth Mexicana was soon manufacturing trailers under substantially the same licensing arrangement as had been made for trucks. Before long, production in Mexicali reached the rate of fifteen trucks and twelve trailers per month.

Production and sales in Mexico continued to improve at a satisfactory level. In 1965 Kenworth Mexicana opened a sales branch in Mexico City. By 1969 the Mexican affiliate had outgrown its leased manufacturing facilities, and on October 1 ground was broken for a new 160,000-square-foot factory and an 18,000-square-foot office building on a 50-acre site, just six miles south of the U.S. border and on the main highway to Mexico City. Capacity of the new plant, completed in 1970, was four or more trucks and two trailers per day.

Kenworth Mexicana, 1970s.

Paul Pigott, 1900–1961

— PAUL PIGOTT'S DEATH —

On two occasions in the fall of 1960 Paul Pigott suffered attacks of vertigo, the second more severe than the first. Concerned, Dr. Jack McVay, his close friend and personal physician, urged him to go to the Stanford Medical School for tests. There his condition was diagnosed as being the consequence of a brain tumor. Some thirty days later, shortly after Christmas in 1960, he was admitted into the Mayo Clinic, at Rochester, Minnesota, for surgery.

Both he and his son Charles were aware that the condition was serious and that the operation would be a touchy undertaking. In the week or so prior to Pigott's surgery, he and Charles had long talks, chiefly about the business of Pacific Car. They spent many hours together in the hospital room, discussing different facets of Pacific Car and Foundry, but mainly the qualities and capabilities of various senior executives. Charles later acknowledged that these talks and the insights they gave him were to serve him extremely well.

Pigott also indicated that he wanted Charles to go on the board if the operation should not succeed or if he himself became incapacitated, a very real danger. Pigott called one of his confidants on the Pacific Car board, mentioning his fears that he might not leave the clinic alive.

He expressed his feeling that O'Brien should succeed him as president of the company, a position for which Pigott had been preparing him for some time. O'Brien at that time was the sole executive vice president of the company, and appeared to be in the natural line of succession, which was typical of Paul Pigott's careful planning for the future. He also mentioned that he would like to see Charles Pigott become a director and the leading member of the family in the company.

Paul Pigott had taken over the reins of the company as the second son of the founder, William, and now was urging a similar future for his own second son. Charles himself had a simple explanation for this turn of events. On each occasion there had been another family business that had seemed more promising than Pacific Car. In the case of the founder, there was the Pacific Coast Steel Company, for which he had marked his oldest son, William Jr., as the successor and which was, indeed, the principal source of the family's early wealth. As for Paul, he had steered his oldest son, Paul Jr. (Pat), toward the family-owned Seaboard Lumber Company, which at the time appeared to be a more profitable long-term business.

Paul Pigott was operated on early in January of 1961, and thereafter he had very few lucid moments before slipping into a coma, from which he never recovered. He died on January 23. At the time of his death he was a director of Boeing, of Standard Oil of California, and of the Seattle-First National Bank, and a trustee of the Washington Mutual Savings Bank. In addition to holding leadership positions in business organizations, he was a member of the Stanford board of trustees and a regent of Seattle University, where he was largely instrumental in having the William Pigott Auditorium dedicated to his father's memory. For his interest in Seattle University and his work on behalf of Catholic education, Paul Pigott was named a knight commander in the Order of Knights of St. Gregory by Pope Pius XII, as was his father before him. He was a founder and director of the United Good Neighbors Fund, and had been a president of the Seattle Community Chest and Council, co-chairman of the building fund of Children's Orthopedic Hospital, president of the board of the Associated Boys Clubs of Seattle, and chairman of the Employ the Handicapped Committee.

In a holiday message to the employees of Pacific Car before going to Rochester, Pigott had said:

> Personal dedication was never more timely. The free world looks to this nation and its people for leadership. This responsibility rests on all of us. Individual initiative and accomplishment are still the measure and strength of our free democracy. . . .
>
> What can we do? We can continually strive to raise our personal standards . . . to work harder at being active, full-time citizens. . . .
>
> I feel that a Greeting to our Pacific Car family should contain a reminder of the rights and privileges we enjoy as citizens. Only by sacrifice and complete acceptance of our responsibilities . . . will we successfully oppose the forces working throughout the world to destroy our way of life.

Toward the end of January the directors of Pacific Car elected O'Brien president of the company. Charles M. Pigott, then assistant general manager of the Renton Division, but not listed in the company's reports as an officer, was elected to fill the vacancy on the board of directors.

O'Brien, then forty-seven, had been educated at Seattle schools and the University of Washington, where he studied accounting before joining Standard Oil. Rather than accept a transfer that required moving from Seattle, O'Brien resigned. While job hunting in 1943, he called on John Holmstrom, who hired O'Brien as a parts expediter for the M-1 wrecker. He was later promoted to the sales staff of Kenworth Motors, and in 1953 succeeded Vernon Smith, who was retiring as general sales manager. O'Brien was elected a director of Pacific Car and vice president and general manager of the Kenworth Division in 1957. The following year he was appointed vice president in charge of sales for all of Pacific Car, and in 1960 he was marked for the top operating post when he was appointed executive vice president.

Those who worked closely with O'Brien thought of him as affable, personable, gentlemanly, and a great salesman. They were most impressed by the brilliance of his retentive memory and lightning-fast mind. "His mind was faster than my slide rule," recalled Don Pennell. At one Pacific Car senior management meeting, he sat quietly in the back of the room, taking no notes, while the heads of the various divisions reported on their sales projections for the coming period. When they had all finished, Charles Pigott recapitulated the projections for the entire company. Later, after a meeting break, Charles rose to make a correction: O'Brien had pointed out to him, he said, that he had failed to add in one figure.

The first annual report to shareholders signed by O'Brien was for the year 1960, reflecting the final year of Paul Pigott's stewardship. Sales of $128 million and net profit after taxes of $3,698,000—including earnings of $244,000 by the non-consolidated truck finance companies— were at new record highs. A good part of the sales increase resulted from a large backlog of unfilled orders accumulated during the mid-1959 strike period, and new orders fell off during 1960, the report noted. Dividends rose with the higher earnings, and a year-end extra of 30 cents was paid, in addition to four quarterly payments of 30 cents per share.

— KENWORTH SURGES AHEAD —

Pacific Car's willingness—almost eagerness—to acquire heavy-duty truck manufacturing firms was undoubtedly influenced by the continuing growth and success of the Kenworth Motor Truck Company. Kenworth production had passed the 1,500 mark in 1955 and again in 1956, before dropping off for the next few years, but the truck manufacturing operation was consistently profitable. Output touched a low of 1,095 units in 1959, partly because of that year's strike and partly because some of what had been U.S. production was shifted to Canada and Mexico. Then, as backlogs were worked off, production surged to a record 1,920 trucks in 1960, then slipped to a still respectable 1,500 in 1961.

As Kenworth prospered, so did most of its dealerships, including those owned by the company itself. Texas Kenworth Corporation, which served as a factory outlet for the sale of Kenworth trucks and handled repair services, was dissolved at the end of 1959, when it became a division of Pacific Car, under the name of Texas Kenworth Company. Colorado Kenworth, which had been merged into Texas Kenworth in 1958, was separated back, also to be run as a division of Pacific Car.

By 1962 it was evident that Kenworth was in need of new and larger facilities. Because of the increased demand for durable, lightweight parts, the company added a special fiberglass shop in Seattle. A new sales branch building was put up in Omaha, Nebraska, to strengthen the company's sales penetration in the Midwest. And that year, when it became evident that the KW-Dart facilities could not meet the current and anticipated demand for Kenworths, plans were made for a $4.5 million factory at Kansas City, adjacent to the KW-Dart plant.

Built to provide a better base for Kenworth's growing sales and service needs in the mid-continent and East, the new plant was begun in March 1963 and completed in November.

The first trucks came off the assembly line in December, but full-scale production did not start until February 1964. Murray Aitken was put in charge of the operation, which added 50 percent to Kenworth's total capacity. Because of the shorter truck length laws of many eastern states, the Kansas City plant concentrated on cab-over-engine models.

Also in 1963, ground was broken for a new engineering and accounting building at the Kenworth plant site in Seattle. The construction was completed on schedule the following April, providing much needed space for the consolidation of engineering personnel and for the installation of a new computer for inventory control and for handling engineering releases to the plant. New company-owned truck sales branches were opened in Houston, Texas, and in Des Moines, Iowa. The warehouse in Chicago was expanded, and Peterbilt's need for more room initiated a 25 percent increase in Newark's production area and an expansion of their office space in 1965.

Mounting sales of Kenworth trucks posed additional record-keeping problems. Kenworth customers had always made up their orders from a list of design options available for each basic model—engine, transmission, differential, cab, radiator, etc. To avoid using a mountain of paper for each truck, Kenworth initiated a "Chassis Record" to show major assemblies and components for each vehicle; these were sent out to places where they were needed, and also filed in a permanent "Chassis Jacket" at Kenworth.

Kenworth continued to develop and build trucks for a great diversity of uses. In addition to the special vehicles built for the desert and for Hawaiian cane plantations, regular production models performed a variety of jobs in logging, construction, and over-the-road hauling. Ninety Kenworth trucks were shipped from Canadian Kenworth to Zambia, in central Africa, to carry bulk liquids, copper ore, and heavy machinery across 1,500 miles of the continent's "Hell Run."

Because of length laws common in the eastern states, Kenworth's Kansas City plant concentrated on the production of cab-over-engine models.

As the Alaskan oil fields were opened in 1970, a new Kenworth model, the 953-S, was delivered for sale to Sourdough Freightlines of Anchorage, Alaska. The mission was to haul supplies along the 400 miles of ice road between Fairbanks and the North Slope. Engineered to operate in temperatures as low as 70 degrees below zero Fahrenheit, the trucks carried 1,000 gallons of fuel and were able to haul payloads of 100 tons. Another model, the 849RFD, produced by Canadian Kenworth, was the biggest logging truck ever built, designed at 500,000 pounds. It went into service in British Columbia to haul loads across some of the roughest terrain in the Pacific Northwest.

One of the more unusual hauling jobs was performed in Mexico by standard Kenworth trucks. The assignment was to move the thirteenth-century Aztec idol Tlaloc from its ancient home in the village of Coatlinchan to Mexico City, 30 miles to the west, for the 1964 opening of the National Museum of Anthropology in Chapultepec Park. Tlaloc was a 154-ton monolith, carved from a single stone, 14 feet wide, 13 feet thick, and more than 24 feet long. The villagers were against having their god of rain and harvest taken away, and they attacked and damaged the steel scaffolding and cables put up for the move. The Mexican government managed to appease them with promises of electricity, a school building, and a paved road to the main highway six miles away.

To handle the move, a 50-ton trailer, 65 feet long and almost 20 feet wide, was built and equipped with seventy-two tires, each having 11-inch treads and twelve plies of nylon. The trip began at six in the morning with two Kenworth trucks pulling the platform and idol along a special road built to the highway, and ended at two o'clock the following morning. Along the route, fifteen hundred telephone and electric cables had to be raised or cut. In Mexico City there was a long pause for televising the procession. And it rained throughout, apparently reflecting Tlaloc's own displeasure, drenching the twelve hundred soldiers assigned to the move, along with an estimated one million spectators.

Kenworth's sales grew during the 1960s on a fairly consistent and strong uptrend. In 1962, volume rose to 1,851 trucks, and then it reached a record 1,976 units in 1963. The 1964 results were slightly higher at 2,037, and in 1965 there was a sharp 50 percent upturn to 3,049. New records continued to be established, with sales of 3,906 in 1966, 4,549 in 1968, 6,240 in 1969, 7,550 in 1971, and 10,519 in 1972, more than five times as great as sales had been just eight years earlier.

All of Pacific Car's truck-building divisions tended to be proud of their own products and jealous of their own prerogatives. Although this made for high morale within the divisions, it also manifested itself in the "NIH," or "not invented here," syndrome. An engineering change in one division was likely to be disregarded, or even reversed, in another. It made for healthy competition, as dealerships of the different divisions would sell hard against each other in the same markets.

The basic business philosophies of all the divisions, however, were very similar, principally because of the interchange of key personnel. In 1959, for example, Robert Norrie was Kenworth's general manager; Donald Pennell was moved from Canadian Kenworth to be general manager of Peterbilt; W. J. Ferguson Jr. was installed as president of Canadian Kenworth; and J. H. Connors was general manager of KW-Dart. He was succeeded in 1962 by Murray Aitken. In 1963 John Bodden took over as general manager of Peterbilt from Pennell, who had by then become group vice president and later a member of Pacific Car's board of directors. And in 1970 Bodden replaced Murray Aitken as general manager of Kenworth, when Aitken took on corporate responsibilities in truck manufacture; Robert Holmstrom was then moved from the presidency

In 1964 Kenworth trucks moved the thirteenth-century idol Tlaloc from the village of Coatlinchan to Mexico City.

of Canadian Kenworth to be general manager of Peterbilt. Holmstrom, John Holmstrom's nephew, started in Kenworth engineering in 1946, became plant manager of KW-Dart in Kansas City, production manager at Kenworth-Seattle, and assistant general manager of Kenworth-Kansas City, before taking on the Canadian post. All of this made for considerable uniformity in the understanding of sales goals, engineering, and manufacturing operations, as well as in approaches to profit margins and product quality.

The rate of sales growth for Canadian Kenworth kept pace with that of the U.S. truck division. In 1959 the British Columbia plant was expanded to 60,000 square feet, increasing manufacturing and storage areas by almost 40 percent. A truck sales branch was built at Nanaimo, British Columbia, in 1965, in addition to other branches in Calgary and Edmonton in the Canadian province of Alberta. There were also independent distributors throughout most of Canada. Another factory expansion was started in 1965.

Canadian Kenworth continued to devote a good deal of its energies and engineering capabilities to the development of specialized products for the logging industry. One of these was a pre-loading trailer, designed so that the driver could drop off an empty trailer for loading and then pick up another already loaded. So well was this idea received that fifteen orders came in before the first one was built.

On April 1, 1961, Pacific Car acquired all the stock of the Westfall Equipment Company, of Portland, Oregon. Westfall was then developing an all-wheel drive, rubber-tired tractor, principally for logging work, and the purchase became a means of entering the field of logging and agricultural tractors. The new subsidiary was first named KW-Westfall Company, and then renamed Kenworth Manufacturing Company. It offered several models for log-skidding and loading. After a little more than a year, operations were transferred from Portland to Pacific Car's Structural Steel Division. The skidder-loader models were eventually discontinued and the larger front-end loaders were transferred to KW-Dart.

Growth of Pacific Car's truck sales in time also required better capitalized organizations

KW-Dart first developed a log stacker in 1962 with technology acquired in the purchase of Westfall Equipment Company.

to finance those sales. With the acquisitions of Dart and Peterbilt, the name of the Kenworth Finance Company was changed to Truck Acceptance Corporation. In Canada, Kenworth Finance Limited changed its name in 1960 to Overland Acceptance Corporation.

Early in 1961 Pacific Car organized a third wholly owned finance company, Carco Acceptance Corporation, investing $4.5 million in capital and lending it $1.5 million to finance the domestic truck sales that Truck Acceptance had been handling. Truck Acceptance then confined its activities to financing foreign sales, principally for Mexico. Information on the credit of potential purchasers would be collected in Mexico by an employee stationed there, and the Seattle office would make a careful credit analysis before offering the transaction to the lending bank for appraisal. When no trade-ins were involved, Mexican sales would generally be made on the basis of a 20 percent down payment.

Carco Acceptance borrowed its funds from a group of U.S. banks in a conventional manner, with parent company recourse or guarantees. Carco helped finance sales of Kenworth, Peterbilt, and KW-Dart equipment, although purchasers of KW-Dart's mining and earth-moving vehicles ordinarily obtained their own financing directly. Distributors were encouraged to develop their own sources of financing, and were helped in doing this as much as possible. Since the sales of new trucks usually involved trade-ins, the financing of used truck sales also became a part of the overall program.

In 1962 Carco Acceptance negotiated a new fifteen-year loan of $6 million with the Prudential Insurance Company, providing $4.5 million of senior funds to reduce bank loans and a $1.5 million subordinated loan, used to liquidate the similar advance from Pacific Car. In 1970 Carco Acceptance Corporation changed its name to Paccar Financial Corp., but its mission and operations remained unchanged.

Results of Pacific Car's first full year of operations under the presidency of Robert O'Brien were not as bad as the fears he had expressed in the 1960 report to stockholders. Sales and earnings were down only a few percent from the previous year's record levels, at $120 million and $3,513,000, respectively.

Truck sales clearly dominated total results, amounting to $70 million, compared to $50 million for all other products. The dividend policy remained as conservative as ever, and common stock payments for the year were cut by five cents to $1.45 per share. The higher level of activity required more working capital, and a term loan with Prudential Insurance was increased from $8.4 million to $13 million.

In 1962 sales shot up to $142 million, while net earnings reached $4,636,000, equal to $9.51 per share. Dividends were increased in the second quarter to thirty-five cents per share, and a year-end extra of 55 cents a share lifted total payments for the year to $1.90. A 10 percent stock dividend paid early in 1963 increased the common stock outstanding to 538,134 shares. The pension and profit sharing plans took a total of $602,000 for the year, and contributions made in 1962 included a sizable payment to a new Paul Pigott Scholarship Foundation, which awarded twelve academic scholarships, each for a year, to children of company employees.

Sales in 1963 rose by $53 million to $195 million, and net profit increased to $7,530,000. Dividends remained at thirty-five cents a quarter, but the year-end extra was increased to $1 a share, and a 20 percent stock dividend was voted near the close of the year; the new shares were also paid the extra dividend. The backlog of unfilled orders increased from $55 million at the end of 1962 to $100 million a year later.

In the list of corporate officers, Charles M. Pigott, whose name had appeared as assistant vice president in the 1962 report, moved up to the post of executive vice president that December. George M. Lhamon advanced in 1964 to vice president and treasurer, on the forthcoming retirement of Donald Douglas from those posts and from the board. His place on the board was taken by John W. Pitts, a business executive from Vancouver, British Columbia. Douglas still remained as president of two of the wholly owned finance companies, with Lhamon taking over as president of Carco Acceptance.

Military work increased very briefly in the early 1960s, as Army Ordnance felt the need for additional self-propelled guns. In 1960 the company was awarded $2.2 million in contracts for engineering, services, and supplies, in connection with three vehicles. This was followed by a development contract from Army Ordnance for self-propelled artillery, and then by orders for 235 units of the M-107 gun vehicles and M-110 self-propelled howitzers, for a total of $17 million, in mid-1961. This new family of guns was to replace equivalent vehicles built by Pacific Car during the Korean War, but which weighed nearly twice as much. To work on this order, the company spent more than $1 million to rearrange and modernize the steel casting foundry.

Production began in the fall of 1961, but few of the vehicles were delivered before 1962. The entire contract was completed by July 1963. Pacific Car bid aggressively on contracts to build more of the gun carriers, but the award went elsewhere.

With military orders confined primarily to research and development in 1964, and with substantially all production volume going to commercial customers, total sales nevertheless rose 21 percent to another new record at $237 million. Earnings of $10.8 million were also at a new peak. Dividends totaled $2.50 per share on the increased number of shares outstanding, including a year-end extra of $1.50. Investment in plant and equipment for the year totaled almost $3 million.

Pacific Car's sales in the mid-1960s placed it among the top 250 or 300 industrial corporations in the nation, and its sales and earnings growth compared very favorably with that of major competitors. Between 1956 and 1964 the company's sales rose 144 percent, as against 65 percent for International Harvester, 16 percent for Mack Truck, and 3 percent for Pullman. Some of this gain was the result of acquisitions, but earnings per share fared just as well. While they tripled for Pacific Car in the same period, they increased just 59 percent for International Harvester, and dropped 34 percent for Mack and 54 percent for Pullman.

In October 1963 Canadian Kenworth Limited acquired the Gearmatic Company, Limited, a manufacturer of power winches that were generally smaller than those built by Pacific Car. The acquired company was owned by Frank Lawrence, who had started manufacturing boom winches and boom stick boring machines in Canada in 1934. He sold his business in 1940 and moved to Renton, where he went to work for Pacific Car and Foundry. Unable to develop his

Ted Monson (second from left), Bob O'Brien (fourth from left), Charles Pigott (second from right), and Ellis Hendrickson (right) presented the M-110 to U.S. Army representatives in 1963.

In 1952 Gearmatic developed a very successful mechanical winch for the log skidder market in Canada.

own ideas, including a three-speed quick-change transmission, at Pacific Car, he left in 1945 to go out on his own again. He returned to Vancouver and founded Gearmatic.

In 1952 he introduced a mechanical winch that sold well to the logging industry, and in 1957 Gearmatic put up a new 30,000-square-foot building in Surrey, British Columbia. Eventually the company was supplying 75 percent of the winches for the log skidder market. Lawrence in 1961 introduced a hydraulic winch useful in logging, construction, mining, fishing, oil exploration, pipeline, and other industries, and it came to account for more than half of Gearmatic's original winch equipment business. Nearing retirement age, Lawrence decided to sell his company to his old employer, and Pacific Car purchased the business as a base for expanding their winch sales in Canada.

— CHARLES PIGOTT AS PRESIDENT —

From the time of Paul Pigott's death, everyone connected with Pacific Car and Foundry assumed that his son Charles would in due course become the principal figure in the company. Just how this was to come about was left largely in the hands of the two outside directors on the board, Tom Gleed and William Reed. The arrangement they had in mind was for Charles to take charge of the company after about three years.

Charles Pigott had wanted to be associated with Pacific Car as far back as he could remember. "I happen to be one of those fortunate people who always knew what I wanted to do," he once said. "I wanted to go to work for Pacific Car." His working career there began when he was a teenager, on summer vacations from high school. In the summer of 1945 he worked at the Kenworth plant, hauling parts, swinging castings, and doing various jobs in a barn being used as a warehouse. Then he worked in the foundry and other departments at Renton. When the union refused to permit him to work in the machine shop there, he got his machine shop training at the Everett Pacific shipyards after he graduated from high school in 1947.

Once, when he worked at the foundry, a carload of 50-pound sacks of a compound for the furnace arrived. Harold Prentice, the assistant superintendent, said to him, "Okay, Pigott, go over there and unload that car." The first hour or two went easily, but by the eighth hour, Charles began to discover some new muscles. He went home, skipped dinner, and crawled into bed, but with youthful resilience he was able to bounce back the next day. Prentice thereafter never tired of recalling the incident with some delight. "Remember, Chuck, how I told you to unload that car and you did it!"

Pigott was in the Stanford class of 1951, but he enrolled in the Naval Aviation Cadet Program during the Korean War, so did not actually graduate until the winter quarter of 1956. After taking flight training he was commissioned as a pilot and flew Lockheed Neptune P2Vs first in the States and then on shipping surveillance missions out of the Iwakuni base near Hiroshima.

After his graduation from Stanford he enrolled at the University of Washington, where he took a quarter of only accounting courses, before coming to work for Pacific Car.

Charles Pigott started work in Canada as an industrial engineer, a role that called for both engineering and business skills. He worked with bills of materials, did some drafting, and spent time on the production floor, where trucks were built progressively, moving from one bay to another. He next worked for a while in sales—"I even sold a truck, and that was pretty good for an inside person!" recalled Pigott. He next went into purchasing, completing his education on how a small operation worked. He enjoyed his three years in Canada greatly, especially when he was dealing with production.

He returned to Seattle in 1959, better prepared to make a contribution to the much larger Renton operation. Pennell, he felt, had a natural interest "in all young people and the opportunities to teach them the trade," while Ted Monson would have found no great pleasure in taking time out from his concentration on trying to run a very complex part of the company.

Charles Pigott's three greatest teachers in the company, he felt, were Pennell, Monson, and Murray Aitken. "While I was never reporting to Murray—it was actually the other way around—you couldn't help but learn a great deal from an old master like Aitken," he said. The most sharply etched lesson from Paul Pigott, and one he had absorbed from the time he was at his father's knee, was that of the value of integrity. "Your word should truly be your bond. If you have a good reputation, you have a much easier time in life. I think that lesson has stood me in very good stead." Another valuable idea he got from his father was that of the executive's need to look far down the road, "anticipate what's going to happen a year or five or ten years from now."

After Charles Pigott became executive vice president under Robert O'Brien, he took an increasingly important part in the management of Pacific Car. But he did not feel ready, after three years, to take on the top role, to be the company's front man and public face, to deliver addresses and to be Mr. Pacific Car in the Seattle business community.

As executive vice president, he faced two major challenges. The first was personal—feeling comfortable in a job that required important decisions and carried a great weight of responsibility, at the age of thirty-four. There were the pressures of workers, of the management group, of the community, and especially of customers—many of them the heads of railroads, aged sixty or more. The second was a business challenge—learning how to manage a sprawling, growing company with at least four separate and largely disparate divisions. He needed more years to season himself in those tasks and to develop greater confidence in his own abilities. "Maybe for some people it's like falling off a log," he said, "but it was not for me."

By 1965 Charles Pigott felt he was ready, and he communicated that thought to Gleed and Reed, among others. "I was surprised when this came about," said Reed, "that Chuck wanted to be president. I thought he ought to be chairman of the board and have Bob be the chief operating officer. But Chuck wanted to run the operations, and I think he did very well. He and Bob, I think, always got along well. They found productive ways to get their talents together."

Pigott recognized, as his father had before him, that his talents suited him to be a direct management executive—only figuratively "out on the production floor," but more specifically to harmonize the various facets that, working well together, would make up a successful business. In June 1965, the board elected O'Brien chairman of the board and named Charles M. Pigott the new president of Pacific Car. Some months later Pennell was made a vice president.

Pigott's seasoning included positions on the boards of the Seattle-First National Bank, Crown Zellerbach Corporation, Northwestern Glass Company, and Stanford Research Institute. As for his own management style, he was a solid and sound businessman, who liked to base his decisions on the evidence in front of him and his best judgment of what was likely to happen in the future.

Charles M. Pigott became president of Pacific Car and Foundry in 1965.

The first annual report signed by Pigott as president and O'Brien as chairman showed the best year, by far, in the company's history. Sales were $292 million, and net profit was $15.5 million. Quarterly dividends were increased at mid-year to 40 cents a share, and a year-end extra dividend of $2.50 was declared, bringing total declarations for the year to $4 a share. The truck divisions continued to dominate volume, as the transportation and mining industries came into the market for much new equipment, but the railroad equipment division still accounted for about a third of the company's sales, since many railroads were engaged in modernization and new equipment programs.

— VENTURES NEW AND OLD —

The following year the company made its most emphatic move yet toward extending its operations abroad, across the Pacific. Back in 1958 a group of Australian truck operators had come to the United States to see what they could learn about equipment and methods that might be useful to them. John Holmstrom and R. B. Waggoner made a return visit to Australia to sound out the level of interest in Kenworth products. They helped establish an Australian sales organization, Australian Kenworth Truck Sales Pty. Limited, of Doncaster, Victoria, headed by E. L. Cameron.

The Seattle plant then began manufacturing some right-hand drive models, both conventional and cab-over-engine, for Australia and other Far East locations. The first commercial Kenworth trucks were sent to Australia late in 1962, and were sold there in 1963.

Don Pennell suggested to O'Brien that Peterbilt be allowed to compete with Kenworth for the Australian truck market. O'Brien accepted Pennell's idea and further agreed that the truck best able to penetrate the market should establish an Australian factory. Peterbilt immediately established a distributor in Melbourne. Though Peterbilt argued that they had sold more trucks, it was decided that Kenworth, with greater experience in running foreign facilities, would begin assembling trucks in Australia.

In 1966, Australia increased its tariff rates, so Kenworth Motor Trucks Pty. Limited was registered as a corporation in Victoria, and they began to import completely knocked-down trucks and to assemble them in Australia. This company then purchased the original Kenworth truck distributor in Doncaster, as well as the Peterbilt distributor in Sydney, and these two outlets were set up as retail Kenworth sales branches in the states of Victoria and New South Wales. Peterbilt distribution in Australia was discontinued.

Sales of Kenworth trucks continued to grow in Australia. In 1969, when there were indications that government policies on imports would stiffen, the Australian Kenworth firm purchased 28 acres of land to construct a new truck factory at Bayswater, Victoria, a suburb 22 miles from Melbourne. The new plant, capable of producing three hundred trucks a year, was started in January 1970 and completed later in the year. By the following January the 56,000-square-foot Bayswater plant was in full operation, putting out trucks with 70 percent Australian content. Parts obtained elsewhere were engines, transmissions, front axles, and chassis frame rails, approximately the same ones obtained from outside sources for the U.S. plants. Sales in 1969 were $5.25 million and then moved up rapidly toward $8 million in 1970 and $10 million in 1971.

To meet the more severe operating conditions, including an absence of freeways and good highways, Australian trucks tended to be more rugged than most of those built for use in the United States. One unusual feature of many of the models was a protective guard, known as a

Kenworth Motor Trucks Pty. Limited successfully marketed and produced its first truck fleet in 1971 and has since grown to become the largest producer of heavy-duty trucks in Australia.

"roo bar" or "bull bar," in front, to prevent damage to the radiator from cattle and kangaroos when driven on the huge, unfenced Australian "outback." These bars had to be hinged to swing away before a cab or a hood could be tilted for engine maintenance or repair.

In Quebec, Canada, Pacific Car made an offer in January 1967 to pay $8 a share for all the 652,000 outstanding common shares of Sicard, Incorporated, the company that was already manufacturing KW-Dart off-highway vehicles under license. Almost all of the Sicard stockholders quickly agreed. The Sicard acquisition represented $2.5 million of the company's $8.4 million in capital expenditures for 1967.

While Sicard was known chiefly as a leading manufacturer of high-speed snowblowers and sweepers for airport and highway use, an important aspect of the acquisition by Pacific Car was the opportunity to increase its sales of trucks and establish its own manufacturing facilities in eastern Canada.

Invention had always been the root of Sicard's success. Arthur Sicard in 1907 had observed a new threshing machine that blew away the straw that was separated from grain. Why, he thought, could not the same principle be applied to clearing away snow? He started working on the idea, created a rotating worm, and placed behind it a strong fan to suck up the snow and blow it out through an ejection chute. The following winter he tested it, but it proved to be too weak to handle the heavy drifts of eastern Canada.

Seven years later, Sicard withdrew his savings of $40,000 and left his small construction business to develop a more powerful snowblowing machine. Within three years, he had sold the first snowblower to the city of Outremont, a Montreal suburb. This machine was still in use when it was bought back by the company in 1957 as a museum piece.

Arthur Sicard died in 1946, and a joint venture of Sorel in Quebec and Schneider & Company, of Paris, France, bought a controlling interest in the closely held company. For two decades they managed its operations and growth before the purchase by Pacific Car. After a brief study, Canadian Kenworth sold the legally encumbered snowblower patents to SMI Industries, which took over its manufacture at the original Sicard plant in Montreal.

Not all the ventures of Pacific Car and Foundry went the way of growth and expansion under Charles Pigott. One that moved in the opposite direction was the Structural Steel Division.

The division, ever since the 1936 purchase of the old Hofius Steel interests, had almost always been modestly profitable, sometimes making a little money one year and losing a little the next. But it was able to maintain and gradually expand its workforce.

The basic philosophy of the Structural Steel Division under Paul Jacobsen was to run a precision shop that could fabricate heavy steel members to extremely close tolerances, rather than seek a large volume of low-value, heavy-tonnage business. From Bonneville on, it had built most of the dam gates for power projects in the Pacific Northwest—gates built to operate on a radius of 40 feet and yet hold to a tolerance of .005 inch. For operation around water and turbulence, a great deal of stainless and other special alloys had to be used for gates, guides, special controls, and orifices that would either take in or discharge water. One of the last hydroelectric jobs assumed was for a third powerhouse for Grand Coulee Dam.

The division also did considerable work on commercial buildings, bridges, aircraft hangars, and factories. Pacific Car crews and equipment would handle the erection at the site for such accounts as the Austin Company; Morrison-Knudsen Company, Incorporated; Weyerhaeuser Company; the Guy F. Atkinson Construction Company; and the U.S. Army Corps of Engineers. About 97 percent of this work was done in the Northwest, mainly in Washington State and Alaska, and much of the remainder went abroad. Pacific Car won a contract in 1959 for 16,000

The Structural Steel Division, which purchased Steel Fabricators, Inc., in 1936, was located in Seattle until the division was dissolved in 1973.

linear feet of piling to be used in the construction of a 4,000-foot cut-off seal at the base of Yankee Dam, some 250 miles upriver from Bangkok, Thailand. The competition for this project included Japanese, French, English, and other United States fabricators. The division also produced structural components for the Robbins tunnel boring equipment used in the construction of irrigation systems in Australia and for subways in Paris, France.

One of the more extraordinary assignments undertaken by the division was as a sub-contractor for the structural steel used in the Space Needle for the Seattle World's Fair. The first proposal came in as little more than a back-of-the-envelope drawing of a thin column, 600 feet high, mushrooming out on top into quarters for a restaurant. Preliminary estimating was done mainly on a tonnage basis, with only the roughest idea of the form it would take. The drawings came out of a Los Angeles office, and detail planning had to be done at Pacific Car. Erection started in May 1961 for the fairly spectacular structure that had to be completed the following May. But by November the participants in the construction were able to hold a Thanksgiving dinner of sorts at the top, still open to high winds, so that a number of those present showed very little interest in the dinner itself. The entire job was completed on time in April of 1962 without a "lost-time" accident.

The next major project of the division was for structural steel for the 50-story headquarters of the Seattle-First National Bank. The steel sections, weighing 730 pounds per foot, were rolled by Bethlehem Steel in Pennsylvania and fabricated as a joint venture by Pacific Car and by the Isaacson Structural Steel Company. Pacific Car turned out the four massive exterior columns, while Isaacson handled the core cluster columns.

The capstone of all the company's structural steel work, however, was a $22 million contract for a major part of the bearing walls for the 110-story twin towers of the World Trade Center in New York City. Bids had originally been sought for steel required for the entire construction project. All were rejected as too far above estimates by the Port of New York Authority, which had undertaken the project. The job was then split into a number of smaller packages, and bids were sought from a large number of steel fabricators across the country. In order to reach the volume needed for maximum efficiency, Pacific Car put several packages together and submitted its bid. They won the award for 5,668 steel panels, weighing a total of 58,000 tons, making Pacific Car the largest among thirteen fabricators contributing steel for the towers.

The construction technique, relatively new, was to be similar to that used for the Seattle-First National Bank building. Most skyscrapers up to that time were supported by interior steel skeletons, along with reinforced concrete, but in the Trade Center towers the outside walls were to be the load-bearing members, and most of the steel went to the exterior walls. This and the use of stronger steel made it possible to use 40 percent less structural steel than in previous buildings.

The tower construction was computer designed, and Pacific Car used as many computer-oriented controls as possible, including the production of more than 45,000 shop drawings. The thousands of steel panels, making up the bearing walls of the twin towers from the 9th to the 107th floor, ranged in thickness from a quarter inch to three inches and in weight from 5 to 23 tons. The steel columns and spandrels were fabricated into three-story panels, measuring 10 by 36 feet. During the fabrication there was continual shifting from steel of one strength to another, with yield points ranging from 36,000 to 100,000 pounds per square inch, depending on such stress factors as the direction of prevailing winds.

Work on the contract began late in 1967 and continued into July 1970, when the last of the

The 605-foot Space Needle was completed in April 1962. It required 3,700 tons of structural steel, and at the time it was the tallest building west of the Mississippi River.

steel panels started on its way to New York, three months ahead of schedule. The completion of this work, on time and in line with all specifications, was a triumph for the relatively unknown steel fabricator in the Northwest in every way but one. The winning bid had been figured closely, and costs—particularly special expenses incurred in expanding the plant to handle the Seattle-First National and World Trade Center jobs, along with regular work—had outrun estimates.

The Trade Center project, the largest ever undertaken by the Structural Steel Division, was technically successful and completed ahead of schedule, yet it turned out to be a money loser. When the bid was first developed, company estimators had projected a transportation cost of $32 per ton for shipping the 58,000 tons of fabricated steel from Seattle to New York by barge. This turned out to be impractical, however, when not even Lloyds of London would insure timely arrival of barge shipments that would include up to three floors of fabricated steel. The contract stipulated a $10,000-per-day penalty payment for late delivery. So plans were revised to provide for rail shipment of each steel member—at a cost of $52 a ton, for an overall cost increase of $1.16 million. Pacific Car used 1,600 railcars to ship the steel to the East for the World Trade Center project. The dunnage alone—wood blocks and pieces used to protect the cargo—cost around $100,000.

From that time on, the fortunes of the Structural Steel Division seemed to wane. A strike affecting that and other divisions of the company began in April 1968. After many meetings with the unions involved, in which management pleaded that the settlements sought would be so expensive as to hurt their competitive position, agreement was finally reached. The strike ended after three and a half months with the signing of three-year contracts by ten unions. But the company's management newsletter warned, "The increases . . . far exceed any productive gains that we might hope to achieve, and hence can only be recognized as extremely inflationary. The practical effects of such settlements are to limit our ability to compete in the market place when we have competitors who are able to produce goods more reasonably."

The Structural Steel Division, it was pointed out, had been given increasing opportunities to quote on work located in California and Alaska. But other fabricators from southern states and, most recently, from Japan, submitted lower bids. Added to such negative factors was the virtual ending of all hydroelectric dam work in the West. Finally, Charles Pigott said, "We decided we were just spending too much time for very little return. It was not a growth business. If the job was big, out-of-state firms with better production facilities would move in. When the Japanese started entering the structural steel fabricating market, we didn't see any more future in it."

In 1973 Pacific Car and Foundry finally got out of the structural steel business and sold its facilities. "Looking back on it," Pigott concluded, "it was a very good decision. It allowed us to concentrate on other parts of our business."

— PACIFIC CAR'S NEW VISIBILITY —

Under Pigott's presidency, the sales volume of Pacific Car continued to grow. It reached a record $333 million in 1966; slipped to $319 million in 1967, when suspension of the investment tax credit hit railcar sales particularly hard; climbed again to $344 million in 1968, in spite of a series of drawn-out strikes at U.S. and Canadian plants; rose sharply to $466 million in 1969; dipped to $442 million in 1970; and passed the half-billion mark at $514 million in 1971.

Earnings followed a similarly erratic course to higher levels. Profits in 1966 were up 19 percent to $18.1 million. In 1967 they dropped to $15.6 million, and fell further to $14.1 million in 1968, when strikes made inroads of well over $1 million and an income surtax cost an estimated $1.1 million in net income. Earnings then reached a record high of $19 million in 1969, dipped sharply again to $14.7 million in 1970, and in 1971 soared to a new peak of $24.3 million.

The company's dividend policies became considerably more generous to shareholders in this period. The stockholders approved a three-for-one stock split in June 1966, so that a change in the dividend rate of 40 cents a share in the first two quarters to 15 cents on the new shares in the last two actually represented a 50 percent increase in the payout of dividends. A year-end extra dividend of 95 cents brought the total to an equivalent of $1.52 paid on the new shares, and in each of the next two years dividends totaled $1.50 per share.

The total number of common shares outstanding had risen from 13,477 after the 1943 recapitalization to 2,749,995, as the result of one ten-for-one split, two three-for-one splits, a stock dividend of 30 percent, another of 20 percent, and four of 10 percent each. A person holding 100 shares in 1945 and leaving them undisturbed would have owned more than 20,000 shares twenty-five years later.

Both Kenworth and Peterbilt offer small diesel trucks for use as short-haul delivery vehicles.

The star in all this growth continued to be the sales of heavy-duty trucks. By 1968 these accounted for fully 75 percent of the company's total volume. This resulted in part from the fact that the market for heavy-duty trucks was growing at a more rapid rate than the gross national product, and in part from new records set in sales in eastern parts of Canada and the United States. Industry statistics for 1970 showed that Kenworth, Peterbilt, and Dart held 12 percent of the market for highway trucks in the United States and 16 percent of the Canadian market. Higher levels of inflation in the United States than in other countries, however, meant tougher competition for Kenworth's export sales.

Pacific Car consistently invested the funds needed to maintain its plants and equipment at modern and efficient levels. To these traditional costs were added new ones for meeting new safety and environmental standards, both for engineering and design of the company's products and for cutting pollution generated by manufacturing processes. Beginning in 1969, an extensive new ventilation system was installed at the Renton foundry. This employed telescoping hoods to collect smoke and fumes from the foundry furnaces, and ducts to transfer them to a new "bag-house" built for the purpose, which removed solids in large nylon bags and transferred them to a conveyor at the rate of 22 pounds an hour, for removal to dumps.

In March 1966 John Holmstrom, long a valued executive and member of the board, died. His place on the board was taken by John McCone, chairman of the Joshua Hendy Corporation, who had been a close friend of Paul Pigott dating from their years at college. Another Pacific Car mainstay, T. B. Monson, reached retirement age in 1970. He was replaced as a director by W. J. Pennington, president of the *Seattle Times*. Monson's role as corporate vice president and general manager of the Renton plant had been taken over in 1968 by B. C. Jameson, who was made a vice president at the same time. Also appearing as a vice president for the first time in the 1970 annual report was Murray Aitken. J. A. Chantrey was named vice president and treasurer in 1971, replacing George Lhamon, who became vice president for international finance. W. L. Peterson was named vice president for marketing, and C. R. Bechtol, vice president for industrial relations. Pacific Car's board also lost the services of Donald Pennell when he reached retirement age in March 1972, thirty-six years after he first joined Kenworth.

The board business policies followed by Charles Pigott were recognizably the same as those of his predecessors. He kept his central office staff lean and allowed almost total autonomy to the divisions, run as profit centers. Each general manager was given full responsibility for—and held accountable for—sales, research and engineering, profits, and development of people.

In labor matters Pigott strove to be fair, and he expected fairness from his opposite number on the other side of the bargaining table. Like his father, he was willing to take a strike when he felt a particular union's demands might be excessive, and he was jealous of management's prerogatives. At Dart, for example, once a very small operation in which superintendents and shop stewards could easily get together to decide on shifts and work schedules, this arrangement had worked its way into the union contract. As Dart grew, this clause became extremely burdensome; the union's veto power made rational work scheduling all but impossible. The union was exceedingly loath to give up a "right" that was already in the contract, and management tried desperately for years to rewrite the clause, ultimately succeeding.

A similar struggle involving work, overtime, and shift assignments and absenteeism at Sicard, in Montreal, brought on a strike. When Pigott threatened to move the plant—and meant it—the union came around.

Perhaps unlike his forebears, who operated in a less formal age and manner, Charles Pigott believed in thorough management training and the use of new management tools and methods. A good many of his executives were asked to attend formal programs at Stanford, Pittsburgh, and other universities. And a management development program, designed chiefly to identify and help teach junior or potential management personnel, was inaugurated in 1966.

For some of the older, more skeptical members of management, Charles Pigott had this message in the company's January 1968 *Management News Letter*:

> Many of you have successfully grasped and utilized the various management tools and controls that have been developed in recent years. You who have . . . are to be commended. It is not easy for any of us to discard our old methods of executing our responsibilities, especially when these old methods have served us well. However, many of us recognize that the new methods or tools may serve us better as our business evolves and cost ratios change.

As for new acquisitions, Pacific Car would first seek to evaluate their existing management to make certain it could fit easily into the company pattern. The company did not acquire other companies just to become larger, but rather to complement its own product lines and to help them grow through the best use of their own talent and through the availability of ample capital resources. In some cases, management was strengthened; but most of the existing management proved up to the job at the divisional level, and some people were able to grow into larger corporate responsibilities.

Charles Pigott expressed the company's broad acquisition policy in an interview with a reporter for the *Magazine of Wall Street* in 1968. "We are particularly interested in the type of heavy-duty, specialized equipment with which we have thus far made our reputation," he said, "but any company whose product has an engine, a transmission, and axles we consider to be fair game. We have no desire to become a conglomerate. We would not wish to acquire, say, a

Pacific Car and Foundry
produced steel castings
from the installation of its
first furnace in 1911 until
its closure in 1988.

chemical firm, since we have no expertise in this field, and any company we acquire we want to be able to manage directly."

It was with such public utterances that Charles Pigott began to turn around Pacific Car's long-standing policy of maintaining the low profile so typical of many closely held companies. This reluctance to air its affairs beyond its own industry kept Pacific Car a virtual unknown entity outside of Seattle, and even in Seattle few people were aware of the size and scope of its operations and payroll. This publicity shyness was irksome to many a securities analyst and journalist, who would have to use roundabout means to find the kind of information they wanted. "What are they trying to hide?" one asked.

One securities salesman who liked to deal in Pacific Car stock would go to Renton and sit in a beer tavern when he wanted to find out how many railroad cars the plant was turning out in a day. In many circles it was regarded as a major breakthrough when O'Brien in 1966 agreed to address the Seattle Chamber of Commerce.

Business Week in 1971 decided to do a full-blown profile on Pacific Car and Foundry. Elliott Marple, the Seattle correspondent, decided it would be a waste of time to try to get his story directly from the company. But he had built up his own bank of information over the years, and was able to call on other good sources. He was ready to do his story, and had decided "to make it clear that this was being written over the dead body of Pacific Car." But he felt he should let the company know what he was doing, so he phoned Pigott. When he did, he was dumbfounded to hear Pigott say amicably, "Come on over." Marple found him completely cooperative and helpful in their interview. Later he was asked by several people in the securities business, "How did you ever manage to talk to Pigott?"

One reason was that the "newspeg" for the article itself was the fact that the company was about to make the first public offering of securities in its history, a $15 million issue of sinking fund debentures. The company's annual report said that this was "to provide more flexibility in our financial operations." A look at the balance sheet could make it clear that the company had no real need to sell a debt issue to the public. But trained observers knew that the wholly owned finance companies would need to go to the market for funds as the business of the parent company grew. And since the principal finance company was not well known, it would be helpful to have the parent manufacturing company become better known.

Part of the change was also within Charles Pigott himself. Not only had he overcome some personal reluctance to appear in the public eye, but he was also convinced that it would be good management practice. Better public understanding of the wellsprings and accomplishments of Pacific Car and Foundry and other firms like it, he felt, would be good for the company and, in a broader sense, good for the country as well.

CHAPTER TEN

PACCAR INC

As a name, "Pacific Car and Foundry Company" had once been serviceable and descriptive. And in time it became a prideful, if matter-of-fact, designation for many of those who had devoted their working lives to the company and whose memories reached back to a time when it was the more formal title for what they knew familiarly as "the Car Company."

But it had also become something of an anachronism, redolent of dust and cobwebs and of sparks flying from a blacksmith's anvil. It told only marginally what the company was, what it did, and the manner of its operation. The foundry operation, for example, had become mainly an internal service arm. So in the early 1970s, the executives decided, with all due respect to the name that had served them so well and for so long, that it was time for a change to something more modern and more suitable.

The image-design firm of Lippincott & Margulies was retained to make a study of appropriate new names. They were asked to find a corporate title that was short, nonlimiting, and apt, that would help modernize the company's image and still relate to its past. From the names suggested, the company selected Paccar. A similar name was already being used for one of the company's finance subsidiaries, Paccar Financial Corp. As a corporate title, it took the form of PACCAR Inc, with the letters capitalized and all punctuation eliminated.

As a matter of legal procedure, a new subsidiary, named PACCAR Inc, was incorporated in Delaware, a state long noted for the liberality of its corporation laws. In December 1971, Pacific Car stockholders were sent a proxy statement for a special meeting at which they could vote on a proposal to merge the parent company into the subsidiary, in that way changing not only the official title, but also the state of incorporation.

At the meeting, held on January 25, 1972, holders of more than 95 percent of the outstanding shares were present, either in person or by proxy, and more than 99 percent of the shares were voted in favor of the merger. The merger was put into effect, and the Pacific Car and Foundry Company name was retained by the Renton and Structural Steel Divisions as an integral part of PACCAR Inc.

Coincident with the merger, the 17,378 shares of Pacific Car stock held in the company's treasury were canceled, and after a share-for-share exchange of stock in the new and old companies, directors voted a 200 percent stock dividend. This tripled the number of shares

By 1979, railcar production represented only 8 percent of PACCAR's total sales.

of PACCAR Inc stock outstanding to 8,249,985 shares of the 15 million shares the company was authorized to issue.

In a very real sense, the name change was part of the greater visibility that the executives felt the company needed. PACCAR was feeling a growing responsibility to deal more openly with a number of outside groups, ranging from its own distributor organizations, to those it might wish to recruit as employees, to the investment community of securities analysts and dealers. As PACCAR, the company could more readily establish an accurate image of its business and its character for these special groups and for the public generally.

— A DECADE OF RAPID GROWTH —

Continuing their strong uptrend of the preceding five years, PACCAR sales in 1972 rose more than 15 percent to $594 million. The gains were made in spite of a reduced level of inflation and adherence to the guidelines established in Phase II of President Nixon's anti-inflation program. Earnings, which had dipped to as low as 3.3 percent of sales as recently as 1970, rose to a 5 percent return, and profits rose to $29.8 million, an increase of almost 23 percent over 1971.

In 1973 sales and earnings increased even more sharply. Sales totaled $766 million, and net profit advanced to $42.9 million, for a 5.6 percent return on sales. Shortages of parts and materials plagued much of American business that year, and many companies scrambled competitively for supplies of goods they needed. Late in the year, there were the first disquieting signs of industrial troubles to come as the Arab oil-producing nations laid an embargo on oil shipments to the United States in the wake of the Arab-Israeli war of that year.

PACCAR's business, however, continued strong through the first half of 1974. Capital spending in 1973 had risen to a new high of $30 million, and the new facilities were making higher production possible. Investment in new plant and equipment continued into 1974 at an only slightly reduced rate. Then, as the summer ended, the pace of new orders began to slow down, and the company started to work off its backlog. In the fourth quarter, new business dropped sharply, especially for the dominant truck divisions. But PACCAR optimistically increased its investment in inventories to more than $200 million and expanded its dealer networks to 455 locations in the United States and forty-four other countries. And sales rose again, this time to $907 million. Profits, however, slipped back to $23.3 million, as federal wage and price controls ended and prices could not keep up with the rapid rise in labor and material costs.

By 1975 the effects of the worst business contraction in some forty years were being felt throughout American industry, and sales of heavy-duty diesel trucks fell sharply. Partially offsetting the drop were higher sales of PACCAR's mining equipment and railroad cars, as the nation embarked on a program pointing toward greater energy self-sufficiency. The company's sales volume dipped by almost 25 percent to $690 million, and profits suffered a further drop to $20.6 million. In two years, earnings per share had been more than cut in half, from $5.20 in 1973, to $2.83 in 1974, and to $2.50 in 1975. In the effort to trim costs, production schedules were pared several times, a number of employees were laid off, and the company deliberately cut back inventories by almost $40 million to reduce the need for short-term bank loans and resulting interest expense.

During the 1976 economic recovery, PACCAR's business bounced back strongly, with truck unit sales almost doubling and total volume passing the $1 billion mark for the first time, to $1,001,410,000. Net earnings more than doubled to hit a new high of $50.6 million, equal to $6.14 per share.

Cab design and comfort
have been the hallmark
of both Peterbilt and
Kenworth trucks.

Records continued to tumble over the next three years. PACCAR sales increased to $1.42 billion in 1977, to $1.55 billion in 1978, and to $1.88 billion in 1979. Earnings shot up by 50 percent to $75.5 million in 1977, then climbed to $86.7 million in 1978, and gained almost 40 percent to $120.1 million in 1979. On a per share basis, profits were up to $9.15 in 1977, and to $14.57 in 1979.

Dividend payments to stockholders followed the general pattern of corporate earnings. In 1972 dividends were 68.3 cents a share on the expanded number of shares outstanding after the 200 percent stock dividend. The following year cash dividends were increased substantially to $1.20 a share, but with the 1974–75 business downturn, the directors reduced the payout to $1 a share in each of those years. Dividend declarations then were increased to $1.50 per share in 1976, to $2.25 in 1977, to $2.70 in 1978, and to $3.70 in 1979. Even at that record level, the total amount paid was just over $30 million, or only slightly more than 25 percent of the year's net earnings.

The continuing retention of a major share of profits in the business virtually eliminated the need for borrowing, and gave the company tremendous flexibility and latitude with respect to its finances. At the end of 1979, PACCAR operated fourteen major manufacturing centers in the United States, Canada, Mexico, and Australia, and had nearly fourteen thousand employees worldwide, including a high proportion of engineers, managers, supervisors, and skilled working men and women. And it was eminently capable of financing its own growth as new facilities were needed or suitable acquisitions became available.

As various directors reached retirement age in the early and mid-1970s, there were several changes on the board, tending mainly in the direction of increasing the number and proportion of outside directors. Not only Donald Pennell, but also Thomas Gleed, a thirty-year veteran of the board, reached retirement age in 1972. Taking their places were Murray Aitken and James C. Pigott, a younger brother of Charles Pigott. John McCone left the board in 1974, and Aitken retired as senior vice president and director in 1975, after forty-two years with Kenworth and PACCAR. Added to the board in 1974 were Gordon H. Sweany, president of Safeco Corporation, and T. A. Wilson, chairman of the Boeing Company. The following year James H. Wiborg, president of the Univar Corporation, was elected to the PACCAR board.

John M. Bodden and Robert Holmstrom were named senior vice presidents in 1975. They joined B. C. Jameson and J. A. Chantrey, who already held that title. Chantrey was elected to the board in 1978, on the retirement of board chairman Robert O'Brien. After O'Brien left, the position of board chairman was not filled. J. M. Dunn and W. N. Gross were both named senior vice presidents of PACCAR Inc.

— MORE TRUCK-BUILDING PLANTS —

PACCAR's truck-building divisions continued to play an increasingly important part in the company's overall sales picture. In 1969, the product mix was 61 percent trucks, 23 percent railcars, 7 percent mining equipment, and 9 percent other products, including winches and government research and development. By 1978, the percentage for trucks had moved up at the expense of all the other product lines, and the mix was 82 percent trucks, 9 percent railcars, 4 percent mining equipment, and 5 percent other items.

In that same period, the company's share of the U.S. market for Class 8 heavy-duty trucks inched upward to achieve about 17 percent of the total. While market share had not figured importantly in the company's projections and targets, the increase was an inevitable outgrowth of the reputation that Kenworth and Peterbilt had built for high-quality products and thus for long-term economies in the life cycle of the vehicles.

Another significant reason for this growth lay in new plants and warehouses that enabled the truck divisions to reach more effectively into markets across the country. Peterbilt's second factory, in Nashville, Tennessee, was completed in 1972. That same year, Kenworth started construction of a new plant in Chillicothe, Ohio. PACCAR also started a program of opening a series of regional warehouses to give spare parts support to the distributors of Kenworth, Peterbilt, and Dart equipment. The first, at Renton, was completed in 1973, and another was started that year in Atlanta, Georgia. There were also additions made to existing factories.

Kenworth's new Ohio plant was nearly completed and ready for occupancy, but this posed a labor problem. It was to be a nonunion plant, and hiring of workers was already under way. Union workers in the construction trades were still finishing off their job at the time, and management felt it might be abrasive to have both groups there together. Production was therefore held off until February, when the building tradesmen were gone. Opening of the plant brought Kenworth's total annual capacity to 16,000 trucks.

Actual output by Kenworth had set a record of 12,787 units in 1973. However, when the 1974–75 recession hit heavy-duty truck sales so hard that national volume dropped from a record 192,000 units in 1973 to 106,000 in 1975, Kenworth was similarly pinched. Production slipped to 11,076 units in 1974, and then virtually collapsed to 4,881 in 1975. Sales recovered modestly to 7,761 truck units in 1976, and then surged forward to new records of 14,091 in 1977, 14,128 in 1978, and 15,691 in 1979.

Both Kenworth and Peterbilt sales reflected growing acceptance of the policy of building heavy-duty trucks to the requirements of individual customers, and many fleet operators similarly found this to their advantage. Petroleum, forest products, grocery chains, breweries, and other industrial accounts were in the market for more and more custom-built vehicles.

Construction started for a third Peterbilt plant, at Denton, Texas, in November 1978. The $50 million facility was built to serve the growing markets for Peterbilt products in the Midwest and Southwest, including the large industrial markets of Dallas and Fort Worth. Denton also offered access to a large, skilled labor pool. The first Denton-built truck rolled out on August 4, 1980, from a plant designed for a monthly capacity of twenty conventional (long hood) Class 8 highway and off-road trucks. The new plant enabled Peterbilt to offer truck delivery in forty-five, sixty, or ninety days, depending on the particular model, and for the first time in many years, Peterbilt would have a domestic production capacity equal to that of Kenworth's.

In an issue of *PACCAR World,* Joseph Dunn, then senior vice president, noted an improvement in Peterbilt's market penetration, which he attributed to the company's successful recruitment of new dealers for previously open U.S. territories and to the completion of the Denton plant.

In the minds of some, the energy shortage—and the petroleum shortage in particular—cast a shadow over the future of the trucking and truck-building industries. Yet it was clear that a large part of the freight hauled within the United States would necessarily be moved by trucks. An estimated forty thousand communities were not even served by a rail system, and had to rely on trucks for a large part of their vital goods and supplies.

Kenworth's Chillicothe, Ohio, plant opened in 1973, with an initial annual capacity of sixteen thousand trucks.

Charles M. Pigott with a Kenworth conventional and a Peterbilt cab-over model at the company's Renton, Washington, research and development center.

Page 207: Soon after T. A. Peterman began building logging trucks, Peterbilt had established its reputation as the "toughest truck in the woods."

PACCAR's three equipment finance companies took on added luster as significant profit centers during the 1970s. More and more of the three hundred–plus truck distributors in the United States and Canada decided to take advantage of this convenient source for financing sales. The accumulation of years of experience enhanced the efficiency of the staff, and losses were an insignificant fraction of the total amounts handled. As loan volume increased, more staff was added. A series of regional offices were opened across the continent—in Atlanta, Georgia, in 1972, and Chicago in 1974, and, then, others in both the United States and Canada.

— TAKING STANDS ON POLICY MATTERS —

As PACCAR itself became a more important factor in the industrial universe, its management did not hesitate to express its convictions about policies and practices that affected the national economy and well-being. Charles Pigott used his letter to the shareholders in the company's annual report as his principal sounding board, just as his predecessors had done. Subjects ranged from those as parochial as truck equipment regulations, to those as broad as the scourge of inflation, or as far afield as special taxes imposed on the energy industry.

On the subject of price controls, Pigott wrote in the 1971 report: "It seems that industry has been selected to bear the brunt of our national efforts to bring inflation under control. Therefore, while we expect to do as well as or better than our competitors in profitability, all of us should recognize that increased profits, and particularly increased margins, are going to be hard to achieve in a government-controlled economy." On profits as a fraction of sales, he had this comment in 1972: "Five cents profit on every dollar of sales barely enables us to finance our

Until the construction of PACCAR's Technical Center in 1982, truck testing and research and development work was carried out, in part, on an abandoned airfield in western Oregon.

growth and provide a proper return to shareholders. Unfortunately, too many Americans believe industry earns many times this modest return. If we are going to increase productivity in the United States, efficient producers must earn a satisfactory profit."

When special taxes on energy producers first became a national topic, Pigott spelled out his own well-reasoned dissent:

> . . . legislation in the form of taxes on profits or the elimination of investment incentives for our energy companies serves to reduce the available private capital urgently required to explore and develop new energy resources. Because new energy sources are difficult to find, more costly to recover, and involve substantial financial risk in exploration, such legislative action serves to limit energy-industry capacity and thus raise the basic cost of the fuel we use. The impact . . . is felt by us all—PACCAR customers who require diesel fuel to operate vehicles we produce and their customers, American consumers who must cope with ever increasing costs of the products they buy, of which transportation cost is a significant part.

A favorite and frequent target of Pigott's verbal assaults was inflation. "Many believe that business benefits from inflation," he wrote in the 1974 report, "but history—and particularly our history—proves conclusively that profit margins erode rapidly during such periods, as manufacturers cannot increase prices fast enough to match upward spiraling costs. Several years of Federal Government wage and price controls produced only temporary benefits, and these were more than offset by economic distortions which prevailed after those controls were removed." His position was, if anything, sharpened even after he noted that PACCAR experienced some beneficial effects of the pronounced inflation of 1978. Some of that year's strong truck demand could well have represented hedging against further inflation, he observed. And the weakening of U.S. and Canadian currencies that inflation helped bring about made PACCAR's products more price competitive overseas, so that truck exports increased 44 percent in 1978.

On at least one occasion, PACCAR was willing to put its money where its mouth was. In 1974 the National Highway Traffic Safety Administration promulgated its Standard 121, a braking regulation that quickly became infamous in the trucking industry. It required the use of sophisticated devices that were supposed to enable a truck to come to a full stop from 60 miles an hour within 293 feet and without deviating from a 12-foot lane. The regulation, adding from $2,000 to $3,000 to the cost of a heavy-duty truck, was to take effect on March 1, 1975, and many fleet buyers rushed to make their purchases ahead of that deadline.

"State and federal governments have increasingly taken it upon themselves to act as designers and standards setters," the PACCAR annual report for 1974 wryly observed. "Trucks . . . will . . . cost . . . more because of government-mandated brake changes which many in the industry say are not necessary." One investment analyst, Peter Zaglio, of Smith Barney Harris Upham, noted that the rush to buy in 1974 had contributed to the sharp cutback in 1975 truck orders. "Fleets were anxious to beat not only the cost, but also the anticipated unreliability of the anti-skid unit," he said.

PACCAR then decided to go further. It brought an action in federal court, challenging the new regulation as arbitrary, inadequately tested, and put forward without sufficient regard for true highway safety. The Ninth Circuit Court of Appeals in San Francisco agreed, and ordered a temporary suspension of the rule. The Highway Traffic Safety Administration then appealed to U.S. Supreme Court Justice William Rehnquist, and he set aside the Circuit Court's suspension. The matter was then brought back to the Circuit Court for a hearing on the merits of the case. The court ruled for PACCAR's contention that Standard 121 imposed new and unproven technology on highway vehicles, and failed to show that the air brake systems in use posed a safety hazard. The relevant parts of the regulation were invalidated by the decision. The Supreme Court, in effect, upheld the ruling when it declined to hear a further appeal.

— ACQUISITIONS —

With its ample cash and management resources, PACCAR Inc unsurprisingly stepped up its pace of corporate acquisitions during the 1970s. In finding and purchasing other businesses, the company hewed to its basic policy of remaining in familiar areas of activity and taking on product lines that complemented its own.

In mining equipment, PACCAR already had Dart Truck, which continued to expand its line of vehicles for surface mining, vehicles that could haul the most material in the least time and at the lowest cost. To this business the company in 1973 added the Wagner Mining Equipment Company, a Portland, Oregon, manufacturer of low-profile underground mining vehicles.

The acquisition began as far back as April 1971, when Wagner made its second public offering of stock, and PACCAR purchased some of the shares. Later that year, PACCAR made a tender offer to the holders of Wagner stock and was able to acquire a 40 percent interest in the mining company. Pigott, O'Brien, and Jameson were elected to the board, and Pigott became Wagner's new president.

A few more shares were tendered and accepted early in 1972. But PACCAR did not obtain majority control until August 1973, when the tender price was raised and enough additional shares were acquired to bring holdings to 92 percent of Wagner's outstanding stock. Among those who turned over their interests were members of the dominant Wagner family, who insisted that they be paid for their stock in cash.

The original Wagner family—father and seven sons—were farmers from Potlatch Ridge, Idaho, who moved to Portland and took jobs as cement finishers. In 1924 they started Wagner Concrete Construction Company. All musically inclined, they spent most of the year at their business, then returned to Idaho in the summer to perform with their family orchestra and to work on the harvest.

Some of the brothers were mechanically proficient, and conceived the idea of mounting a two-yard cement mixer on the chassis of a car, and then driving it to their jobs. They kept making more of their "mixermobiles," improving each one enough to make the previous one obsolete. In 1938 a cash buyer purchased one of the machines, for their first equipment sale. Later, one of their cement customers saw one of the machines, and proposed handling sales if they would take care of manufacturing. They agreed, and in 1938 formed the Mixermobile Company, which grew rapidly enough to necessitate a new facility two years later.

As word of the Wagners' design ingenuity spread, people came to them to order pieces of equipment for specific jobs. They would draw plans on a cement floor with chalk, and then fabricate the machines. During the labor shortages of World War II, a fuel handling firm asked the Wagners whether they could build a machine to unload coal from beneath railroad cars. They did, calling it the Scoopmobile. After the war, they contracted with the Kaiser shipyards in Portland to build two hundred Mixermobiles and other pieces of equipment.

In 1955 the family organized the Wagner Tractor Company to build four-wheel-drive, rubber-tired farm tractors, log skidders, and log stackers. They sold this company in 1961, and it ultimately became known as Rayco Wagner. Meanwhile, however, Eddie Wagner had begun to develop a rubber-tired underground mining vehicle called the Scooptram, and formed the Wagner Mining Scoop Company as a partnership with his wife and son in 1958. They branched out, mainly at the request of customers, into other mining vehicles, and moved into a 15,000-square-foot plant and office building near Portland, Oregon. These quarters were expanded in 1963 and again in 1968–69. The firm was incorporated as the Wagner Mining Equipment Company in 1970, when the first public stock offering was made.

By the time PACCAR first bought into Wagner Mining in 1971, the company was making a varied line of mining vehicles, most with such picturesque names as Eject-o-dump Bucket and Teletram, as well as Scooptram. Wagner showed after-tax profits of $1.5 million on some $20 million of sales in 1971, although backlogs were then down and immediate prospects not as bright.

PACCAR put millions of dollars into Wagner for expansion and for added capabilities, and developed a worldwide market. Wagner was made a division of PACCAR Inc in 1976. Toward the end of the decade, Wagner was building more than thirty different models of underground mining equipment, most of them with diesel drives, but some electrically powered. The machines were designed to operate in narrow, low-ceilinged mine tunnels; some units were slim enough to pass each other in tunnels and low enough to work in galleries too low for a man to stand upright. Marketing was done through forty dealer outlets in twenty-seven countries.

In February 1974, PACCAR purchased Hayes Trucks Limited, of Vancouver, British Columbia, a principal competitor in Canada of Canadian Kenworth. Specializing in heavy-

duty trucks used by a number of large forest products companies, Hayes had sales of almost $20 million in the fiscal year ended November 30, 1973. The firm's market was mainly in western Canada, but it had sold units in other provinces, as well as in the United States. The plan was to have Hayes compete with Canadian Kenworth, much as Peterbilt and Kenworth competed for business in the United States.

Hayes had been founded as a Vancouver truck dealership in 1920. Two years later, a group of local businessmen provided the financing needed to design and build a heavy-duty vehicle rugged enough to operate in the western forests, and the Hayes-Anderson Motor Company Limited was organized. They moved to larger facilities in 1928. The trucks became Hayes-Lawrence vehicles when the company merged in 1946 with the Lawrence Manufacturing Company, which made such equipment as winches, hoists, gears, and transmissions. Mack Trucks, Incorporated, took over the firm in 1969, changing the name back to Hayes Trucks, Limited, and expanding the sales organization into eastern Canada. As sales rose from $10 million a year to $20 million, Mack was faced with the choice of financing an appropriate plant expansion or disposing of the company. In 1974 they decided to sell, and PACCAR decided to buy.

Hayes Trucks did not turn out to be a good investment for PACCAR. The acquisition had been made just before the start of a major worldwide recession and a pronounced downturn in the truck sales market. Prospects for long-term growth seemed little better, and thus PACCAR decided to dissolve the company. Its operations ended on September 30, 1975.

Oddly enough, part of the growth pattern of PACCAR Inc was a willingness to shut down operations, either temporarily or permanently, if they failed to show adequate promise of long-term profitability. Thus, a declining market and the entrance of Japanese and low-cost U.S. competition into the structural steel market were major influences in closing down that division in 1973. The Structural Steel Division's assets were sold to Schnitzer Investment, of Portland, Oregon. The Dart Division in 1973 halted sales of heavy-duty trucks for mining activities when they were no longer profitable. All existing orders were filled, and Kenworth moved in to occupy factory areas not being used. When prospects for the truck line later improved, Dart reentered the business, and developed even heavier equipment, such as a 150-ton coal hauler.

Even though railroad cars represented a declining portion of its overall business, PACCAR in 1975 acquired the International Car Company, of Kenton, Ohio, from Nationwide Industries, Incorporated, of Chicago. The purchase price was approximately $2.5 million for a company with annual sales of almost $10 million.

International Car was a small, specialized manufacturer, concentrating on the storied "caboose" cars. The caboose had evolved over the years from a haven where a conductor could come in out of the cold, to the status of a well-appointed office car of a freight train, as well as a comfortable home-away-from-home for the conductor. The old Pacific Car and Foundry had once built cabooses, along with any other kinds of railcars it could sell. In 1973 PACCAR began delivery to the Burlington Northern on an order for fifty caboose cars, the first it had built in a dozen years.

In 1924 International Car had been known as the New City Car Company, which built wooden railcars to transport live poultry to be slaughtered in Chicago. The cars were rented to poultrymen and returned. They would then be cleaned and their contents processed into garden fertilizer. The plant stood idle from 1939 to 1941, when it was purchased by an investor, replaced by a new building, and put back to work building railroad rolling stock, including insulated beer cars. The company began to specialize in making caboose cars, and gradually captured 85 percent of that market, giving Kenton, Ohio, the title of "caboose capital of the world."

International's yearly output of nearly 285 caboose cars was something less than an enticement to PACCAR. More important was the acquisition of a base from which to sell to eastern markets. With freight a major factor in the cost of railcars, both for the inbound shipment of materials and the outbound delivery of finished products, the eastern facility offered opportunities for growth in the railroad equipment industry that the Renton plant could not provide. By 1977 PACCAR was building 60-foot boxcars for hauling automotive parts and paper products at the new International Car Division in Ohio.

In 1977 PACCAR acquired for cash the Braden Winch Company, of Broken Arrow, a suburb of Tulsa, Oklahoma. As the only profitable division of Braden Industries, Incorporated, the firm produced a variety of winches used in construction equipment, petroleum drilling, and on automotive wreckers and special electric utility vehicles. Braden thus became the third of PACCAR's winch lines, after Carco and Gearmatic.

The Oklahoma company's history began in 1924, when Glenn T. Braden, a Pennsylvania oilman, added a line of winches to his company, then engaged in the manufacture of engines fueled by natural gas, for "popping" shallow oil wells. His new product, called the Ryan Braden hub winch, could be operated off the rear wheel of a truck. When it was made obsolete by the rapid acceptance of dual rear truck wheels, Braden developed a horizontal truck winch.

Braden died in 1930 and the Colonial Trust Company, of Pittsburgh, was named executor of his estate, and later became sole owner of the Braden Steel and Winch Company. T. J. Schuetz, chief engineer of the winch division, entered into an agreement with Colonial Trust to sell and service the winches in stock and to make more to meet the demand. He developed a new line of more compact and more easily manufactured winches.

In 1936 Colonial Trust separated the steel and winch divisions, and gave 30 percent of the stock in the Braden Winch Company to Schuetz in payment for his tools, patterns, and inventory. Schuetz then prepared, at Braden's expense, a demonstration project of two of the winch models for a group of officers at the Fort Sill Army Base, Lawton, Oklahoma. Later, during World War II,

Hayes Truck was purchased by PACCAR in 1974, but dissolved in 1975 as a result of the depressed truck market in Canada.

International Car, the largest producer of cabooses in the United States, was purchased by PACCAR in 1975.

Dodge bought thousands of Braden winches for use on military vehicles. Before that time, Schuetz persuaded I. E. Mabee, a wealthy oilman, and Logan Stevenson to buy out the Colonial Trust interest in the company. Another new winch was designed and large quantities were sold to the military during the Korean conflict. Kaiser equipped its famous Jeep with Braden winches. Army Ordnance eventually purchased the design, so that other companies could bid on the manufacture of the winches.

Paul Pigott had briefly entertained the idea of purchasing Braden Winch in the late 1950s. However, Braden was sold in 1959 to Motor Products Corporation, which later merged Braden with Aeromotor Company, a maker of steel windmills. Motor Products, by then renamed Nautec Corporation, spun off Braden Aeromotor Corporation as an independent entity, which was reorganized later into Braden Industries, Incorporated. It was from this firm that PACCAR purchased the Braden winch business.

A less successful effort at a major acquisition was attempted by PACCAR in May 1977, when it made a cash tender offer for the common stock of Harnischfeger Corporation, of Milwaukee, Wisconsin. Harnischfeger, with annual sales of approximately $500 million, was an important manufacturer of mining and heavy construction equipment, including diesel-electric and electric-powered shovels, overhead factory cranes and hoists, and mobile cranes often used at construction sites.

The possible acquisition had been under study by PACCAR for some time, and it was decided that the two companies would fit well together. Harnischfeger had excellent products and good long-term prospects, and PACCAR believed it could bring in needed capital, as well as know-how and a number of complementary lines. The offer, for stock that had been selling not long before for $12 to $13 a share, was for $20 a share, for a total of $180 million, if all the stock was tendered, offered, or purchased. The investment banking firms of Goldman Sachs and Lazard Freres were retained to manage the tender.

But Harnischfeger resisted the offer, and contested it by seeking a restraining order in a Federal District Court. The transaction would violate antitrust laws, they contended, because their hydraulic excavator was competitive with Dart's front-end loader. PACCAR's lawyers regarded this as little more than frivolous. Although both pieces of equipment might be used for excavation, they said, they had different functions, and a customer planning to buy either one would hardly consider the other for the same work. Nevertheless, after a one-day hearing, the judge granted the restraining order. PACCAR appealed, but the Court of Appeals refused to set the order aside.

PACCAR decided not to pursue the case further. A full trial of the issue, they felt, might take years and make heavy demands on the time of its management, as well as its legal department. Moreover, they noted, Harnischfeger's earnings appeared to be in a declining trend.

In another case, PACCAR found itself as the wooed, rather than the wooing, party, and an acquisition was brought to a successful conclusion. The company was Fodens Limited, a heavy-duty truck manufacturer located in Sandbach, England.

Fodens, one of the oldest and most respected names in the British motor vehicle industry, had fallen on hard times. In July 1979 it went into receivership. Not long afterward, Sir Kenneth Cork, one of the joint receivers, wired Pigott to see whether PACCAR was interested in bidding for the company. Pigott, thinking principally "of the U.K.'s bad reputation for labor troubles," thought he would pass up this venture. Later, however, he heard that there had been no labor disturbances at Fodens for more than ten years. Furthermore, he learned that the British firm might be available for much less than the $75 million figure mentioned in the press. He reopened

Braden Winch first began producing winches for the oil industry in 1924.

Fodens Limited, one of the oldest truck producers in the world, built its first truck in 1898. It was incorporated into the newly formed Sandbach Engineering Company in 1980.

the matter and, in October 1980, PACCAR acquired Fodens for less than $40 million. PACCAR transferred the assets into a newly formed subsidiary, Sandbach Engineering Company, to manufacture Foden Trucks.

Pigott was convinced that the investment was a good one, not only in terms of the potential return, but also because of the opportunities it opened. With a good product and plant, and with established markets in Africa and the Middle East, as well as in England, Fodens, Pigott said, could become "a springboard either to export from the United Kingdom or to build a team that will be able to go elsewhere in that part of the world."

With products so ideally suited to satisfy the continuing drive for industrialization in both developed and developing countries, PACCAR's international sales took on increasing importance. These activities encompassed not only export sales, but also manufacturing, in Canada, Mexico, Australia, and England.

With manufacturing plants outside of Vancouver, British Columbia, and in Montreal, Quebec, Canadian Kenworth matched the U.S. sales growth rate in heavy-duty trucks and specialized vehicles. In 1975 PACCAR of Canada Ltd. was formed to create a structure paralleling the company's U.S. format—operating divisions that report to a parent company. The assets of Canadian Kenworth; Sicard Incorporated; and Gearmatic Company were transferred to the new corporation. There was no change made, however, in the structure of the Canadian finance company, Overland Acceptance Limited. The Canadian corporate headquarters were set up at the Sicard offices at Ste-Thérèse. Sicard Incorporated was formally dissolved in 1976, when its Ste-Thérèse plant was turned over to Canadian Kenworth, whose corporate headquarters were moved to Ottawa. A substantial number of the Kenworth vehicles manufactured at the Sicard plant were exported to the States, while the Dart mining vehicles built there were put to use chiefly in Canadian mines.

In Mexico, Kenworths made up almost half of all the heavy-duty trucks sold by a total of eight manufacturers there. One of those held a 20 percent share of the market, and the other

Wagner delivered its first order of Scooptrams to China in 1980.

six divided the remaining 30 percent. By early 1979, Kenworth Mexicana had built its ten thousandth truck, substantially more than any other Mexican manufacturer had produced. At that time, the Kenworth plant in Mexicali was turning out trucks with 92.5 percent Mexican content, already in excess of the 90 percent that Mexican laws were to require by 1981.

Mexican truck production was hard hit, along with the entire national economy, by the 1976 devaluation of the peso. More than half of the Kenworth Mexicana workforce of eleven hundred had to be laid off, and the plant was closed for a time. Parts sales provided the chief source of income for a number of months. Loans from Truck Acceptance Corporation had to be paid off in dollars. This posed a special hardship for almost half of the Mexican buyers, who had financed their purchases and then had to come up with 22.85 pesos for each dollar owed, rather than the former 12.50 per dollar. To help them handle this extra burden, Truck Acceptance extended the repayment periods.

Mexico needed two years to recover from its economic shock. But by 1979, the Kenworth plant was turning out eight trucks a day, production fully 33 percent higher than its designed capacity. Would-be buyers had an eight-month wait for their vehicles. In a nation that was thinly served by railroads, trucks were relied on to haul most industrial and consumer goods. Not only did Mexican truck replacements have to catch up after the long period of curtailed production, but greater transportation demands grew out of the new discoveries of vast petroleum reserves.

Kenworth was similarly well received in Australia. Most Australian companies requiring heavy-duty hauling, as well as departments of the state and commonwealth governments, used

Over the years, Kenworth has grown to be Mexico's largest producer of heavy-duty trucks.

Kenworths, either directly or through subcontractors. As demand grew, a plant expansion was begun in 1977 and completed in 1978, doubling capacity from four trucks per day to eight trucks per day on a single shift.

Australian Kenworth acted also as the marketing and service agency for Dart construction vehicles and Wagner underground mining equipment. In an emergency, the plant managers maintained, they could turn out equipment in Australia to Dart and Wagner design.

In 1972 Murray Aitken and W. N. Gross, then an assistant vice president of PACCAR, noted that Kenworth's international activities kept producing increasing earnings for PACCAR. At their suggestion, the company formed a new subsidiary, PACCAR International Inc. (PACCINT), to concentrate on and coordinate export sales. Headquartered at the company's principal offices in Bellevue, Washington, PACCINT was staffed with a team of experts in such matters as tariffs, shipping rates, domestic and foreign financing, and business practices and conditions in countries around the world. By centralizing the marketing efforts which had been previously handled by the individual divisions, the new unit could work on the export of trucks, mining equipment, and winches not only from the United States, but also from the Canadian and Australian subsidiaries. Its efforts were directed principally at parts of the world not directly served by PACCAR plants—South America, Africa, the Middle East, and Southeast Asia.

PACCINT, however, did not take over the marketing functions from PACCAR divisions that had already established their own selling networks abroad. Wagner Mining Equipment, for example, already had twenty-six dealers around the world handling its products outside the country. Not only were they thoroughly familiar with the unique Wagner line of underground mining vehicles, but many of them had made important contributions to the firm's past growth. Wagner had even established itself with a dealer in the People's Republic of China who was familiar with the level of sophistication that the Chinese market might absorb.

PACCAR International opened sales offices in a number of countries—Colombia, France, Greece, South Africa, and Singapore among them—to promote company exports. Higher export sales, especially of trucks, provided a welcome offset to reduced domestic sales during the 1974–75 recession. PACCAR International's truck sales advanced dramatically, from $17 million in 1973, to $64 million in 1976. PACCAR's total foreign sales, exclusive of those to and within countries that had manufacturing facilities, reached $100 million in 1976, or approximately the same as the company's total sales volume less than twenty years before. Its world market consisted of some ninety countries, with more than one hundred foreign representatives and distributors.

"PACCAR," observed Gross, "holds over 17 percent of the U.S. heavy-duty truck market. . . . I think that we are at a reasonably mature stage right now. Not too much growth can occur in the U.S. [truck] market for PACCAR's portion without some profit deterioration. If the company is going to grow in trucks it is going to have to grow outside the U.S."

An especially noteworthy event was a $3 million order for twenty-two Kenworth trucks from the People's Republic of China in August 1978, four months before diplomatic ties were established between that nation and the United States. PACCAR was one of thirty U.S. companies invited to give technical seminars in the People's Republic of China early in 1978.

When the PACCINT representatives had finished their presentation, the Chinese said, "Now tell us about your trucks." They continued to press David McKay, western region marketing manager for PACCAR International, for more and more details, such as the tensile strength of truck frame rails. "They wanted to see if we knew what we were talking about," he explained. Unable to readily answer some of the technical questions, the marketing group would send a daily telex to Bellevue and return with the answers the next day. The Chinese seemed pleased with the responses. Then, after a planned two-week visit had stretched to five weeks, the Chinese placed their order for eighteen heavy-duty trucks, two small trucks designed for geophysical exploration, and two Super 953s, the biggest brutes built by Kenworth, all the equipment to be used principally in oil field development. Later in the year, a delegation from the People's Republic came to the United States and visited PACCAR.

As William Pigott had discovered some sixty years earlier, McKay learned that China had tremendous reserves of coal. "But they don't have the capacity to transport coal or oil. They need to modernize their ports and highway transport. The rail system is pretty good, but it isn't sufficient. China is a fragmented country because of poor transportation. There's a tremendous opportunity for us there, but it's a difficult market to penetrate. You have to wait to be invited."

Among those invited was a team from Wagner, which went to China to deliver seminars on mining equipment late in 1979. Before leaving, they closed an order—on Christmas Day—for seven electric and five diesel Scooptrams to mine gold in Shandong province, south of Beijing. At the request of the buyers, the usual six-month warranty was extended to a year—hardly a problem, since the Chinese cared for all their mechanical equipment so scrupulously.

In February 1980, a delegation of fifteen high-ranking Chinese officials came to the United States to examine port facilities, coal mines, and coal-mining equipment. Members of the group specifically asked for a meeting with PACCAR, and six visited the Renton plant and Bellevue offices, where the Chinese vice minister of rails displayed great interest in Pacific Car and Foundry technology.

— **ABREAST OF TECHNOLOGY** —

In displaying leadership or in keeping up with the leaders, technology was the name of the game for many an American business and especially for industrial concerns. It was a lesson that Pacific Car and Foundry and Seattle Car and Foundry had learned a long time ago, one that was not about to be forgotten by PACCAR.

Kenworth began marketing trucks in the People's Republic of China in 1978 through PACCAR International for use in China's new oil industry.

From almost its earliest days, the company had operated a metallurgical and chemical laboratory on the plant premises. Carcometal was a principal product of the research conducted there. Experiments were also conducted in the heat treatment of metals and alloys, in order to bring them to the required levels of hardness or to promote other characteristics and qualities. A heat-treating department had special ovens to temper metal for winches or armor plate. Eventually there were three heat-treating departments at the Renton plant, including one that used electrical induction heating.

Computers and the newly developed techniques of systems management were put to work as soon as economies could be effected by their use, principally in minimizing the need for maintaining voluminous written records. This was especially true of truck manufacturing and parts records. In 1972 a corporate manufacturing system was put into place, along with the computer installations required to support it. Its main purpose was to control parts inventories at the factories and warehouses in Seattle, Kansas City, and Chicago. As new plants and parts

Robert Holmstrom (left), John Salathe, and Don Stephens review progress in transforming the Technical Center Concept from its plan to completion.

supply depots were added in different regions of the country, they were worked into the system. The company built a new computer center near Seattle to accommodate the electronic data processing program PACCAR had developed for parts ordering and distribution. Within three years PACCAR had built a larger and more powerful centralized computer center, Management Information Systems, in the Renton area for company-wide use.

As new and more efficient machines and pieces of heavy factory equipment were developed, the company invested in them as replacements for its older and somewhat out-moded machinery. As a consequence of a long series of such changes, the newer equipment was vastly more complex than the old, and various kinds of special training were required for its use and maintenance.

At one time, Pacific Car's entire maintenance department consisted of three or four carpenter-mechanics and perhaps five or six electricians. Over the years, this grew to a department of seventy-five people, mostly specialists. A carpentry crew took care of building maintenance and woodworking; the machinery was watched over by a mechanical crew; an electrical contingent handled a variety of assignments involving electrical installations and problems; and many of the new automated machines required the specialized services of a group of numerical control technicians. Virtually all of the newer machine tools were computer-controlled, and new generations of equipment would make the old obsolete more frequently than ever before.

All of this required a continuing program of training and retraining for many members of the maintenance department. There were three such programs at PACCAR: one mechanical, one electrical, and the third for numerical control, the latter usually conducted at the manufacturing plant of the machine builders in Chicago, Cleveland, or Cincinnati.

Trucks and mining equipment required their own special kinds of research activities. In 1972 two types of gas turbine engines were tested by Kenworth. One, a Ford unit, was installed in a truck at Seattle, for testing in Canada by Canadian Kenworth. This program was dropped after two months, when the early results indicated poor fuel mileage.

In 1980, PACCAR began construction of a new Technical Center in Skagit County, Washington. A major step forward in truck research, the facility was to include the latest equipment in testing and product evaluation, including an environmental dynamometer, a ride simulator, electronics instrument calibration, and failure analysis laboratories, as well as an outdoor proving ground with more than a mile of banked and level test track. Aimed primarily at the development of superior Class 8 trucks, the new center was also designed to solve some of the thornier research problems encountered by any division or plant in the PACCAR family.

— SUCCESS STORY —

By virtually any definition of the term, PACCAR Inc was a successful business enterprise as it rounded out its first three-quarters of a century.

On *Fortune*'s list of the 500 top industrial companies in the United States, PACCAR ranked 180th in sales in 1979, having moved up eight places from its position in the preceding year. Had there been a classification for companies-doing-the-most-with-the-least, PACCAR undoubtedly would have placed very high, since it stood 275th in assets, and 238th among the leading 250 companies, and 291st in total employees.

In net income for 1979, PACCAR was 159th among the 500; in net income as a percent of

"You're squinting into a blizzard, shifting with both hands, steering with both knees, pulling a 110-wheel trailer. . . . Then you begin to feel ice on the road. That's when you thank the Man upstairs that you're driving a Kenworth."

stockholders' equity, it was 35th; and in growth in earnings per share, it ranked 4th. *Fortune* noted that it was surprising to find companies in mature industries among the top ten in the important growth-in-per-share-earnings list. The magazine pointed out that PACCAR had once done well with railcar manufacturing and then switched to more profitable heavy-duty trucks, without commenting on the fact that both these industries were at least fairly mature.

Long-term stockholders could hardly have been happier with the company's record. "If you had bought one share for $75 in 1943," Senior Vice President Chantrey observed in 1979, "through stock splits and dividends you would now have 617 shares with a current value of $35,452. In addition, you would have received $7,800 in cash dividends."

The $10 billion heavy-duty truck manufacturing industry had suffered from chronic overcapacity for a number of years, the *New York Times* said in September 1980, and such names as Diamond Reo, Brockway, and Chrysler had all given up the business, leaving only seven manufacturers in the field. Even General Motors announced in 1979 that the heavy-duty Chevrolet line would be discontinued. And when heavy-duty truck sales suffered their worst slump in five years in the early 1980s, White Motor declared Chapter 11 bankruptcy. PACCAR, described by the *Times* as "perhaps the strongest and most efficient of the lot," was preparing to open the newest Peterbilt plant in Denton, Texas, just as this slide got under way. Asked whether he was particularly concerned about this, Pigott took the long view. "A recession is not necessarily the worst time to bring on a new plant," he said. "It's not good for P & L, but they are able to train people more carefully. . . . Quality is so important."

CHAPTER ELEVEN

EVOLUTION OR REVOLUTION

Not far into the 1980s, rapidly rising interest rates, plunging economic indicators, and major competitors seeking Chapter 11 bankruptcy protection jarred PACCAR's confidence, but not its determination. The company once again examined how it conducted its business, assessed its strengths, and looked at appropriate areas for change.

PACCAR entered the decade from a position of financial strength and flexibility. With sales of $1.735 billion and earnings of $85 million, 1981 had been a record year. Still, the company chose to retain most of its earnings, a philosophy based on decades past when its fortunes were tied to the rise and fall of the railcar business. PACCAR was virtually free of debt, and in a cyclical business like trucks, the availability of cash and the absence of debt had proven to be key to its continued development.

Some PACCAR executives describe their company as "conservative" (as in inconspicuous, thrifty, and Spartan), but that does not mean they seek to maintain the status quo, which at PACCAR is unacceptable. The company is not at all conservative in reshaping and reinventing itself, whether that requires discontinuing or selling divisions, adjusting its workforce, moving into new businesses, or acquiring cutting-edge technology.

The recession of the 1980s had a profound impact on PACCAR and its competitors. The winch business was down, and railcar orders slowed after a record year. Production schedules were rearranged. The Class 8 market had crashed, but PACCAR's share of it increased to 18 percent, and it moved from being the number three to the number two domestic truck manufacturer. International Harvester's long strike that year led to its filing for Chapter 11 protection and its eventual reorganization as Navistar.

The recession itself was no surprise, but its depth and duration were. Maintaining a long-standing PACCAR policy of only building to order, plant output dropped. Peterbilt and Kenworth were forced in 1982 to lay off several thousand employees. PACCAR's equity uncharacteristically fell from its 1981 high of $602 million to $548 million by the end of 1982 due to adoption of a new rule for foreign currency translation accounting. Under the new accounting rule, a devaluation of the Mexican peso resulted in a substantial writedown of PACCAR's investment in VILPAC, S.A. However, the company's chain of operating profits— unbroken since 1938—continued.

Three generations of Kenworth trucks, from 1924 to 1995.

Peterbilt's Denton, Texas, plant opened in 1980 with a daily production rate of twenty conventional trucks.

Despite the recession, PACCAR had the financial resources to develop new products, and the ability and capital to upgrade its facilities. During this slow period it completed major renovations at its Chillicothe, Ohio, and Nashville, Tennessee, plants.

Some U.S. factories were operating at 25 percent of their capacity. PACCAR was able to maintain a minimum production level, but its 1982 sales fell to $1.223 billion, with earnings barely exceeding $37 million. In 1983 sales improved slightly to $1.41 billion, and equity recovered to $604 million. PACCAR was able to maintain a ratio of assets to liabilities of 2.14:1, and long-term debt of only 2.3 percent of equity.

Late in 1983, the Class 8 market began to recover, and the efficiencies PACCAR had developed during the recession began paying dividends. Truck sales rose above their low-water mark of 1982, but the market had become intensely price-competitive. PACCAR's share increased to 20 percent, third behind International Harvester and Mack.

From the perspective of PACCAR vice chairman Mark Pigott, great-grandson of PACCAR's founder, "The whole industry changed during the last decade. The type of product that's sold has changed, and the customers have changed, and the dominant manufacturers have changed." Cab-over-engine trucks dropped from 45 percent of the market to less than 6 percent in 1995. The big freight haulers, like Consolidated Freight, Yellow, PIE, and others, dominated their industry, but following deregulation, these firms had been over-shadowed by the nonunion truckload carriers. In 1980 International Harvester represented 30 percent of the Class 8 market, PACCAR 14 percent, and Freightliner 10 percent. Fourteen years later, Freightliner production represented the largest share of the Class 8 market, and its parent company, German-owned Daimler-Benz, was the largest truck manufacturer in the world.

— DEREGULATION AND TRUCK DESIGN —

The passage of the Motor Carrier Act of 1980 deregulated and reshaped the trucking business, setting in motion an era of market changes that would result in a leaner, more efficient truck transportation industry. Private fleets—owned and operated by companies in industries such as petroleum, forest products, and retail—were freed to carry any commercial load they could find.

Trucks, stacked three deep, en route to a Peterbilt dealership.

As a result, these operators had fewer empty return trips and made more productive use of their equipment. By the mid-1980s, private carriers were hauling 60 percent of intercity freight and 90 percent of loads within city limits. Much of that private fleet growth came at the expense of common carriers. (A common carrier is a person or company in the business of transporting goods for a fee, at uniform rates available to all parties.)

The effect of deregulation on truck manufacturers was at first positive, but the buying trend was slowed by the recession and by interest rates above 20 percent. The shakeout from deregulation had resulted in a demand from the owners of aging fleets for new trucks that were more cost-efficient and fuel-efficient, and had longer warranty protection.

Fuel efficiency was a hot topic following the oil shocks of the 1970s. When Peterbilt introduced the Model 362 cab-over-engine in 1982, its selling points included 10 percent fewer parts than its predecessor, the 352, and an aerodynamically designed cab that reduced air drag by nearly 9 percent, contributing to improved fuel efficiency. Using new lightweight materials reduced weight and increased payload capacity. And, following a trend in the industry, the 362 was Peterbilt's first all-metric product.

The recession eased, and by the end of 1984 PACCAR posted record sales of $2.25 billion and profits of $125 million. Its annual report for that year noted that the company had paid income, sales, excise, use, and personal property taxes in excess of $131 million, far more than its net profit for that year.

In 1986, Peterbilt introduced new models including the 357, 375, 377, and 379. Dubbed "The Successors," the new trucks offered improved fuel efficiency and strength with only a limited departure from the traditional "long nose" Peterbilt design.

T600 look-alikes, Peterbilt retained the traditional styling of its trucks, concentrating instead on increased driver comfort, maneuverability, reliability, and ease of maintenance.

Model 379, the classic-nosed Peterbilt, was an update of the 359 that was targeted for the more traditional segment of the Class 8 market, the owner/operators who wanted their trucks to be "out there in front."

These new models were well timed. Deregulation of the trucking industry six years earlier had had a delayed effect on sales, as many operators stayed out of the market until the uncertainties associated with deregulation were replaced with facts.

The Successors were followed in 1987 by another series of new models, including what Peterbilt called premium "Light 8" vehicles. Model 376 offered a standard low-horsepower, short-distance truck, targeted at the buyer whose needs fell somewhere between a medium-duty Class 7 and a heavy-duty Class 8. Another new model, the Model 378 conventional, was designed for inter-city short-haul and highway operations, and its target market included leasing companies and fleet operators.

In 1988, in spite of the 1982 Surface Transportation Assistance Act's effect on the market for cab-over trucks, Peterbilt introduced Model 372, an aerodynamic cab-over-engine tractor developed in response to an anticipated increase in the COE market due to some state length restrictions and the increased popularity of 53-foot trailers. Unfortunately, the 372 didn't sell very well and was ultimately dropped. By the end of the decade, conventional trucks represented 88 percent of the market.

In 1990, when Peterbilt celebrated its fiftieth anniversary, the division became the only Class 8 truck manufacturer in North America to offer air ride on both front and rear suspensions, when it introduced an exclusive front-axle air-suspension system. In later models, Peterbilt innovations reduced the total number of components in its trucks by two-thirds, which lowered its parts inventory costs for owners, dealers, and fleet operators. Equally important, newly designed cabs could be assembled in half the man-hours, and maintenance was greatly simplified.

Unlike Kenworth, with its fleet-owner clientele, Peterbilt engineers were faced with the challenge of changing the aerodynamics of its cabs without changing its "trucker" appeal to customers who appreciate Peterbilt's styling tradition. It was not until 1991 that Peterbilt launched its Model 377A/E (Aero-Enhanced) truck. It offered a conventional-type tractor with dramatically improved fuel efficiency.

By the end of the 1980s, PACCAR had developed a reputation as a low-cost producer of high-quality trucks. In 1987 it produced a record number of Class 8 trucks, and it did so after closing two plants, Peterbilt's Newark and Kenworth's Kansas City plants. The effect was more than a bolstered ego for the company. That year, sales jumped to $2.4 billion, and net income jumped 107 percent from the previous year to $112.5 million.

The question of whether Kenworth or Peterbilt represents PACCAR's higher-quality line of trucks is more a matter for outside speculation than internal contemplation. Each truck appeals to a different market. The lines generally have different customers: Kenworth is preferred by cost-conscious fleet owners, while Peterbilt is the choice of owner/operators. And because of the owner/operator market, Peterbilt trucks command a higher resale market price. Peterbilts have metal hoods, while Kenworth uses fiberglass. Both truck companies use similar drive trains. Each offers engines from three different makers, two axle manufacturers, and two transmission builders. "The competition between the two has served the company very well, but each is expected to be the best," observed Michael Tembreull.

By 1989, combined Peterbilt and Kenworth sales represented 24.5 percent of the U.S. Class 8 market, making PACCAR the largest manufacturer of Class 8 trucks in the United States that year.

— DIVESTMENT PHILOSOPHIES —

In describing the PACCAR diversification philosophy, Charles Pigott said, "We recognize that circumstances change, so from time to time, businesses should be sold."

In 1984 PACCAR sold the Dart Truck Company, its above-ground-mining and log-handling-equipment division, to Unit Rig & Equipment Company, of Tulsa, Oklahoma. Unit Rig, which was owned by Kendavis Industries International, bought all manufacturing rights for Dart loaders, trucks, and log stackers. The transaction did not include the factory and parts warehouse, adjacent to Kenworth's Kansas City plant, which was instead converted for additional Kenworth production.

As Charles Pigott described Dart Truck's fall from grace, "Dart management failed to keep promises to the customer, and warranty costs soared." It also failed to keep up with its competitors in developing and broadening its product lines, and it became unprofitable. "Dart was an unfortunate chapter for PACCAR, but we learned a lot from it. We had a perfectly wonderful company, but the management lost sight of the fact that they had to do what they said they were going to do, and they had to keep the quality at absolutely top level." The quality slipped. "There was no way that we could resurrect the company in the absence of spending several hundred million dollars."

The year 1988 marked the end of an era. PACCAR announced the closing of Pacific Car and Foundry, the eighty-three-year-old manufacturer of railcars and military hardware. Production of railcar and military equipment, including highway-speed earthmovers and military equipment, in its foundry had stopped. During World War II, Pacific Car had produced more than fifteen hundred Sherman tanks. Railcar manufacturing was the foundation of the company when it started in 1905, and railcars had been produced at the Renton site since 1907. The company had prospered, first in railcars for the logging industry, then in ice-cooled cars for transporting Pacific

In 1988, after careful evaluation of the future for railcar manufacturing, Pacific Car and Foundry was closed.

Northwest fruit to eastern markets. In 1932, the Car Company developed the Carco winch, which became the foundation of PACCAR's winch division in 1980. The company boomed with the railroads and suffered during the industry's downturns.

During the 1970s, PACCAR increased its stake in the railcar business when it acquired International Car. For a time it had been the nation's largest manufacturer of cabooses, but when railroad regulations changed, the caboose was no longer required. As a result, PACCAR began to divest itself of the railcar business. The division posted record sales in 1980. Then the industry's annual production plummeted from its peak of 125,000 cars, railcar production overcapacity created a buyer's market, and margins disappeared.

"We recognized that we weren't going to be very busy," said Charles Pigott, "and that because so many railcar components come from suppliers in the Midwest, the Car Company was poorly located in the Northwest. If we were going to continue in the business, we would have to relocate to the Midwest." At that time, PACCAR was expanding its truck manufacturing capability, and it chose to close the Car Company in order to concentrate on what had become 90 percent of its sales—trucks. (It turned out to be a wise decision, because in the mid-1990s the railcar market shrank to an annual production of 20,000 to 30,000 cars, and there were four large U.S. manufacturers competing for that meager market.)

PACCAR Defense Systems shared the Renton facilities with the Car Company, but defense contracting had become a source of more aggravation than profit. There were times when funds were committed for military equipment acquisitions, but contracts would never be signed. On one Defense Systems research and development contract for a highway-speed earthmover, one that could keep up with tanks, funds had been allocated, but the U.S. Army never delivered a signed production contract. The division had developed other military hardware, including a missile-loader and a missile-launcher. PACCAR Defense was also responsible for developing what became known as the Bradley Fighting Machine. Defense projects had been good for PACCAR, as they had become a source for new technology, but the Defense Division was gradually dissolved in the late 1980s.

It was not always a lack of sales or profit potential that led to a company's sale. Wagner Mining Equipment was the sole U.S. manufacturer of both diesel and electric underground loaders and haulers, and it had prospered during the 1980s, when coal and gold mining experienced a resurgence. In 1988 Wagner's sales represented nearly a third of the world market for underground mining vehicles. It was the largest manufacturer of rubber-tired underground mining equipment in the world when it was sold by PACCAR in 1989. It was also profitable, but its product line was narrow, and the development of new products would be expensive. Acquisitions were considered, but because of inflated prices they were declined. Instead, Wagner was sold to Atlas Copco of Sweden, one of the world's largest mining equipment companies.

"Wagner was turned around and was very profitable for us in the last few years that we had it," said Charles Pigott. "But we chose to sell it because the division occupied a very narrow segment of the total mining equipment business, and we did not think it would be economically feasible to broaden its product lines."

The sale of Wagner gave PACCAR a $52.4 million after-tax gain, which enabled the company to end 1989 with a 37 percent increase in net income to $242 million. Sales increased 28 percent to $3.1 billion. Equity exceeded $1 billion for the first year in the history of PACCAR.

In 1997, PACCAR sold Trico Industries, Incorporated, its San Marcos, Texas, pump and petroleum-extraction equipment manufacturing company. Trico, a producer of technically advanced "down hole" pumping equipment, had been acquired by PACCAR in 1987. Trico was expanded with the acquisition of Baker Lift Systems in 1989 and National-Oilwell in 1994. At the time of its sale, Trico was the only oil-field equipment company to produce and service all major types of artificial lift systems: sucker rod, hydraulic submersible, and electric submersible pumping systems.

Although highly respected, Trico's product line was narrow, and additional product development or further acquisitions were considered expensive by PACCAR management. The valuation of oil-service equipment manufacturing companies was high in 1997, and rather than invest additional capital in the industry, PACCAR instead chose to sell Trico to Houston-based EVI, Inc., for $105 million. The sale produced a one-time $35 million after-tax gain for PACCAR, which was identified for investment in its "core business activities."

— ACQUISITION PHILOSOPHY —

"Acquisition," according to Charles Pigott, "is among management's most important responsibilities, because when we put dollars into a division or company, those dollars are likely to remain there for ten to twenty-five years." Although the truck manufacturing business has been the heart and soul of the modern-day PACCAR, the company invested in other industries where it saw opportunities. The decision to acquire a new business was based on several factors, including whether PACCAR felt it could make a difference by adding management, investing money, or putting a product into some underutilized facilities. On the other hand, PACCAR rejected investments that looked like they might require too much management time or assistance outside PACCAR management expertise.

In a 1995 interview, PACCAR president David Hovind said that the company "looks for companies where there's good synergy. We prefer a company that has some management team, that is either short of cash, or needs an infusion of capital equipment or better internal control. One of the real strengths of PACCAR is its internal control. It's an off-balance-sheet asset."

PACCAR executives generally rely on their own due diligence in evaluating a potential acquisition, without investment bankers. "Before we make large investments, we walk around them several times and make sure we know what we're doing," said Don Hatchel, vice president and controller.

In 1987, PACCAR entered the fiercely competitive retail auto parts business with two separate acquisitions—Al's Auto Supply and, in 1988, Grand Auto, Incorporated. Al's operated 25 outlets in Washington State, and with Grand Auto's 130 stores scattered throughout Alaska, California, and Nevada, PACCAR became the fourth-largest auto parts retailer on the West Coast and the eighth largest in the United States. Al's Auto Supply was PACCAR's first auto parts acquisition, and though the business was promising, it was no overnight success. "We thought we knew more about the business than it turned out we did when we acquired Grand Auto. That was a real eye-opener for us," recalled Chairman Pigott.

PACCAR vice chairman Mike Tembreull noted that the acquisitions of Al's and Grand Auto were done without consulting investment bankers. "In doing that, we had to rely on our own due diligence. We brought the key people out of the [Al's and Grand Auto] organizations and spent a lot of time evaluating what we were acquiring." The retail auto parts business was a marked departure from PACCAR's core business, but the auto parts did offer some synergy to

PACCAR entered the retail auto parts business in 1987, and in 1988, it acquired Grand Auto.

the company's truck parts distribution business. The 1987 Chairman's Letter said, "We believe some of the retail merchandising knowledge perfected by Al's Auto Supply and Grand Auto management can be shared with our truck dealers."

The two chains were joined under the division title of PACCAR Automotive, and a new management team was brought in to reevaluate every aspect of the operations. The Los Angeles–area units were abandoned because there were too few desirable locations and too many competitors, while new locations were opened in Washington and Idaho, leaving the company with 120 surviving units. The new division installed a sophisticated point-of-sale computer system that enabled Al's and Grand Auto to communicate among all of its stores. This system allowed management to merchandize stores according to geographical and seasonal differences and to adjust inventories between stores.

A large number of PACCAR's truck-part suppliers also produced auto parts, which increased the company's overall buying capacity. In addition, the acquisition offered Dynacraft, a PACCAR company that manufactures hoses and belts, an opportunity to sell in a new market. The acquisition also expanded the company's ability to merchandise truck parts through its auto parts stores.

Unlike PACCAR's other interests, the auto parts business tends to hold steady during recessionary times, when consumers are more apt to buy replacement parts for their older cars than buy new vehicles.

As the 1990s progressed, PACCAR Automotive began to show a profit, and planning for its future became more aggressive. "You have to be involved in the business with a long-term perspective," noted Tembreull.

— LARGEST INDUSTRIAL WINCH MANUFACTURER —

Winches had been an important part of the company since the Carco winch was developed by Alex Finlayson and other Pacific Car and Foundry engineers in 1932. The company's first winches were sold to the Pacific Northwest logging industry for use with cleat tractors and logging arches. The success of Carco helped the company stay afloat during the dark days of the Depression when there was no railcar business to be found. The company added to the winch line with its acquisition of the Canadian winch maker Gearmatic Company, Limited, in 1963, and later the Braden Winch Company, in 1977.

In 1980, the company formed the PACCAR Winch Division, with sales and manufacturing of winches consolidated in Broken Arrow, Oklahoma, in 1985. By 1986, PACCAR was the largest commercial winch manufacturer in the United States. And by 1989, PACCAR Winch had become the world's largest manufacturer of industrial winches.

In 1993, PACCAR Winch purchased the design and manufacturing rights to the Caterpillar line of winches. The agreement included a contract to supply Caterpillar with winches and parts for Caterpillar factories and its dealer network.

One year later the Winch Division signed a ten-year distribution agreement with OMNI USA, a large manufacturer of planetary drives. OMNI's smaller winches were designed as wheel drives for smaller mobile cranes and other lifting equipment.

By 1994, PACCAR's Winch Division was not only the largest but likely the most profitable industrial winch manufacturer in the world.

Throughout the 1980s, PACCAR had built on its strengths, its management, and its financial condition. In 1989 its long-term debt, outside of PACCAR Financial bond obligations that were sold to finance purchases and leases at low interest rates, was barely $33 million.

The decade ended on a high note. PACCAR's 1989 income before taxes exceeded $363.3 million, about $301.6 million from domestic sales and $61.7 million from international sales. Income taxes, before deferments, consumed $128.6 million, more than half of PACCAR's net profit of $241.9 million.

With 92 percent of its sales and profits derived from truck manufacturing, PACCAR's performance during the 1980s followed the up-and-down cycles of the industry. But the company cushioned the financial troughs by staying true to the philosophy it developed in its cyclical railcar manufacturing years: maintain a strong cash position, build only to order, never sacrifice profit for market share, never trade quality for profit, and never operate at a loss.

Throughout the 1980s, PACCAR paid increasingly handsome dividends and split the stock several times: 10 percent stock dividend in 1981, a two-for-one split in 1983, and another two-for-one split in 1988. At the same time, the company was able to develop new products, offer new services, build new plants, and enter new businesses. By comparison, many of the company's domestic competitors did not fare as well. International Harvester, the largest U.S. truck manufacturer during the 1980s, ultimately sought Chapter 11 protection from its creditors, and White, Freightliner, and Mack were acquired by foreign competitors.

The decade also saw a changing of the guard within senior PACCAR management. In the early 1980s, Senior Vice President Robert A. Holmstrom retired, and another senior vice president, B. C. Jameson, died prior to retirement. Gerry A. Robbins, Pacific Car and Foundry's longtime leader and senior vice president of manufacturing, retired in 1985. The year 1987 saw the retirement of Executive Vice President William N. Gross, a charismatic manufacturing man with a gift for marketing. Senior Vice President Robert Dickey, a young attorney with a penchant for the trucking industry and deregulation, left the company to assume the top job with the American Trucking Association. Jack A. Chantrey retired from the company in 1989 as senior vice president, and in March 1991, Leonard A. Haba, the company's chief financial officer, retired.

Thus, by early in the 1990s, senior officers Charles Pigott, PACCAR's chief executive officer, and Joseph Dunn, president, were joined by a wave of young, talented, and markedly enthusiastic senior managers who have led PACCAR into a new era of growth and change.

PACCAR Winch Division was rooted in the 1932 development of the Carco winch. By 1994, PACCAR had grown to become the largest manufacturer of commercial winches in the world.

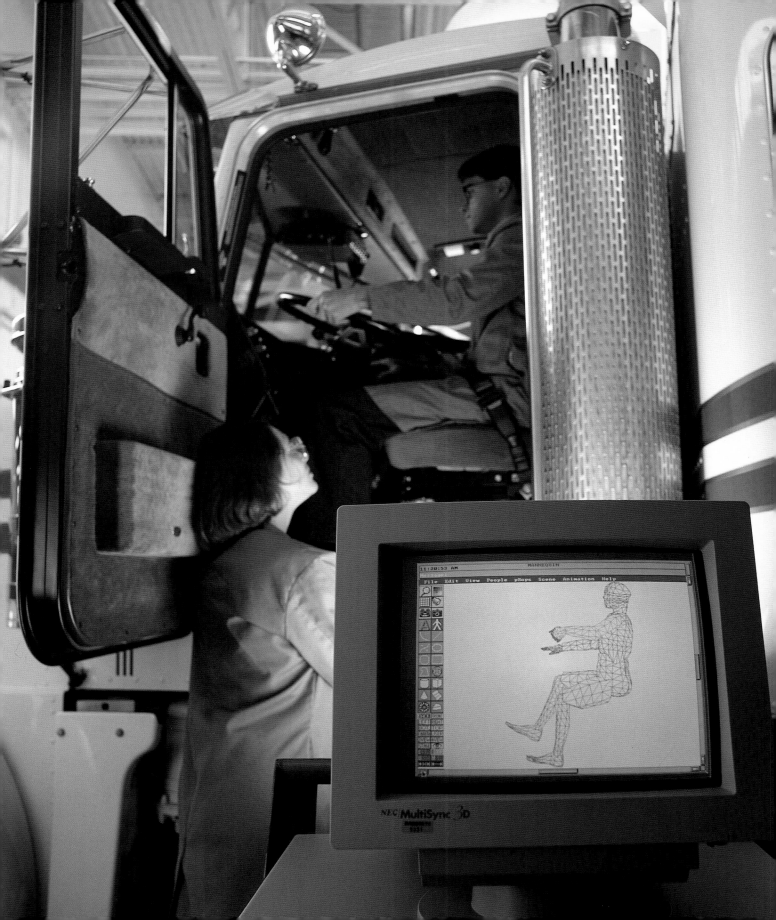

CHAPTER TWELVE

GUIDING PRINCIPLES

PACCAR's trinity has always been ethics, integrity, and quality, and each of the company's interests is guided by the same strong principles.

— PACCAR'S DEALERS —

Kenworth and Peterbilt are the only truck manufacturers in the United States to sell exclusively through dealerships. That makes the capabilities and quality of those dealerships very important to PACCAR.

Kenworth and Peterbilt established their own networks of independent dealerships, and by 1995 PACCAR's trucks and services were sold at 418 North American locations. The company's oldest dealership was Portland, Oregon–based Roberts Motors, which had become a Kenworth dealer in 1938. That year, custom "heavy-duty" trucks sold for less than $5,000. Roy T. Williams established the Spokane, Washington–based Williams Equipment Company, the first truck dealership formed after PACCAR's acquisition of Kenworth in 1945. By then the cost of a new Kenworth had increased to more than $8,000.

Coast Counties Truck and Equipment Company, Peterbilt's oldest dealer, was established in a shed on a vacant lot in San Jose, California, by Austin Archer in 1949. In 1950, when the cost of a two-axle Peterbilt was roughly $13,000, Archer managed to sell nine. (At the time, Peterbilt produced only five trucks a day.) In 1995, Coast Counties sold more than three hundred Peterbilt trucks—some worth over $150,000—and had expanded to three Bay Area locations run by the second generation, Robert Archer.

The firm has a history similar to that of many of the company's dealers. It began as an order taker, expanded into multiple locations, and over time developed a broad base of services: first, parts and accessories, then, PFC financing and PACCAR Leasing programs.

Since the advent of the computer age, dealership management has become more complex, and in 1981, PACCAR developed Dealer Management Consulting (DMC) services. Its first director was Mac Phares. Consulting services included dealership management and operations, financial and insurance planning, human resources, and computer systems management. By the mid-1990s, under the direction of Carter Baker and Jim Moore, DMC had trained more than eleven hundred dealer-personnel in business dealer management techniques.

In 1991, PACCAR, at its Technical Center facilities, became the first truck manufacturer to study human factors engineering. Its findings were incorporated into improved Kenworth and Peterbilt designs.

The first Dealer Councils were formed in the late 1970s. Council formats encourage a free exchange of ideas, which contributes to the development of new truck models, better parts distribution and marketing, and a wider selection of financial services. In 1992, Kenworth formed the Driver Board, made up of five hundred owner/operators and fleet drivers. About half drove Kenworths and the balance drove trucks manufactured by Kenworth competitors. Councils and the Driver Board are two-way streets, where dealers and drivers share their experiences and observations. The result often has been a better truck design. Along with research and development, as well as purchasing procedures, the councils and board have greatly assisted PACCAR in its pursuit of quality.

With the advent of computers and on-line communications, PACCAR developed a computer-based engine diagnostic system similar to that used in automobile dealer service centers. Computer-based technology also was developed to help truck sales representatives evaluate, specify, and price custom trucks in minutes.

— A BROADER LINE OF TRUCKS —

PACCAR's pursuit of the Class 6 and 7 markets began in 1986, when it contracted with Volkswagen do Brasil S.A. for trucks manufactured in São Paulo. These 19,501- to 33,000-pound trucks incorporated advanced German technologies with North American components.

Joseph Dunn, who became the company's president in 1987, explained the reason for PACCAR's involvement with Volkswagen in a 1986 article in *PACCAR World.* "Cummins introduced a new engine designed for lighter trucks. Volkswagen was building a quality vehicle and agreed to build to our specifications. Our goal was to offer the best truck, not to be the first."

The "Mid-Ranger" line of trucks carried either Kenworth or Peterbilt nameplates and were marketed through a new subsidiary, PACCAR Sales North America (PSNA). By 1992, PACCAR had begun production of newly engineered cab-over Class 7 trucks in Kenworth's Ste-Thérèse, Quebec, factory. The North American–built trucks offered improved cab access and payload capacity. They were marketed as Kenworth K300 and Peterbilt Mid-Ranger 200.

"What we ultimately learned was that instead of a cab-over vehicle, a conventional vehicle was really what the market wanted," observed Charles Pigott. In 1994, Kenworth and Peterbilt introduced conventional Class 7 models, and within a year they represented about 85 percent of PACCAR's medium-duty truck market.

The potential—and the dilemma—for PACCAR's small trucks was critiqued in a 1995 interview with Mark Pigott. "The future of Class 6 and 7 is very exciting. . . . Together, they represent about 130,000 units. If we can get a 10 percent market share, and that's less than half of what we have in the Class 8 market, that will be another 10,000 to 15,000 trucks we can sell each year. We will need a new factory for that. We'll produce 1,000 trucks this year, but we're making them in a Class 8 factory where for every Class 7 we make, in effect, we're giving up a Class 8 truck."

— TRUCK PARTS —

PACCAR Parts began in 1973 as a means to support truck sales and service through Kenworth and Peterbilt dealers. The first warehouse/distribution center was opened in Renton, Washington. A year later, another distribution center was opened in Atlanta, Georgia. In 1986, Kenworth's and Peterbilt's after-market sales and parts distribution efforts were united to become PACCAR Parts.

By 1988, PACCAR Parts distributed its goods through more than five hundred dealerships, including fifty international dealerships in forty countries around the world. By the end of the decade, PACCAR Parts had become a significant source of revenue for the company, distributing not only Peterbilt and Kenworth parts but also parts for all makes of heavy-duty trucks.

The division opened a new distribution facility in Rockford, Illinois, in 1991. The 263,000-square-foot Midwest Distribution Center—as large as most truck manufacturing plants—inventoried parts from nearly five thousand manufacturers. The company's 1991 annual report noted, "During the last five years, PACCAR Parts Division has grown over 35 percent, far exceeding the U.S. industry average."

The division opened a new headquarters building on part of the Pacific Car and Foundry site in 1992. And, in an effort to be more strategically placed, PACCAR Parts closed its Newark, California, warehouse in 1995 and opened a new facility in Las Vegas, Nevada. The Las Vegas warehouse was 40 percent larger than the Newark facility it replaced.

PACCAR Parts took orders and delivered parts on a twenty-four-hour-a-day basis, and by 1994, it had designed and installed sophisticated software that allowed its dealers direct access to its inventory. "The whole emphasis of PACCAR Parts is to give dealers one-stop shopping for any part they need for any truck," noted PACCAR vice chairman Mike Tembreull.

PACCAR designed a new line of Class 6 and Class 7 trucks for both Kenworth and Peterbilt to include conventional models such as the T300 shown above.

PACCAR Financial Corporation (PFC) was organized in 1961 as a service to its truck dealers, but it remained a small subsidiary until the 1980s. By then, PACCAR managed three financial subsidiaries, PACCAR Leasing Corporation, RAILEASE Inc., and an insurance company. These financial services were offered through the dealer network, which then numbered over three hundred.

PFC capitalized on PACCAR's strong financial position and was able to obtain funds at favorable rates through banks and insurance companies. When interest rates soared above 20 percent in 1981, PFC offered special interest rate financing that was, at times, as much as 3 percent lower than market rates. That year, PFC became the first in the industry to offer customers the option to refinance at lower rates should market rates fall. By the end of 1982, Charles Pigott's Message to Stockholders noted, "About one-third of all Kenworth and Peterbilt trucks sold in the United States during 1982 were financed by PACCAR Financial Corporation. . . . These subsidiaries help dealers sell new equipment and generate business for PACCAR manufacturing divisions during difficult economic periods. As profit centers, they also contribute significantly to corporate revenues." Financial services were also offered in Canada, Australia, Mexico, and the United Kingdom.

Beginning in 1983, PFC received approval for the first of several shelf registrations from the Securities and Exchange Commission. The first medium-term notes were for $250 million. This allowed PFC to borrow funds directly in the public bond market at lower than bank interest rates. By the end of that year, its assets were in excess of a half billion dollars, and its net income represented nearly 30 percent of PACCAR's consolidated income.

PACCAR Inc stood behind PFC debt, guaranteeing minimum ratios between income, interest payments, and assets. PACCAR did not guarantee PFC's indebtedness, but rather it insured the finance company's ability to pay its indebtedness. On that basis, when PACCAR Financial goes to the markets, it really carries the strength of PACCAR behind it in its ratings.

Following years of double-digit growth, PFC products and management needed some refinements. In the past, a lot of business had been done based on the guarantee of the dealers, but PFC's competition no longer required dealer guarantees and it became a non-recourse market. As a result, PFC established rigid credit standards and created a delivery system to service its dealers in a timely fashion.

In 1992, the truck industry experienced a strong surge. To keep up with demand, PFC filed a new shelf registration for $1 billion in 1993. A year later, its net revenue exceeded $205 million and its assets topped $1.7 billion. PFC financed approximately 25 percent of Peterbilt and Kenworth truck sales in 1994. An additional $1 billion shelf registration was approved in 1996.

PACCAR Leasing Corporation was formed in 1980 to provide the legal, financial, and marketing framework for leasing-dealer franchises. In addition to trucks, leases could include insurance, fuel, maintenance, and multistate tax reporting and vehicle licensing.

Leases were sold through PacLease dealer franchises. PACCAR Leasing Corporation purchased trucks from franchise dealers and leased them back to them for short-term rental or long-term lease to end-users.

By 1990, approximately 35 percent of U.S. Class 8 sales went into service as leased vehicles, and by the mid-1990s PACCAR's lease fleet had increased to 6,620 trucks and nearly 1,400 trailers. PACCAR Leasing Corporation had become one of the ten largest full-service leasing companies in North America.

— GLOBALIZING PACCAR —

PACCAR's international marketing was formally organized in 1972, when the company established PACCAR International. The division sold PACCAR trucks and truck parts, and offered PACCAR financial services to Kenworth's and Peterbilt's international dealers. By 1995, PACCAR International had become one of the largest exporters of capital goods in North America. (PACCAR's Winch Division, and later Trico Industries, managed their own offshore sales because of the expertise required to sell their products.)

The International Division's business was directly affected by the rise and fall in value of the U.S. dollar, and PACCAR's advantage was sometimes its ability to produce trucks in Canada,

PacLease was introduced to PACCAR dealers in 1981. Custom leases included insurance, fuel, maintenance, tax reporting, and licensing. By 1997, the PacLease fleet had grown to more than ten thousand vehicles.

In 1992, nearly three hundred Kenworth trucks were loaded on two ocean-going barges for delivery to two PACCAR International dealerships in Colombia.

Mexico, Australia, or the United Kingdom. The company's 1980 annual report stated, "While the U.S. economy was troubled, demand in much of the world remained strong. PACCAR shipped more than twice as many vehicles abroad as in previous years." In 1984, when the dollar was strong, trucks produced in the United Kingdom proved more competitive, and 35 percent of the International Division's sales that year were Foden trucks.

PACCAR was sometimes at a global disadvantage for reasons other than a strong dollar. In a 1995 interview, Vice President/General Counsel Glen Morie lamented, "We could have done a marvelous amount of business in Iran, but there was an embargo; we couldn't do anything there. So, who is building in Iran today? Daimler-Benz, Iveco, Scania, all of our competitors." Still, by 1990, PACCAR International was marketing trucks in more than forty countries.

A Kenworth K953 was exhaustively tested by the Chinese National Petroleum Corporation in 1991. China had acquired its first K953 trucks in 1978, but by 1991 it required its new trucks to have more cab room and improved forward visibility. PACCAR International worked with Kenworth engineers to create a new cab-over design, the "K953S Shamo-Wang (Desert King)," for operation in one of the world's harshest environments—China's Taklamakan oil fields. The company's relationships in China continued to develop, and in 1996 PACCAR International signed a joint venture assembly agreement with Xuzhou Construction Machinery Group to produce Kenworth T800s in China.

In 1992, PACCAR International shipped nearly three hundred Kenworth trucks to Industrias Ivor of Bogotá and Kenworth de la Montaña of Medellín, the division's Colombian dealers. The shipment required two seagoing barges and represented the consolidated orders of more than 150 customers, the largest single international order ever received by PACCAR.

Russia and other eastern European countries became promising markets following the collapse of the USSR in 1990, and in 1992 the International Division opened its first office in Moscow. One year later, the division joined with Caterpillar Incorporated in a joint venture with ZiL, Russia's leading truck manufacturer, to build trucks for eastern Europe. PACCAR also planned future production of Kenworth trucks at the ZiL factory. However, in 1996, due to ongoing economic turmoil in Russia, the venture was dissolved.

"Most countries have become much more sophisticated in their joint venture legislation, the percentage of foreign investment, local content, and labor relations," noted Glen Morie. In 1984, PACCAR began to ship trucks in "kit" form, for assembly in countries with local content laws. The trucks were then built with local labor, often using locally produced batteries, tires, glass, and other components. This approach to local content laws was later expanded to other joint ventures. Building on a decade of experience in licensing truck assembly in Malaysia, in 1993, PACCAR entered into an arrangement to assemble Kenworths in Zimbabwe, through a mutual agreement with Canadian Kenworth and T.A. Holdings Limited, of Zimbabwe. The Canadian International Development Agency provided some of the funds.

Because of Kenworth's and Peterbilt's proven utility in the extractive industries, PACCAR International focused its early marketing efforts on countries where mining, petroleum exploration and extraction, or logging flourished. During the 1980s, the division extended its reach to sell to countries where large construction projects, such as airports, oil pipelines, and hydroelectric dams, were planned. "There has been an exciting shift in PACCAR International," said Mark Pigott. "For many years, their primary focus was natural-resource exploration and development within such countries as Indonesia, Thailand, or China. Those countries are developing infrastructure, a middle class, and they're talking about construction of houses and freeways and office buildings, hauling produce, and manufacturing goods within the country. They have become new markets for our International Division."

— WORLDWIDE MANUFACTURING —

By 1994, international truck manufacturing (exclusive of Canadian Kenworth) provided approximately 14 percent of PACCAR's total truck revenue.

Canadian Kenworth moved its headquarters from Ottawa to Toronto in 1985, at a cost of $9.5 million. The principal benefit of the move was substantially lower operating costs. Management operations were consolidated with those in the United States to create a truly integrated North American organization in 1993. The plant in Ste-Thérèse, Quebec, operated without a general manager, and plant management reported to Kenworth headquarters in Kirkland, Washington. The Ste-Thérèse plant, along with Kenworth's Chillicothe, Ohio, plant, produced trucks for the eastern Canada market and for the growing northeastern United States market, while the Seattle and Renton plants produced trucks for western Canada as well as for U.S. and export markets. The Canadian plant also produced Class 7 trucks for Kenworth and Peterbilt until a prolonged strike in 1995 led to its closure. Class 8 production was increased at Kenworth's United States plants, and Class 7 production was moved to VILPAC.

In 1998, PACCAR announced plans to reopen the Ste-Thérèse plant and invest $75 million to modernize and expand the Canadian Kenworth factory.

With Foden, PACCAR began to benefit from its increased globalization. Led by a team of PACCAR people, Foden disposed of obsolete inventory, much of it leftover parts from its days as a vertically integrated manufacturer. Mark Pigott recalled, "Foden, almost up to the point where we took them over, was making rails. It even had its own engines and transmissions, so we brought the whole concept, one of being an assembler, to Foden." By 1982, for the first time, customers could order a Foden built to their specifications, and this move enhanced Foden's reputation among truck buyers. By 1983, 35 percent of PACCAR International's sales came from Foden's product line of highway tractors, garbage trucks, snowplows, and on- and off-highway dump trucks for private business, government, and the military.

Foden afforded PACCAR a window for observing the European market and its competitors there, and the connection exposed the company to European suppliers of quality truck parts. Foden also contracted to produce trucks for Ford during the middle 1980s, and later it began building Kenworth trucks for the Middle East markets. At that time, Kenworth trucks produced in the Foden plant cost 10 to 15 percent less than comparable models produced in the United States and shipped to the Middle East. Mark Pigott remarked, "I think Foden, to some extent, gets part of the credit for pushing our boundaries outside of North America."

By 1987, Foden, which had 57 dealerships in 46 countries, had its best year since its acquisition by PACCAR. The new Foden 4000 Series was well received, and the division's unit sales increased 20 percent. In 1990, PACCAR U.K. Ltd. opened a new headquarters and engineering complex, another commitment to Foden's future.

PACCAR had acquired Fodens out of bankruptcy, and it was still in the midst of reorganizing when Mark Pigott, great-grandson of the Company's founder William Pigott, was given operating responsibility for it. For him, Foden represented what he considered his most interesting learning experience.

PACCAR U.K. Ltd. opened new headquarters and an advanced engineering complex in 1990 near its Foden plant in Sandbach, England.

"Foden has been a good investment for us, not solely because we have made some money with it, but because it has given us firsthand knowledge of the European market and even some of the export markets that they used to have," said Charles Pigott.

Kenworth Australia's plant produces trucks for the Australian market as well as for markets in New Zealand and Papua, New Guinea. Truck designs are modified not only for right-hand steering but for the Australian environment as well. "Australian Kenworths have heavier frames, heavier suspension, and a lot of severe service components on the cabs," observed PACCAR vice president Gary Moore. "There is more on/off highway driving than there is in North America."

Kenworth is the largest manufacturer of Class 8 trucks in Australia's very competitive market. Its 1993 market share was 20 percent. New models, such as the T440 and T480, offer more horsepower and more hauling capacity. Kenworth Class 7 models were introduced to the Australian market in 1994.

In 1994, Kenworth Australia was recognized for its quality manufacturing when the company was granted ISO 9001 certification—an international quality standard rating.

Kenworth Mexicana traditionally represents over half of Mexico's sales in heavy-duty tractors, but in 1993, Mexico's economy slowed the truck market. That year, PACCAR received Mexican government approval to purchase additional shares in VILPAC, S.A., and the transaction was completed in 1994, when PACCAR increased its ownership in VILPAC from 49 percent to more than 55 percent. By the fall of 1995, PACCAR had purchased complete ownership of its Mexican operation.

The 1994 North American Free Trade Agreement, which covered trade relations between Canada, the United States, and Mexico, had a minimal short-term impact, but it held the promise of more trade in the future. Michael Tembreull pointed out that "even though we always had a strong share of the market, our ability to trade across borders will provide an even stronger market for our products."

The 1995 currency devaluation caused the Mexican economy to stagnate. At the time the value of the peso began to drop, PACCAR had invested much of its cash in U.S. dollars, so the devaluation did not have a significant impact on its balance sheet; however, production slowed to a standstill.

Devaluations of the Mexican peso have occurred several times in recent history, but that, according to David Hovind, was not PACCAR's principal concern. "Business in the future will be very different and a lot more difficult. But, it has nothing to do with the peso. With tariffs coming down, more people are finding the Mexican market attractive, so we see a lot more competition. . . . But we've been there for thirty-five years. The names 'Ken-Mex' and 'Kenworth' [both names are used on those trucks] are to durability what Kleenex is to tissue. The names are generic."

In spite of the effect of Mexico's depressed economy, in 1995 PACCAR acquired full owner-ship of VILPAC. In so doing, the company demonstrated its belief in the long-term health of Mexico's trucking industry, one that the Ken-Mex nameplate had dominated for thirty-five years.

— A NEW PLANT IN RENTON —

In the trough of a truck market downcycle, PACCAR announced in 1991 that it would build a 300,000-square-foot plant for Kenworth on the old Pacific Car and Foundry site in Renton. This decision was based on the company's belief that the Pacific Rim export market would continue

PACCAR acquired
100-percent ownership
of Kenworth Mexicana
in 1995. In 1997,
Ken-Mex produced
more than 5,600 trucks
for the Mexican and
export markets—
a record.

to grow and that North America's aging truck fleet would soon need to be replaced. (At the time, the average fleet tractor in service was eight years old.)

The decision to build in Renton was otherwise complicated. Before construction could begin, the property needed to be cleaned up. The Environmental Protection Agency (EPA) declared the location a federal Superfund cleanup site, not so much because of contamination, but rather because of a points system used to determine toxic risk. The EPA considered the site in relation to a source of the city of Renton's drinking water, the Cedar River, which was about 1,700 feet from the plant site. The fact that the water flows off the property away from the river made no difference to the EPA.

"The real story with Renton was that we embarked voluntarily to clean up that site without any government involvement," said General Counsel Morie. "We spent a lot of money in Renton on cleanup rather than hassling with the government, and to the government's credit they supported us. It's worked out very well."

PACCAR's goal in planning the new plant was to make it the most cost-effective in its history. Before a design line was drawn on paper, the company considered every detail. When completed, the facility was considered one of the most efficient in the country, with state-of-the-art insulation and lighting systems, and the latest in paint technology, ergonomic assistance, and environmental monitoring and control systems.

On June 4, 1993, PACCAR officially dedicated the new plant. It was designed to build twenty trucks a day, which accelerated Kenworth's delivery schedules. Along with Kenworth's other U.S. factories, the new plant contributed to PACCAR's 5 percent profit margin, the highest in the industry.

In 1993, PACCAR's net income rose 118 percent to $142.2 million on record sales of $3.379 billion. Increased sales and profits in all divisions contributed to the surge. The improved

In order to meet the growing demand for trucks in western North America and around the Pacific Rim, Kenworth opened a new plant on the Pacific Car and Foundry site in 1993.

business climate was fueled by pent-up replacement needs and lower interest rates. The U.S. Class 8 market rose to 155,000 units, and PACCAR's 34,100 trucks represented a 22 percent share of the market. International truck manufacturing added another 9,900 units to the company's total production.

The company set more records in 1994, with sales of $4.285 billion and earnings of $204.5 million. The year ended with a backlog sufficient to keep its truck plants operating at full capacity through 1995. In fact, the Seattle plant, which had been scheduled to close after the Renton plant's start-up, was kept open to meet demand.

— ISO 9001 —

In 1995, PACCAR became the first truck company in the world to have all of its domestic factories simultaneously certified by the International Standards Organization (ISO). ISO is a documented approach to ensuring a quality product. It includes all phases of product development and manufacturing, from design and design review to production and product support. What ISO ensures through its independent auditing groups is that a certified company has established ISO standards and has maintained ISO practices. Because PACCAR's interest always has been in quality, the company's standards and procedures were well advanced when it applied for ISO certification.

A significant step toward what became the company's ISO certification was instituted in the shadow of the Dart Truck demise, when PACCAR formed a corporate quality department that reviewed everything from purchasing to assembly. In addition, it developed what became known as PACCAR Integrated Quality System (PIQS). PIQS standardized quality procedures and processes so that PACCAR trucks would meet the same standards no matter where they were manufactured. Although the primary emphasis was on the truck divisions—each manages its own quality affairs—every division benefits from PIQS.

In his 1990 Chairman's Letter, Charles Pigott announced the expansion of PIQS. "Along with PIQS comes the renewal of our central message: the foundation for the Company's success—both past and future—evolves from the integrity of the PACCAR name and the quality of our products."

The company formed a corporate purchasing group in 1987 that consolidated Kenworth's and Peterbilt's buying functions. PACCAR was a systems integrator, buying components that were designed into its products from more than twelve hundred suppliers. During a mid-1980s study, PACCAR determined that about half of the company's warranty expenses had been caused by failure of vendor-supplied parts. PACCAR's Technical Center began a rigorous parts testing program, often establishing benchmarks for measuring quality. The Purchasing Group inspected its suppliers' facilities, audited their quality programs, and established a rating system and a preferred supplier group. Over time, the number of suppliers dropped to six hundred. Mark Pigott observed, "Quality enhancement has just been astounding, and we can show a 50 percent improvement in our truck building efficiency over the last decade." The life expectancy of a Class 8 truck increased from one to two million miles.

— PLANNING FOR THE FUTURE: COMPETITIVE PRODUCTS AND PROFITABLE ACQUISITIONS —

"The truck was a mature product and generally low-tech compared to an airplane. But we needed high-tech solutions to be a winner," noted David Hovind. Advancing technology mandated more frequent truck design updates. The Kenworth W900 design had sold well, with little modification, for more than a decade before it was replaced with the W900B. A third redesign of the T600 had been developed by the end of its first decade.

PACCAR invested in a worldwide common engineering computer-actuated design (CAD) system, the only one of its kind. With advanced software, every PACCAR truck division, whether

Introduced in May 1996, the Kenworth T2000 was developed over three years at a cost of nearly $100 million.

in Australia, the United Kingdom, Mexico, the United States, or Canada, had access to the same truck design system. This greatly improved communications among the company's design engineers.

The company also invested in computer software that involved a process known as stereo lithography. The end product was a wax-like mold of a newly designed part accurate down to one one-thousandth of an inch. The likeness could be produced in thirty-six hours instead of six to eight weeks. Chrysler had used this system to develop its Viper engine. With these and other systems, PACCAR greatly improved the design time and cost required to produce a new model truck.

One of the most visible new PACCAR products, the Kenworth T2000, was introduced in 1996. The T2000 concept was born in 1992, when the company committed to what became a $100 million research and development budget to create the next generation of advanced trucks.

Kenworth had clear design objectives and ambitious goals for the truck: Reduce wind drag. Improve fuel economy. Increase driver comfort and visibility. Reduce weight and increase payload by using new lightweight composite materials. Reduce the frequency and cost of maintenance. And substantially increase the new truck's life expectancy.

The T2000 was developed by a cross-discipline team. Design and manufacturing engineering got on board along with representatives from Kenworth service, purchasing, parts, and marketing. Eight people began work in May 1992—but by January 1994, more than seventy people were directly involved, including T600 veteran engineer Larry Orr, Kenworth chief engineer Paul Middlehoven, and Rob Chopp, who managed the truck's development.

While some engineers created a mock-up of the cab, others built models for wind-tunnel testing. The mocked-up cab toured truck stops, where company personnel inter-viewed more than twelve hundred drivers. Scale models of various shapes were evaluated following countless hours of wind-tunnel testing. Driver suggestions and test results were incorporated into a concept truck that featured a well-tested diesel engine, a redesigned cab climate control system, new electronics, and a state-of-the-art suspension system. It was called the "Green Truck."

Suppliers were included in the research and development process. A new wheel seal design increased the part's life expectancy to 350,000 miles, almost twice the lifetime of those used on existing trucks. A technologically advanced driveline decreased the need for drive-line lubrication by a factor of ten. The life expectancy of a new water pump was double the expected service of existing models.

Prior to its introduction, the T2000 had proven itself in more than 60,000 hours of testing at the PACCAR Technical Center under the direction of the center's general manager, Jim Bechtold. It completed the equivalent of 5 million miles of durability evaluation before it got the green light for production.

The T2000 was introduced to Kenworth dealers in May 1996 with an impressive list of advancements, including a 6 percent improvement in drag coefficient, resulting in a 3 percent improvement in fuel economy. The advanced suspension system helped reduce the truck's weight, which substantially increased its potential payload. Its cab and storage space was larger than that of any previous Kenworth model, and it offered improved visibility and an impressive climate control system. In all, the truck had 30 percent fewer parts than previous models.

PACCAR announced its acquisition of DAF Trucks N.V., an innovative Netherlands-based manufacturer of medium- and heavy-duty trucks, on November 15, 1996. DAF was Europe's seventh-largest truck manufacturer. Its sales represented 8.6 percent of the European market, a heavy-duty truck market approximately the same size as North America's and one that tended to be counter-cyclical to the North American market. It was a $550 million acquisition, the largest in PACCAR's history.

The acquisition greatly expanded PACCAR's European truck manufacturing capability. DAF's two plants were large and modern. Axles and cabs were produced in a 920,000-square-foot plant in Westerlo, Belgium. Company headquarters, engine production, parts fabrication, warehousing, and truck assembly were located in a 2.7-million-square-foot facility in Eindhoven, the Netherlands. There were nearly one thousand DAF dealer and service locations in Europe.

PACCAR and DAF shared similar operating philosophies, including the policy of only manufacturing trucks to order and selling them at a profit through independent dealers. Both companies had well-defined customer service policies and strong reputations for integrity and quality. And like Kenworth, Peterbilt, and Foden, DAF factories were ISO 9001 certified.

DAF's 1996 sales of $1.58 billion produced a profit in excess of $49 million. That year it sold more than 17,000 Class 6–8 trucks throughout Europe, the Middle East, and Africa. And under an assembly agreement, DAF sold nearly 8,000 Leyland Class 4–5 trucks. (DAF had sold its interest in Leyland as part of a reorganization in 1993.)

The company, founded in 1928 by brothers Hub and Wim van Doorne, became known as van Doorne's Aanhangwagenfabriek—DAF for short. Before World War II, DAF began developing vehicles and bus prototypes for the Dutch government. In addition to manufacturing automobiles, the company invented the first variable-speed transmission. It began producing trucks in 1949.

DAF was more vertically integrated than PACCAR's other truck companies, manufacturing its own engines and axles. The company began producing diesel engines during the 1950s, and in 1959, it became one of the first manufacturers to apply turbocharger technology to diesel truck engines. DAF again advanced diesel engine technology in 1973, when it introduced a turbocharged engine with intercooling, which extended engine life and improved the truck's power/weight ratio. DAF produced 21,000 engines in 1996, including the Euro 2 engine, to meet Europe's stringent emission requirements. Its development of strong, lightweight axles began in 1973, and by 1996 annual axle production exceeded fifty-six thousand units.

DAF won the prestigious 1998 International Truck of the Year award for its heavy-duty DAF 95XF. The award derived from evaluations by leading truck journalists from fourteen European countries. Their decision was based on the truck's contribution to efficiency standards, specifically the truck's operating costs and driver comfort. The jurors lauded DAF's diesel engine for its economy and superior emission standards and added that it demonstrated an exceptionally low noise level, which was due to the stout construction of the engine block. The jury's report stated, "A light chassis for a high payload and increased service intervals to 100,000 km further improved the economy and efficiency of the truck."

PACCAR acquired DAF Trucks N.V. in 1996. In 1998, the DAF 95XF was named International Truck of the Year in recognition of its efficiency, driver comfort, low noise, and low exhaust emissions.

In 1987, Charles Pigott led an effort to acquire Leyland Trucks, the legendary United Kingdom–based manufacturer of civilian and military trucks. When PACCAR lost in the bidding to DAF, Pigott used the General MacArthur quote "I shall return." DAF reorganized in 1993 and sold Leyland to a group of investors, and in 1998, PACCAR acquired Leyland Trucks from that group, Kepacourt Limited.

Leyland Trucks became the second-oldest company in the PACCAR family. It was formed in 1896 as Lancashire Steam Motor Company, in Leyland, England, and its first truck was a steam-powered van with a capacity of 1.5 tons. It adapted its line to internal combustion engines and produced trucks for the British Army during World War I, when the company changed its name to Leyland Motors. Prior to World War II, Leyland was the world's largest bus producer and the largest fire truck manufacturer in the United Kingdom. During World War II, Leyland manufactured a wide range of military equipment, including the Centurion tanks used in Africa by British Field Marshal Montgomery's Eighth Army. Before a series of divestments, including that of the respected Range Rover nameplate, Leyland was ranked as the world's fifth-largest producer of commercial vehicles.

The city of Leyland had long been known as a great motor town because of the trucks manufactured there. By 1998, Leyland employed 760 people in its modern 600,000-square-foot plant, located in central England. The facilities, which included two parallel assembly lines, produced light and medium (6- to 50-ton) trucks. It had a single-shift capacity of 20,000 vehicles.

Leyland Trucks began as Lancashire Steam Motor Company in 1896. Shown is a Lancashire 6-ton "tipper" steam wagon.

During 1996, Leyland truck sales totaled 8,747 units, including military 4 × 4, 4-ton vehicles and military DROPS (Demountable Rack Off-loading Pick-up System) trucks for United Kingdom and other defense forces.

In addition to manufacturing trucks, Leyland adopted the Japanese "Best Practice" system of management principles, which became known in Europe as "Team Enterprise," a practice described as "empowered people working toward mutually beneficial objectives." As consultants, Optima Personnel Services, a Leyland Trucks subsidiary, has lectured on Team Enterprise principles to diverse business groups and government institutions.

Like PACCAR's other truck companies, Leyland operated on a build-to-order philosophy and had the manufacturing capacity to build vehicles in virtually any weight range. It produced trucks for both its own and DAF's network of European distributors, and it sold its line world-wide, both directly and through specialist export distributors such as Leyland Exports Ltd. and Leyland Asia Pacific.

— ETHICS AND MANAGEMENT —

When Charles Pigott became president in 1965, PACCAR's annual income was just over $15 million; by the time he retired, in 1996, company profits had increased almost thirteen-fold to $201 million. Sales had grown during that time from about $320 million to more than $4.3 billion, and shareholders' equity increased from $60.6 million to well over $1.3 billion. During each of those years PACCAR recorded a net profit. Pigott also directed the PACCAR

Foundation, which distributed millions of dollars to nonprofit organizations and communities where PACCAR does business.

If anything exceeded Pigott's interest in growth and profit, it was his attention to the company's image. Company reports often point out PACCAR's concern for the way it conducts business. Pigott once wrote, "Our reputation for ethical conduct and management opportunity has attracted many young people to the company's various operations. We recognize that we must prepare today for the managers and senior executives that we will need tomorrow."

Another hallmark of PACCAR's story is its corporate ethics. According to Charles Pigott, "The company's culture starts with a very high level of ethics. I think that has been a hallmark of PACCAR forever, and people who have similar values are attracted to that kind of a group."

In the past, the company's ethics have been tested at great expense. During the early 1980s, it took its position on mandatory installation of ABS brakes all the way to the United States Supreme Court. In 1988, when a vendor-supplied steering gearbox began to fail, PACCAR took the initiative. It was the first truck manufacturer to say, "Park the trucks." By then, Kenworth and Peterbilt had already installed more than eleven thousand of the gearboxes. PACCAR's action was followed by other truck manufacturers, and it was ultimately supported by the component's manufacturer.

Another contributing factor to PACCAR's culture is the longevity of its chief executive officers. Paul Pigott directed the company from 1934 until his death in 1961. Charles Pigott became the company's senior officer in 1965, and continued to serve as the company's chief executive officer until 1996. One advantage to their extended tenure is consistency of direction over a very long period of time.

General Counsel Morie observed, "We had a consistent philosophy, a clear focus. This is a conservative company; everyone knows that. A lawyer couldn't work in a better place. I mean, we have the former president of the Boy Scouts of America as our chairman, and as a lawyer you're never asked to deal in a gray area."

Yet another reason has been the personal strength of PACCAR's chief executives. Each of the Pigotts who led the company has been Irish, Catholic, and driven by his own set of high values. They have demonstrated a strong sense of family responsibility and a demanding work ethic.

Other factors contributing to the company's strong ethics are its tight internal control and its short lines of communication. Centralization of functions, such as legal, financial, and insurance matters, as well as public, government, and media relations, also has contributed to its consistent standards.

Mark C. Pigott became PACCAR's chairman and chief executive officer following his father's retirement in 1996. During a 1995 interview, Mark Pigott remarked, "To become a successful manager at PACCAR requires the pursuit of profits—not just profits, but ethical profits, which come with furnishing the customer with a quality product. We want to be able to look people right in the eye and say we did it squarely, ethically, and to the best of our ability, and these are the results. That's exciting. They don't teach you that at business school."

In many ways, David Hovind, Mark Pigott, and Mike Tembreull were typical PACCAR senior executives. President David Hovind was a University of Washington business administration graduate with advanced schooling at Stanford and Northwestern universities. He began his career in 1964 with Kenworth and witnessed PACCAR's transformation from a manufacturer of primarily railcars to one of trucks. He joined the company's corporate management team in 1987. Mark Pigott worked for Kenworth during his college summers,

PACCAR's 1997 senior
management (from left):
Vice Chairman Michael A.
Tembreull, Chairman
Emeritus Charles M.
Pigott, President David J.
Hovind, and Chairman
and Chief Executive
Officer Mark C. Pigott.

then graduated from Stanford University and later Stanford's Sloan program. He started
with the company in 1979 and held several positions before being transferred to Foden Trucks,
where he served as managing director for four years before returning to the United States.
Vice Chairman Mike Tembreull, like Hovind, graduated from the University of Washington,
and like his peers completed the Sloan program at Stanford. He joined the company in 1970
and filled a variety of management positions, including general manager of Peterbilt, before
becoming a part of corporate management in 1990.

Charles Pigott has often pointed out that PACCAR's executives work Saturdays with
great frequency, and because of the company's Pacific Northwest location, they often are
expected to travel on weekends. "Our executives recognize that we are in a very competitive
business, and that requires a lot of personal dedication." Other senior management
characteristics include graduate degrees, depth of experience, and lifelong careers with the
company.

International experience is part of PACCAR's upper management training. "Observing
the foibles and genius of our country from abroad improves our objectivity, and it's necessary
if we are going to be a strong international competitor," noted Mark Pigott.

The lean management policy was strengthened under Robert O'Brien during the early
1960s, and the company's early application of computers and its continued thirst for technology
allowed it to remain lean. Today, PACCAR is considered to be a model of efficient manufacturing.

Without the company's use of technology, it would not have been possible to generate products valued in the billions of dollars with a workforce of seventeen thousand. The company has continually invested in new hardware and software and in training its employees.

During the 1980s, women became major contributors to PACCAR's success, playing key roles as senior executives, plant managers, foreign office managers, chief engineers, purchasing directors, commodity managers, and line workers. "We've cast our recruiting net wide to make sure that we are able to do that," said David Hovind.

The company's current and future executives are offered a wide variety of advanced educational opportunities, including PACCAR Institute, which was organized in the late 1980s as a means to institutionalize PACCAR's management principles and skills. The full-week course was developed by key managers who worked in concert with Battelle Institute. Institute courses teach the management principles of PACCAR. In a 1995 interview, Tembreull observed, "There are programs where we send people to universities or for other types of training, but PACCAR Institute has just been spectacular. It teaches us how to be better managers within the PACCAR system."

The second half of the 1990s began with PACCAR's North American factories running at full capacity, and the company still had room to grow.

Domestically, West Coast markets represented PACCAR's greatest penetration, and the Northeast—home to two of the company's three principal competitors—offered the greatest opportunity for PACCAR's future growth. The company's offshore sales had been stellar, and PACCAR continued to develop its potential for international sales with its Foden, DAF, and Leyland truck nameplates.

In 1981, writer Alex Groner concluded the first edition of *PACCAR: The Pursuit of Quality* with the observation that "Charles Pigott was not too much different from his father and grandfather before him." The same is true of Mark Pigott.

Groner's conclusion to the first edition was as salient then as it is now. "As PACCAR entered the final quarter of its first century it was very much involved with the present and more than a little concerned with its future. That future probably depended less on an endless supply of Pigotts (although something might have been said for that) than on a continuing dedication to the exercise of intelligence and craftsmanship, along with devotion to service. Such qualities were surely important ingredients of a successful business, if not indeed the measure of greatness in a civilization."

In terms of vehicle quality, innovation, efficiency, and technology, PACCAR's Kenworth T2000, DAF 95XF, and Peterbilt 379 represent the pinnacle of accomplishment in heavy-duty truck manufacturing.

PACCAR Inc

Quality Technology Innovation

CHAPTER THIRTEEN

GLOBAL FOCUS

PACCAR continued its global focus on being the quality leader in all aspects of the business as it entered its tenth decade in 1995. Its processes became faster, its manufacturing more efficient, and its quality standards were raised still higher. It had become a company respected as much for its technology and processes as it was for its quality products and financial strength.

In 1997, when Mark Pigott became chairman and chief executive officer, those who counseled him were trusted and experienced. The list included senior officers who had spent their entire careers at PACCAR. Vice Chairman Michael Tembreull joined the company in 1970, and his career included five years as Peterbilt's general manager. Vice Chairman David Hovind began with Kenworth in 1963, when PACCAR's principal business was railcars. President Thomas Plimpton was a controller and former general manager of Peterbilt who had worked at Foden Trucks for four years. Senior Vice President Gary Moore had managed Kenworth before moving to PACCAR, where he established the company's Preferred Supplier program. And Vice President and General Counsel Glen Morie had joined the company's legal department in 1973. They had worked together for years, and they brought a unified sense of teamwork to the senior management level. "Management longevity has always been a strength at PACCAR," Tembreull observed. "In so many companies, leadership changes every five to seven years. PACCAR has had four chairmen in a hundred years, and there is a consistency of purpose and direction that has served PACCAR well."

Outside directors on PACCAR's strong board included Delta Air Lines' Gerald Grinstein, Volkswagen's Carl Hahn, Chevron's Harold Haynes, Univar's James Wiborg, Fluke Capital's John Fluke Jr., and MacDonald, Dettwiler and Associates' John Pitts, the longest-serving outside board member. Added continuity came from Charles Pigott, who remained on the board after his retirement, and James Pigott. After serving on both the Foden and DAF subsidiary boards in Europe, Friends Provident Plc Chairman David Newbigging became a PACCAR director in 1999. Air Products and Chemicals, Inc. Chairman Harold Wagner joined the board in 1999, as did Simpson Investment Company Chairman William G. Reed, Jr., whose father, William G. Reed, had served as a PACCAR director from 1946 to 1971.

The trend toward diversification had changed, and by the mid-1990s PACCAR had sold most of its non-core businesses, choosing geographical rather than product diversification. The sale of Trico in 1997 made available millions for reinvestment, as did the divestiture of the

PACCAR's family of international brands. *From left:* Peterbilt, DAF, and Kenworth.

company's retail automotive business two years later. The sale of these businesses allowed PACCAR's senior managers to focus on initiatives that would enhance quality, reduce costs, develop new products, and employ new technology in their core businesses.

The challenges faced by PACCAR included increased competition from foreign-owned businesses and an array of computer-driven processes that would need remarkable expertise to realize their potential. A successful future would require substantial capital investment in information technology (IT), manufacturing and engineering design tools, factories, financial services, and aftermarket customer support.

—INFORMATION TECHNOLOGY—

In 1997, Patrick Flynn was hired as PACCAR's chief information officer (CIO), leaving a job at Fruit of the Loom. He found a management information systems (MIS) group working on a diverse list of projects. "They pretty much operated independently," recalled Flynn. "Each division had operating system preferences, and cross-company communication was complex. There were six different vendors supplying hardware and multiple network types. We had three different e-mail systems, and four engineering design programs. We could not share documents with any degree of reliability." He likened the system to a "big company scattered all over the world with operations to run where everybody spoke a similar, but not the same, language."

Years of intense competition between Kenworth and Peterbilt had created fertile ground for innovation and technology, but interdivisional sharing of information was not characteristic of PACCAR's culture. Information technology was not easily shared, and subsequently, what worked well in Peterbilt's Nashville plant might not be replicated at Kenworth's Chillicothe facility.

"There is still a lot of competition between our divisions, but there is an understanding now that when we create a system to optimize a factory, PACCAR is making that investment for the good of the shareholders. Moving a good idea from factory to factory as fast as we can is the name of the game. It doesn't matter whose idea it was. This change in mind-set took us a while to implement," said Tom Plimpton.

The cost to update and standardize PACCAR's information technology was significant. David Hovind described the company's historical view of technology-related costs, especially information technology: "We used to see management information services as an overhead cost and consider how it could be reduced. As an example, we would say, 'We are paying $213 a truck for MIS; now how do we recover this?'

"That view changed, and the Opcom [Operations Committee] offered a different view of the expense when Mark Pigott suggested, 'Why don't we consider information technology as a competitive weapon? If we do it better than our competitors, we will reduce cost, we will have more information, and we will be able to make better decisions.'"

The opportunity to take a close look at the company's extensive computer systems came as a result of the Year 2000 compliance issue, which became internationally known as simply Y2K. It was feared there would be a catastrophic failure for many of the company's computer systems. When the threat was tackled in the mid-1990s, PACCAR had five thousand desktop computers, as well as product-design supercomputers and mainframes around the world. The task required more than 150 man-years to complete. Flynn recalled it as "a time of great investment. We developed a much greater understanding of our technology assets. We had to invest in upgrading and modernizing hardware, networks, and software." Systems were tested and rechecked for reliability before the new millennium, including those that interfaced with dealers and many suppliers. Still, it was a sleepless New Year's Eve for the company's MIS staff, and as the new year dawned, the group was both relieved and satisfied that its reprogramming had been successful.

MIS was elevated to divisional status in 2001 and renamed Information Technology Division (ITD). Symbolically, the brass letters of MIS were removed from the concrete wall at the division's entrance and the new name Information Technology was installed. Every person in PACCAR had a stake in utilizing technology to make the company more efficient.

Objectives for "real-time information" included quicker response time and more production control. Results were sometimes dramatic. As Hovind recalled, "Twenty-five years ago, if we were turning our inventory twelve times a year, that was good. Now Leyland, DAF, Peterbilt, and Kenworth turn their inventory over fifty times. This saved hundreds of millions of dollars and could not have been done without systems and real-time information."

During the 1990s, the dot-com industry boom captured the imagination of the Pacific Northwest, and the area became a technology hotbed. Newspapers regularly reported on start-up software companies that in less than a year of public trading had a stock market value surpassing that of the region's old-line businesses. PACCAR was intrigued by the promise of technology, but only as it applied to its business.

In 1999 the company formed two new divisions as part of its e-commerce strategy. One was PACCAR.com. It was started as a venture-capital fund that invested in start-up companies developing technologies applicable to PACCAR's core business. The other was ePACCAR, designed to coordinate all of the company's Internet and intranet activities.

PACCAR.com's aim was to get access to new technology, and in some cases early access to developing technology so that PACCAR could leverage it sooner than its competitors. The company also wanted to shape the technology to better suit its own applications. In Plimpton's view, "in some cases it turned out to be tuition where we learned what would and would not

The PACCAR ITD control room was completed in 2004. It is used to monitor system functions and information flow worldwide.

New to Kenworth and Peterbilt in 2004: sophisticated luxury interiors with electronic gauges, simplified dashboard wiring, GPS, and enhanced reliability. The multiplexed system was also important for accurate remote monitoring of truck performance.

work. There was so much new technology developed during that period. We look back and shake our heads at the stock-market side of that period, but the real fact of that era was that it fundamentally changed the technology landscape, and through PACCAR.com we were able to participate in that evolution."

The intent of PACCAR.com investments was not to be the next eBay or Amazon.com. Some PACCAR.com investments enabled the company to gain a better understanding of the technological requirements of onboard telematics, which was fast becoming the focus for new truck technology. It was envisioned as an array of high-tech equipment that would monitor and transmit everything about a truck's performance and its location. It could enable drivers to accurately estimate arrival times, an essential tool for just-in-time inventory control.

In a 2004 interview that appeared in the British publication *Truck,* Mark Pigott said, "Our vision is to have enough electronics on a truck to diagnose just about everything. And when that diagnostic equipment detects something that may need to be improved, it sends a wireless message to our call centre, which does the analysis automatically and then electronically contacts the dealer, checks if the parts are available, allocates the service bay, picks the technician and gets all that information back to the driver, who did not even know there was anything wrong! . . . It will do that in minutes, not hours. That is the type of service we are close to providing, and I think many of our customers will be over the moon with it."

Aware that the array of onboard technology had to be fully integrated, PACCAR's Information Technology Division established the Truck Technology Center. There, technicians worked to find the most promising practical technology in development and integrate it into a reliable, cost-sensitive platform. This group became highly proficient at identifying technology with promise for the future.

ePACCAR was developed to be what Flynn called the company's "air-traffic control." It directed each of the company's Internet activities to the right destination. It created the www.PACCAR.com and Truckxchange Web sites.

In 2002, PACCAR introduced what became known as an electronic dealership, or eDealership. The original concept came from Mark Pigott, who informally presented his vision to a few ITD engineers from handwritten notes and a couple of illustrations. The Electronic Dealership demonstration site was assembled in a 30-by-60-foot room at ITD, in Renton, Washington. It included a representation of many functions found in a typical dealership and incorporated state-of-the-art hardware and proprietary software created by PACCAR.

The eDealership systems were able to access and print chassis-specific bill of materials, service manuals, parts catalog pages, inventories, engine diagnostics reports, radio frequency identification (RFID), bar-coding, and warehouse-receiving and inventory-control reports. They could provide a weather report or check road conditions. They also provided quick access links to PACCAR Financial and PacLease. "It is a place for dealers to see where we are headed," said James Poff, director of parts and dealer systems. A second unit was constructed and installed at DAF in 2003. Since then, the eDealerships have been installed in PACCAR-owned facilities, and made available to independent dealerships throughout Europe and North America. More than ten thousand customers, dealers, and suppliers have toured the sites to learn firsthand about technology that is available and how it could be incorporated into their businesses.

The origin of the electronic dealership was a study in creativity. Pigott was aware that dealers were not applying ITD-developed technology, and the company was looking for the means to demonstrate the value of its new systems to both dealers and customers. ITD had constructed a factory mock-up so that its systems engineers and others could see how and where their work was being applied. PACCAR managers regularly toured Microsoft's Home of the Future and Office of the Future. The centers were hands-on demonstrations of both practical and theoretical technology. The idea of embedding digital information such as a chassis number into

PACCAR's Electronic Dealership was created in 2002 and continuously updated. It served as a proving ground and demonstration center for current and new technologies for PACCAR dealers and customers.

an ignition key came from Pigott's viewing of a science-fiction movie; the customer kiosk was adopted from outdoor equipment retailer REI; and the electronic shopping cart was adapted from Amazon.com's Web site. These dissimilar elements led to the presentation to ITD engineers, and from that meeting came the eDealership.

"These developments have helped throughout the company," said PACCAR Senior Vice President James Cardillo. "ITD has given PACCAR managers more tools to do their job and do it better. We use 80 percent less paper now and that is a big move in the right direction. We communicate with our suppliers better, and it is all through systems connections. When product comes from a supplier, it is loaded on the trailer. We know exactly where it is by serial number for the axle or engine or whatever so that it can go right to the point of use. Instead of handling parts two and three times, we have launched a 'Single Touch' process throughout the company. This could not be done without IT."

Hovind observed, "This use of technology started with Chuck Pigott, but it is continuing at a rapid pace with Mark, where we want to be a one-stop shopping place. We want our premium reputation to be related to truck products, parts, and to financial services."

PACCAR was recognized as the number-one technology company in North America in 1999 by *PC Week,* and it is interesting to note that Hewlett-Packard, IBM, and Lucent were ranked two, three, and four behind PACCAR.

Business journalists who once quipped that PACCAR was a bank that made trucks now wrote about PACCAR as a technology and financial services company that made trucks. Actually, it had become both.

Mark Pigott, shown here in the ITD Truck Technology Center, championed PACCAR's development of advanced yet practical technology.

To get the most out of every process at the company, it was necessary for PACCAR to employ a variety of new tools, and the most significant was Six Sigma. Six Sigma statistically measures performance. It requires a rigorous analytical approach to defining and then lessening or eliminating the root source of error. It became a part of PACCAR's business philosophy in the late 1990s. Managers referred to it as a toolbox for improving quality, lowering costs, increasing productivity, and enhancing customer satisfaction.

Six Sigma was developed at Motorola in 1987, but it didn't gain much attention outside that company until 1995, when General Electric Chairman Jack Welch acknowledged that dramatic improvements in quality and cost savings at the conglomerate were due to Six Sigma. As a result, it quickly caught the eye of other businesses, including PACCAR.

At PACCAR, it would be a broad-based initiative, and it required highly trained people for it to make a significant contribution to the company's quality standards and its bottom line. Hovind was advised not to hire consultants. "Train the trainer and then train your own people." Then came the warning, "If senior management is not trained, nothing will happen." The first group to be trained was PACCAR's Opcom.

PACCAR championed Six Sigma, and its expectations were high. The company believed it could reduce defects in everything PACCAR did, from engineering, services, manufacturing, and sales to customer service. Glen Morie observed, "It's a mind-set that says 'good quality' is no longer good enough, and that only excellence, or the virtual elimination of all defects and process inefficiencies, will do."

In 1998, PACCAR hired Helene Mawyer to establish an in-house Six Sigma program. Mawyer, a Ph.D. mathematician, was a GE–trained Six Sigma expert and a member of that company's management before joining PACCAR. By the end of 1998 more than 850 PACCAR employees had been trained in Six Sigma to evaluate everything from engineering design and assembly procedures to sales ordering and financial transactions. That year's annual report noted, "PACCAR's financial returns already are benefiting from Six Sigma." By the end of the next year, more than 2,000 company employees had been trained, and PACCAR had begun to offer its Six Sigma expertise to dealers and suppliers. A year later, more than 5,000 PACCAR employees had been trained, and 560 active projects related to Six Sigma were under way. During that year, Six Sigma projects contributed more than $25 million to the company's operating profits.

The big difference between traditional quality programs and Six Sigma was that in addition to setting goals and objectives for improving quality, it defined and documented quality procedures. Previous programs such as Total Quality and PIQS were instrumental in improving quality. However, as Mawyer observed, "each new program brought us to a higher level of quality, but once that level was attained, further improvements became difficult to achieve." Unlike other programs, Six Sigma accurately defined defects, non-value-added processes, and other inefficiencies, and then focused on reducing or eliminating their root cause.

Laurie Baker, retired human resources vice president, said of those with advanced training in Six Sigma, "They not only learn a new set of technical tools, but they also increase their leadership skills as they work with people in a variety of functions. This is an opportunity to take some of our most talented employees, give them a brand-new set of skills, and then promote them back into the business."

PACCAR's objective was to reduce its rate of error to a Six Sigma level, or 3.4 defects or fewer per million. Mawyer used household electricity as an example to illustrate the difference between a three and a six sigma. "A three sigma electricity provider would fail to deliver power for almost seven hours each month," she said. "A six sigma provider would fail to deliver power only one hour every thirty-four years."

A Six Sigma process puts all the elements together in a well-defined, disciplined, data-driven process and focuses on achieving results that last. Coupled with a set of statistical-analysis tools that identify the root cause of defects and errors, it helps find ways to eliminate problems and improve quality. New employees were introduced to it during PACCAR's orientation. It became a part of PACCAR Institute's managerial leadership session on change management. Beyond basic training, "Green Belt" and "Black Belt" designations were given to employees who underwent additional training.

Green Belts were assigned transactional projects in their areas of expertise. Black Belts became the backbone of the company's Six Sigma program. Candidates for that distinction were selected from PACCAR employees who exhibited strong analytical ability. They worked through a sixteen-week course focused on defining problems, then were assigned to cross-divisional, cross-departmental projects that required the use of complex statistical tools. A data-driven approach was considered the cornerstone of Six Sigma.

PACCAR's Product Quality Inspection (PQI) was established to monitor the finished quality of its trucks. The system identified any imperfections and assisted in the elimination of the root cause of the defects.

Design for Six Sigma (DFSS) was introduced to PACCAR in 2001. It was a tool used by engineering in product concept, development, and implementation. It was later extended to PACCAR suppliers, whose early involvement in the development of a new product enabled them to supply new products, already tested to predetermined specifications, with a shorter lead-time.

Gary Moore, retired senior vice president of PACCAR Purchasing, described some of the considerations raised by Design for Six Sigma. "With Design for Six Sigma, at the same time that you design the product, you clearly identify the critical parameters and the requirements for that design and the tolerances the supplier must hold and ask the question, 'Am I going to make the investment in the tooling required to hold this tolerance?' In the past, the engineer designed a part, but we didn't necessarily put enough money into the tooling, so it wasn't optimized, and by the time it was manufactured, there were many compromises. You can't do that and hold quality."

The ultimate goal of Six Sigma and Design for Six Sigma is to eliminate non-value-added tasks. "We used to spend a lot of time doing things over," said George West Jr., Vice President Manufacturing. "With Six Sigma, we reduce that wasted effort and rework. Employees have more time to do the important things. We want everything we do to be done right the first time."

— CONTINUING EDUCATION —

The rule of thumb at PACCAR regarding employee education—anything from training on the safe operation of Direct Current (DC) tools to studying for an MBA—was straightforward. It was expected that a minimum of 2 percent of every employee's time would be spent acquiring or improving skills and knowledge. New employees began with a weeklong orientation to acquaint them with the company's systems, benefits, compliance program, and expectations for its quality products and processes.

Whether mounting an engine onto frame rails or detailing a sleeper, most PACCAR factory employees were specialists, and between ongoing safety training and frequent classes in the use of computers and the Internet, meeting the company's expectations for advanced training occurred in the course of the job. Increased levels of technical expertise required more classroom and hands-on instruction.

"We have to make sure that our managers are either teaching or learning every year," observed PACCAR President Thomas Plimpton. "We invest a lot of money in continuing education. Every month, one or more divisions present to the Operating Committee their staff depth reviews. In addition to reviewing their key people, including developmental plans, they present their educational budget and how they are going to use it."

As the level of technology increased, so did PACCAR's budget for education. When the Renton Kenworth plant installed a robotic paint system, implementation included months of training. The paint-room supervisor and a crew of four joined company engineers for training classes provided by the robotic-equipment supplier. They returned with many books, an operating manual, specifics on maintenance, and a three-inch-thick error codebook that were assigned reading for the weeklong class in the system's operation. Additional weeks were spent in hands-on training. This was followed by a trip to Peterbilt's plant in Denton, Texas, where a similar system was already in operation. The Renton team condensed what they had learned into an abbreviated operating manual and created a position of "paint trainer," who was assigned to instruct additional system operators.

Computer-directed robotic paint systems provided high-quality finishes for PACCAR trucks in controlled environments, seen here at Peterbilt Denton.

As the complexity of assignments increased company-wide, so did the scope of training. PACCAR Institute was created in the early 1990s. It was designed to increase management skills and also to provide leadership training. Previously, training in leadership skills had been received only by those few who had mentors. "We didn't feel that there was a purchased curriculum available, so PACCAR created its own," said Tembreull. "Management and leadership are different from one company to another. It's how to be successful in your company. PACCAR created the PACCAR Institute." The Institute was offered four to five times each year, and by 2004 it had trained more than two thousand employees.

"It's easier to train somebody in management than leadership," said Plimpton. "Training can help them understand what key qualities are." During team decision-making sessions, groups worked on actual projects. Their work was videotaped and scored. The video enabled the individual to see how he or she handled group dynamics. Other exercises helped train PACCAR employees in the decision-making process so that they knew when they should be making a decision themselves or bringing in another person to help make that decision. The Institute also taught managers how to deal with different personalities. Such training helped managers become more effective in working with their teams.

Outside the company, PACCAR encouraged its employees to attend college to complete degrees or pursue advanced degrees. "We have a tremendous tuition-reimbursement program for earning a bachelor's or a master's degree," commented Nick Highland, human resources director. "PACCAR has paid for many employees to receive degrees, and the employees and the company have benefited."

PACCAR, the PACCAR Foundation, and the Pigott family invested heavily in education. William Pigott was one of several founders of Seattle University, and the company and the Pigott family continued to contribute to the development of that institution's engineering programs and business school. The Paul Pigott Scholarship Fund granted up to twenty-five scholarships each year to children of company employees. In 2004, PACCAR contributed $2 million to the University of Washington's capital campaign, and each year the company had presented the largest monetary award for graduate business school teaching excellence granted in the United States. The $25,000 annual award was given to a University of Washington Business School professor selected by students for his or her ability and commitment to teaching.

— PROGRESS REPORT —

During his first eight years as the company's chairman and chief executive officer, Mark Pigott managed two divestitures and two acquisitions, a period of steep sales and production increases, significant growth in Europe, and a rapid contraction and recovery of the North American truck industry. Through it all, and unlike any of its global competitors, PACCAR remained profitable. The senior management team continued to improve the company's products and processes, benchmarking, and integrating proven Best Practices. Some of the new executives contributing to the company's success were Senior Vice President James Cardillo, Vice President and Controller Ronald Armstrong, Vice President–Facilities Richard Bangert II, Vice President Robert Christensen, Chief Information Officer Janice Skredsvig, Vice President Kenneth Gangl, Vice President Timothy Henebry, Vice President William Jackson, Vice President Thomas Lundahl, Vice President Helene Mawyer, Vice President Daniel Sobic, Vice President George West Jr., Treasurer Andrew Wold, Secretary Janice D'Amato, and Aad Goudriaan, who was named president of DAF Trucks in 2004. The company had become more complex as it approached its one hundredth anniversary in April 2005.

Mark Pigott described the scope of knowledge and characteristics common to the company's senior officers: "All of PACCAR's senior executives know the specific details about what it takes to be world class in their area of responsibility. They also know what the competition is doing worldwide, and what different governments are doing that could impact our business. These are bright, motivated, engaged leaders and managers."

"Company management regularly briefs the board on their areas," said director James Pigott. "And it is not always the same group. One time they might have the credit team, quality control, and insurance. The next time, it might be the general manager of a division such as Peterbilt or DAF. Board members also get a look at the up-and-comers who are not management members of the board."

In 2002–2003, board retirements included Charles M. Pigott, Carl Hahn, John Pitts, and Harold Haynes. They were succeeded by Boeing Company's Chief Executive Officer Harry Stonecipher and United Technologies' Stephen Page. Retired Chief Executive Officer and President of the Federal Reserve Bank of San Francisco Robert Parry was named to the PACCAR board in 2004.

Charles Pigott's parting counsel to company employees when he retired in 1996 outlined the company's future. "PACCAR will increase its quality leadership by maintaining strong investment programs aimed at improving productivity, through enhanced products, systems, and process tools, as well as embrace technology to assist our distribution network and our customers." PACCAR incorporated his advice and generated excellent financial results in the intervening years.

PACCAR posted record revenues, net income, and stockholders' equity in 1998 and 1999, managed profitably through the market decline of 2001, and by 2004 again posted record sales, profits, and gains in stockholder equity. In 2004, PACCAR won the International Stevie Award for Best Multinational Company in the first-ever International Business Awards. PACCAR also received a Certificate of Finalist Recognition in Best Overall Company and Best Facility categories. The company also gained recognition as one of the nation's best-run companies, according to *Fortune* magazine, which ranked PACCAR second in shareholder return among all companies on the *Fortune 500* list for the last fifty years. A $1,000 investment in PACCAR in 1954 would be worth $5.2 million fifty years later. The company won every J.D. Power and Associates award category within the Class 8 truck manufacturing industry in 2003, and DAF models were twice recognized by European industry writers as International Truck of the Year, in 1998 and 2002.

Quality awards such as the J.D. Power and Associates recognitions confirmed PACCAR customers' satisfaction with Peterbilt and Kenworth trucks' build quality, performance, and aftermarket support.

PACCAR Trucks Awarded Highest Customer Satisfaction.

PACCAR thanks its customers and dealers for their wonderful support. Peterbilt and Kenworth design and produce the Class™ of the industry by delivering The World's Best™ products and superior aftermarket service.

PACCAR Inc

CUSTOMER INITIATIVES

PACCAR's commitment to superior aftermarket dealer and customer support included PACCAR Financial Services (PFS), PACCAR Parts, PacLease, and Customer Call Centers. These services were developed to provide focused support to dealers and customers in Australia, Canada, Europe, Mexico, and the United States.

PACCAR's quality emphasis was dramatically exhibited in its technical centers in North America and Europe. PACCAR Purchasing, in tandem with supplier quality, defined and controlled the quality of every part assembled into a PACCAR truck.

Collectively, finance, parts, purchasing, and the technical centers were integrated elements of the PACCAR brand worldwide, which was increasingly emphasized in all markets, raising awareness within the financial community and among dealers, customers, and suppliers. The DAF 4- and 6-liter engines used in the DAF LF and CF series, and some Foden models became the first components to wear the PACCAR badge, establishing a trend toward branding other components with the PACCAR name.

— PACCAR FINANCIAL —

In 2003, PACCAR Financial Services (PFS) had more than 116,000 trucks and trailers in its portfolio, a fourfold increase since 1996. Combined with PACCAR Leasing's fleet of more than 17,000 vehicles, PFS's assets exceeded $5.6 billion. PFS financed nearly 30 percent of PACCAR's worldwide production in 2003. Its principal advantages over its competitors were quality products, market knowledge, and its ability to borrow money at low rates, which was based on PACCAR Inc's superior debt rating of AA-, the highest of any truck manufacturer in the world.

Established in 1961, PFS became increasingly aggressive in pursuit of financing for PACCAR trucks. This provided a ready source of funds for dealers and customers during all phases of the business cycle, and additional profit for PACCAR.

PFS's abilities were tested and strengthened in the face of the deep economic recession of 2001, when freight tonnage dropped and fuel prices soared in North America. As a result, the truck companies' failure rate increased dramatically. The North American new-truck market plummeted from a peak of 305,000 annual registrations in 1999 to less than 174,000 two years later. The price of used trucks fell from 25 to 40 percent below the projected residual value.

PACCAR Leasing, a part of PACCAR Financial Services, doubled its previous record sales in 2004.

PACCAR Financial
Services, including
insurance and
service contracts,
were offered
by PACCAR
dealerships
throughout
North America.
In 2001, PACCAR
Financial Europe
was established.

Industry losses on repossessed trucks were as high as $22,000 a truck, although Kenworth and Peterbilt trucks continued to earn premium prices.

PACCAR Vice President, Financial Services, Kenneth Gangl described the period as challenging. "When many finance companies abandoned truck financing, PACCAR Financial continued to support the sale of Kenworth and Peterbilt Trucks." He explained that PFS worked with its clients to keep them in business. "We looked at payment-relief options, as those are the types of credit decisions PFS has to make during a downturn."

PFS employees were experts in the truck finance business. They understood the business and they were empowered to create custom contracts that reflected the specific needs of their customers. As an example, Gangl described a unique contract written to accommodate the needs of seasonal haulers in which "payments were lower during the off-season and higher during a customer's peak season."

In the following year, 2002, truck industry conditions improved slightly. Nevertheless, more than 2,500 fleets went out of business in North America. But PFS had improved its collection and credit procedures at the depth of the recession. It also had enhanced its ability to resell trucks by adding lists of used trucks, their condition, and photos on both Kenworth and Peterbilt Web sites. PFS also opened a used-truck center in Chicago that enabled the company to maximize the resale price of every PACCAR product. Before the market turned upward, PFS had remarketed nearly four thousand used Kenworth and Peterbilt trucks.

During 2003 and 2004 business continued to improve, and PFS's philosophy of providing support throughout the business cycle resulted in greater customer loyalty. PFS had a record year in 2003, reporting a pre-tax profit of $124 million, and continued on a record pace into 2004.

When PACCAR acquired DAF in 1996, it assumed DAF's 49 percent interest in a joint venture with Rabobank that provided retail financing for DAF customers. That changed in 2001, when PACCAR established PACCAR Financial Europe (PFE) and entered the European market. Initially, PFE operated in seven western European countries—the Netherlands, Great Britain, Germany, Belgium, Italy, Spain, and France. Two years later, PFE's assets had grown to exceed €1 billion. During 2004, PFE expanded operations to Ireland, Portugal, Austria, and Sweden.

PACCAR trucks, including the increasingly popular DAF products, were sold in more than one hundred countries through PACCAR International. When financing was a condition of the sale, PFS worked with the Exim Bank to facilitate the transaction or assisted the customer in negotiating with other finance companies that had a greater understanding of local conditions.

PACCAR Leasing Company (PLC) had become a significant part of PFS since it was established in 1980. The truck-leasing business in North America was dominated by two large competitors that constituted nearly 70 percent of the industry, but PACCAR Leasing posted record profits every year since 1993, and its fleet had shown steady growth.

Automobile leases were typically based on a use rate not exceeding 12,000 miles a year, but the standard for a truck lease was 100,000 miles a year, and lease terms could be for a period of up to seven years. PACCAR Leasing's ability to compete with industry giants came from its understanding of the value of PACCAR trucks—the lowest operating costs and highest residual values in the industry.

In 2004, PacLease President Bob Southern presented a plan to sell five thousand trucks, double PLC's record year. PLC increased its national sales force, instituted advanced IT systems, added new locations, and systematically expanded customer relationships to increase the business. The sales target was based on the recent performance of Peterbilt and Kenworth truck sales in North America, especially the growing Class 7 market. There were skeptics, but by October 2004 the leasing company had already sold more than five thousand trucks, and would meet its ambitious goal.

Transaction speed was critical for dealers closing a sale, and PFS created a credit-processing system called Online Transaction Information System (OTIS). With OTIS, PACCAR dealers could submit credit information online, allowing PFS to process an application and respond to the dealer within two hours, or within thirty minutes if the credit application was from an existing PFC customer. This was significantly faster than previous service levels.

—PACCAR PARTS—

At the end of 2004, the company's aftermarket truck parts division, PACCAR Parts (PPD), had posted record profits every year since 1991. The growing number of PACCAR Parts distribution centers and expanding markets worldwide provided the opportunity, but market penetration and profits were a result of innovative applications of technology and grass-roots marketing.

By 2004, PPD was operating eleven parts distribution centers (PDCs) strategically placed throughout PACCAR's markets. The North American centers accounted for 825,000 square feet of distribution center space. An 80,000-square-foot, $10 million center was constructed in San Luis Potosi, Mexico, in 1998. European centers included a 485,000-square-foot facility at DAF in Eindhoven, and a 100,000-square-foot facility was opened in England at the Leyland plant in 2003. The Australian PDC added another 100,000 square feet to the distribution system. The warehouses stocked everything from bolts to axles and transmissions, as well as DAF engines in Europe, Australia, and Mexico. PACCAR Parts shipped over nine million orders in 2003, with an accuracy rate above 99.7 percent.

Market focus and technology offered a framework for its future growth. PPD's first edition of its electronic catalog was released as a CD, leading the industry in the 1990s. Its operating system allowed the user to identify a part as large as a transmission or as small as a lug nut with the click of a computer mouse. Updates were frequent, and revised CD editions were constant and costly. In 2001 the electronic catalog, named "Smart Search," became Internet-accessible. In Europe, DAF took the system a step further to include service manuals online, with similar information later instituted for North America.

The most revolutionary PACCAR Parts initiative was called "Managed Dealer Inventory" (MDI), and it was introduced to company dealers in 1999. It combined software technology and forecasting with parts delivery that offered efficient dealer inventory management and restocking 365 days a year. MDI was championed by PACCAR Vice President Robert Christensen during his tenure as the Parts Division's general manager. By 2004 there were more than seven hundred dealer locations worldwide using MDI.

Vice President and PACCAR Parts Division General Manager William Jackson observed, "The system is similar to a retailer such as Wal-Mart managing the inventory in its stores across the country, yet few companies have been able to transfer the technology into the capital goods industry."

In 1999, PACCAR opened a twenty-four-hour Customer Call Center. It was located in Renton, Washington, and its services were offered to PACCAR customers in North America. It was modeled on the DAF International Truck Service (ITS) Call Centers in Europe. The facility looked like one of NASA's mission control centers. Operators had up to three monitors at their fingertips, showing service center locations, parts availability, maps, customer and supplier contacts, and other information that might be required to provide roadside assistance. In its first full year of operation, the PACCAR Call Center received over 300,000 calls, and in 2001 the North American and European call centers responded to more than one million calls. By 2003 that number had increased to 1.6 million calls.

The call centers put PACCAR in direct contact with its customers on a continuous basis, and this generated a philosophical change. Christensen viewed the division's past as being focused on dealers. "We assumed that dealers would transfer whatever was offered by PACCAR Parts to our customers, the actual owners of the trucks or fleets. What the call center did was to focus our attention directly on the customers." What followed this epiphany was an initiative called Managed Dealer Marketing (MDM), for which PACCAR developed custom-designed flyers and e-mail promotions that were sent to truck and fleet owners either directly or through dealers. The benefit to dealers was more service business. By 2004, the Parts Division was custom-producing up to five-hundred thousand promotional pieces a month. The promotional material offered unique parts and service programs created by PACCAR and its participating dealer organization. Successful in North America, MDM was introduced to Europe in 2003. Call

centers were also considered key to telematics-based communication between the customer, dealer, and manufacturing facility.

PPD developed maintenance contracts that were sold through dealers. These offered a measure of operational security to PACCAR truck owners, and brought them to its dealerships for contract maintenance as well as services.

—PACCAR PURCHASING—

The genesis of PACCAR Purchasing was a move in the 1980s to consolidate and expand the company's global purchasing reach and expertise. Retired Vice President Louis Cattaneo was the first executive to lead corporate purchasing. The principal objective of the division was to control the quality, cost, and availability of items purchased by the company and its manufacturing and aftersales units globally.

The quality of purchased parts was essential to building quality products, as nearly 80 percent of the content of a Kenworth, Peterbilt, and Foden truck was purchased from

PACCAR Parts opened the 100,000-square-foot Leyland distribution center to supply parts to the United Kingdom and European markets.

outside suppliers. DAF, because of its engine and axle manufacturing, purchased only 70 percent of its parts from suppliers.

An early initiative was to establish purchased-parts quality guidelines and quality tolerance levels based on the number of non-conforming parts (NCP) per million. It was initially set at 2,500 NCP, and then lowered to 1,000 NCP. Increased quality standards were projected in 2004 to further improve tolerance to 750 NCP. The ultimate goal was to reach the Six Sigma quality standard: 3.4 NCP per million.

In 2004, PACCAR purchased custom-designed door pads from an automobile-interior supplier that was selected in part because of its 2003 record of delivering seats and door pads for Toyota with near Six Sigma quality. Such consistent quality drove PACCAR's other door-assembly suppliers to meet the standards of the manufacturer, and the end result was a better door. "It is a continuous improvement loop that is driving the quality of our products," observed Thomas Lundahl, Vice President, Purchasing.

A heavy-duty truck contains about 8,500 parts, and one of Purchasing's objectives was to ensure ease of assembly by acquiring complex modules that fit into a truck without additional on-site subassembly. In the past PACCAR had assembled intricate modules on the factory floor before their installation, but as parts became more complex and factory processes faster, that practice became too time-consuming and expensive.

When PACCAR realized that it needed additional expertise to design a new engine-cooling module, it involved its suppliers at the beginning of the design process. This relationship was enhanced by using Design for Six Sigma processes that decreased development time and cost, and increased quality. As an example, Lundahl explained, "We specify the cooling module, and describe the performance specification and the space that it must fit into. Our tech centers supply the parameters and how to measure them, and in the end the supplier assumes full responsibility for delivering the product to us."

PACCAR started its Preferred Supplier program in the early 1990s, under the direction of Senior Vice President Gary Moore. The program was expanded to Europe in 1997. It was meant to recognize suppliers that consistently met the company's quality requirements. The designation was a three-stage process that began with an audit to assess a proposed supplier's ability to deliver a part. Then came certification based on the supplier's meeting PACCAR quality requirements. The final measure reflected its delivery performance, engineering, training, and even marketing support. By 2004 there were 122 PACCAR Preferred Suppliers worldwide.

Corporate purchasing also initiated programs to control indirect costs, such as those incurred in gathering and disposing of packaging materials. In 1994, the company managed the disposition of approximately 1,100 pounds of packaging material for every truck it built. In 2001, that amount was reduced to 500 pounds, eliminating 105 tons of dunnage every day from its manufacturing facilities worldwide.

Cost was only one of the considerations when selecting a supplier. PACCAR Purchasing developed a comprehensive system to calculate a part's total value. Total value was based on quality, proximity of the supplier, delivery time, and cost, and it became the basis for the selection of PACCAR's suppliers. Lundahl counseled, "Shortchange any of those elements and you're impacting total value. Quality is the key factor in the selection process. We may pay more for something than if we had purchased it from another supplier if it delivers better overall value."

PACCAR Purchasing worked with suppliers to improve quality and lower costs. One aspect of this effort was a program initiated in 1994 called Cost Management Partnership (CMP), which continued to reap benefits a decade later. Suppliers were required to provide ideas on increasing efficiency and lowering cost. In addition, the company brought suppliers into the development process earlier to determine which ones would be able to manufacture the parts and provide the best value.

Another change in PACCAR's buying processes was the implementation of an electronic purchasing computer system. It was faster and provided more and better information to potential suppliers. Specifications for a proposed part were supplied electronically to suppliers, enabling them to respond within hours and days rather than weeks or months. The PACCAR Purchasing System was a software program developed in conjunction with ITD in 2004 that simplified the purchase process and enhanced communication between PACCAR and its suppliers.

Dynacraft, a PACCAR division, began as an in-house manufacturer of air and hydraulic components for Kenworth and Peterbilt trucks, and for the aftermarket. The subsidiary manufactured subassemblies in Algona, Washington. Dynacraft expanded its production and opened a 120,000-square-foot logistics facility in Louisville, Kentucky, in 1999, the same year it was recognized as QS9000 certified. It traditionally had supplied fan belts, radiator and fuel hoses, and battery cables, but in the 1990s Dynacraft began providing increasingly intricate door assemblies, radiators, and other assemblies consistent with the factories' "Single Touch" material-handling philosophy.

"Dynacraft's ability to add value to PACCAR branded trucks increased during the late 1990s," said Thomas Plimpton. "Dynacraft was able to concentrate on complex parts like radiator assemblies common to PACCAR trucks that increased quality and reduced their unit cost. The subassemblies were delivered to Kenworth and Peterbilt plants ready for installation, and that eliminated much of the need for in-plant high-bay storage."

Dynacraft's ability to manufacture parts and assemble kits for efficient factory installation enabled PACCAR factories to utilize floor space more effectively for truck assembly.

In 2004, PACCAR operated two Technical Centers, one in North America and the other in Europe. The two Centers shared a similar mission: test products to ensure that they meet rigorous standards for quality, durability, and reliability; analyze materials and help suppliers determine product improvements; and eliminate defects. The Centers field-tested vehicles under all conditions, winter and summer, either static or on the test track, using either actual or simulated parts to prove or improve the product.

In the 1990s, the DAF Technical Center at Eindhoven tested parts that were responsible for the success of the 95XF, and the CF and LF models that followed in rapid succession. The DAF Center also developed and tested the DAF Euro 3 engines, including the 12.6- and 9.2-liter engines, and the PACCAR-branded 4- and 6-liter engines. In 1999 it developed and tested the Servoshift system, a pneumatic-assisted shift system that shortened gear-lever travel and reduced effort.

In 2002, the DAF Technical Center completed research and development work for what was called an "ultra-silent" tractor. Its purpose was to assist customers in meeting after-hours noise restrictions within European cities. Drivers could switch to "whisper mode" when entering an urban area at night, limiting maximum engine speed to 1,100 rpm, which reduced engine noise by a remarkable 10 dB. PACCAR Senior Vice President James Cardillo described the truck as a research project, a joint venture with the government that was tested in Rotterdam. "It was

PACCAR's Technical Centers used severe shake tests to evaluate vehicle durability and record points of stress and strength.

Page 289: DAF and Foden truck components were developed and tested at the DAF Technical Center in Eindhoven, the Netherlands.

more of an experiment, but it is clear that in Europe, cities are going to be restricted in terms of the time a truck can operate. If we are restricted to only being allowed in at night, then we will need to have a much quieter vehicle. That test vehicle was 65 dB, very quiet. It had modifications so that you didn't have to slam the door. It was similar to the hydraulic trunk latches on some cars, where you put the lid down and it is pulled in place automatically."

The PACCAR Technical Center near Mount Vernon, Washington, evolved from a durability and reliability test facility in 1982 into an advanced laboratory for technology investigation and innovation. Among its facilities was a state-of-the-art ergonomics lab for testing everything from visibility to comfort. During the 1990s the Center expanded its focus beyond testing and validating quality to become an integral partner in the development of design processes, helping each manufacturing division improve its competitive advantage in the marketplace. In 1997 the Center initiated a study of virtual reality in association with Washington State University. Its inventions included the FlexAir/AG 380 rear air suspension, which provided a significant weight savings as well as an improved ride.

In addition to durability studies, both Centers studied materials, coatings, simulation techniques, corrosion, electronic systems integration, power-train integration, and reliability planning and growth. They also provided aerodynamic testing, strength analysis, and other guidance to the company's manufacturing divisions. The Centers shared their expertise. DAF provided engine data and testing experience to PACCAR's Mount Vernon Center, which in turn provided advanced ergonomic testing and rapid prototype capabilities to the Eindhoven Center.

The most challenging studies carried out at the Technical Centers in recent years were in preparation for the 2002 engine requirements for North America and Euro 3 in Europe. The 2002 engine reduced nitrogen oxide emission by 50 percent, but the mandated engines ejected 25 percent more heat, and that necessitated development and testing of new radiators and charge air coolers, as well as cab insulation. The front chassis brackets were redesigned to make room for new radiator and charge air coolers, and a simulation test for radiator shake after 750,000 miles was completed.

Since then DAF developed a 12.9-liter PACCAR MX engine that offered up to 560 hp and maximum torque of 2,750 Nm. Equipped with a "DeNOx" catalytic converter, the new engines were able to meet both Euro 4 and Euro 5 emission standards. "The drive to improve," commented Bob Morrison, General Manager Technical Center, "is constant. PACCAR can always do better."

Truck engine emission restrictions set to begin in 2007 were already a focus of both Centers by 2004. An engine test laboratory was constructed at the PACCAR Technical Center, and the DAF Center's engine laboratory was expanded to jointly research the design parameters necessary to deliver the required performance.

PACCAR Technical Centers test vehicles to verify that quality and longevity meet PACCAR's rigorous standards.

CHAPTER FIFTEEN

PRODUCTS AND PROCESSES

PACCAR is a consistent, process-driven, highly focused, and detail-oriented company, guided by long-standing, uncompromising, well-defined relationships with and responsibilities to and between its principal constituents: employees, customers, dealers, communities, stockholders, and suppliers. In addition, PACCAR is agile and quick to embrace new technology and processes, especially those that enhance the quality and profitability of its products and services.

PACCAR's financial performance placed it prominently on *Fortune* and *Forbes* magazines' lists of U.S. companies ranked by sales and profits. In 2004, PACCAR was recognized by *Fortune* as one of America's Most Admired Companies. PACCAR was named to the 2003 Honor Roll of *The Wall Street Journal's* ninth-annual Shareholder Scoreboard of one thousand major U.S. companies. The *Journal's* Honor Roll listed companies that earned straight-A ratings, ranked on five-year average compound annual total return to shareholders through 2003. Companies had to be in the top 20 percent of firms ranked for the previous one, three, five, and ten years to be considered. Only seventeen companies earned the Honor Roll distinction. PACCAR ranked twelfth. The placement was based on PACCAR's one-year return to shareholders of 89.8 percent, three-year return of 41.5 percent, five-year return of 30.3 percent, and ten-year average return of 22.7 percent.

In PACCAR's 2003 annual report, Chairman/CEO Mark Pigott noted the company's "consistent record of earnings through all phases of the economic cycle, achieving annual profits for sixty-five consecutive years and paying dividends since 1941." Consistent profits were the result of discipline and constant attention to details.

Goals were aggressively set annually for every part of the business, and then closely monitored. Quantifiable measures—unique to PACCAR—such as the time it took to assemble a truck, pack and ship a part, or process a lease were reviewed monthly by many levels of management: first by the division controller, then operations controllers, and finally PACCAR Vice President and Controller Ronald Armstrong, before being sent to the Operating Committee.

"My predecessors, including Len Haba and Don Hatchel, defined our oversight system," Armstrong said. "Financial controllers know what the measures are, and we ask questions and get into the details. . . . We have our finger on the pulse of the key heartbeats around the company. We can spot a trend and react to it quickly. We monitor each performance measure very closely."

PACCAR continually invested in its products and processes, including a new Kenworth Research and Development Center that was completed in August 2004, more efficient handling of parts world-wide, and manufacturing floor assembly processes.

The company's objectives and values were unchanging, but the products and processes were continuously reinvented to deliver the highest quality and remarkable life-cycle cost to customers.

— EVOLUTION OF THE WINCH DIVISION —

In 2003, the PACCAR Winch Division represented less than one percent of the company's annual sales, but it was the world's largest commercial winch manufacturer. The winch business began in 1932, and it represented the sole product legacy of Pacific Car and Foundry. Winches were manufactured in a 230,000-square-foot plant in Broken Arrow and its 83,000-square-foot facility in Okmulgee, Oklahoma.

Winches were engineered for the smooth delivery of turning-power-based products for a variety of industries, such as utilities, logging, and fishing. There were two types of winch drives, worm- and gear-drive. Each had different benefits and limitations. Both could be powered by electric, air, or hydraulic motors that impel a drum equipped with either cable or auger. By mixing and matching these elements, engineers created new products and applications.

"PACCAR is focused on improving all its products and utilizing technology to create better solutions," counseled PACCAR Vice President of Manufacturing George West Jr. "A winch is basic, but with RFE [radio frequency emitter] technology, a winch can send data to a sensor indicating a scheduled oil change or, more critically, shut itself down before it reaches the last wraps of cable on the drum."

One design exercise was based on the use of a computer-controlled auxiliary brake. Engineers applied current technology to a safety feature that revolutionized the offshore winch business. Winches designed for use on drilling platforms performed like elevators to lift and lower human and mechanical cargo to and from the decks of supply vessels. Engineers coupled RFE, a computer, and auxiliary brake technology to create a safer system with increased control that allowed the drum speed to quickly but smoothly adjust, enhancing performance when working on the deck of a pitching supply ship. Similar technology was applied to tower winches used in the construction of high-rise buildings.

— BUILDING A BETTER TRUCK —

PACCAR's products and processes evolved to meet the demands of the marketplace. Its managers knew the difference between what could be changed and what should be improved. As a result, PACCAR's trucks evolved from relatively simple vehicles of the 1940s into complex trucks designed as much for comfort and strength as for incorporating the latest electronic components.

After climbing down from a Peterbilt Model 379 in the mid-1990s, Mark Pigott suggested that the quality and comfort of its interior could be improved. He was aware that when a driver goes to work, he or she often moves from a comfortable, quiet, easy-to-handle car or pickup to the cab of a commercial truck. Because of that transition, he thought, "trucks should be like the highest quality cars and offer amenities similar to those of luxury automobiles, but with the strength and reliability of a commercial vehicle."

Peterbilt and Kenworth engineers accepted the challenge. They studied top-of-the-line autos, such as Lexus and BMW, and took turns driving them. They disassembled them, paying careful attention to every detail. They applied what they had learned and integrated the findings

In 2003, Peterbilt introduced a 70-inch sleeper that offered a luxury automotive interior and 77 cubic feet of storage space.

with data from ergonomic studies conducted at the PACCAR Technical Center. Then they began the design process that resulted in a more comfortable cab and a better-handling truck. New cab design and assembly processes led to a new level of comfort, fit, and finish. Handling was improved, engine and drivetrain efficiency was enhanced, and a new proprietary suspension system was added.

—THE ASSIMILATION OF DAF—

By 2004, DAF had become PACCAR's largest division, and its recovery from bankruptcy a decade earlier had been decisive. In 1998, barely two years after PACCAR's acquisition, DAF trucks received international recognition for their performance, innovation, comfort, and quality. The International Truck of the Year award was presented to the heavy-duty DAF 95XF. The light-duty DAF LF received the International Truck of the Year award in 2002, and the DAF medium-duty CF placed second in the 2003 balloting. The DAF CF85, Britain's most popular tractor model, earned the Fleet Truck of the Year award from readers of *Motor Transport* magazine for the third time in four years. In 2004, for the fourth consecutive year, the DAF LF was named "Best 7.5 tonne truck" in the import category by the readers of Germany's leading trucking magazine—a first in the history of the award.

Among the largest DAF customers in the United Kingdom was the Royal Mail. It operated a fleet of twenty-eight thousand trucks and was one of the largest commercial vehicle operators in Europe. Royal Mail awarded DAF "First Class Supplier" recognition in 1998 and again in 2003

James Cardillo and Stuart Heys accepted the DAF LF award. The LF was launched at the 2001 Brussels Motor Show and earned the Truck of the Year Award.

Page 297: DAF XF is the flagship of the DAF product range and the quality leader in the European market. The original DAF 95XF was introduced at the Brussels International Motor Show in 1997 and voted International Truck of the Year in 1998.

for its trucks and its customer support, including spare parts, technical assistance, and priority access from DAF dealerships in the United Kingdom.

DAF's history of innovation included building the first prototype (a front-wheel driven two-axle rigid) and its first production truck in 1950, and then its own engines in 1957. In 1962 DAF Trucks set new standards in European international transport with the introduction of the 2600 series. A decade later, DAF established International Truck Service (ITS), a roadside assistance system. ITS provided the first central call center in the European truck business with operators capable of speaking a number of languages. As central Europe became a more significant part of the transport network, ITS set up six mobile workshops equipped with satellite communication facilities that could be dispatched from its ITS Control Center in Eindhoven.

A concern of DAF employees after the company's acquisition by PACCAR was the fact that North American truck manufacturers did not have integrated powertrain manufacturing. It was feared that PACCAR would no longer support the manufacture of DAF engines or, worse yet, turn DAF into what Europeans referred to as a "screwdriver factory." Cor Baan, retired DAF President, commented, "I knew that DAF and PACCAR would be a strong combination that would challenge the largest OEMs. The financial strength, design ingenuity, and hard work made the acquisition a winner." PACCAR took an immediate interest in DAF's engine technology and funded development of Euro 3 engines. In the first years of the new millennium PACCAR invested in the total renewal of DAF's engine plant in Eindhoven at a cost exceeding $100 million. Further evidence of PACCAR's integration of engine technology came in 2004, when the company announced that the PACCAR Technical Center would construct a complete engine-test laboratory in Mount Vernon, Washington, similar to the DAF Technical Center's

The DAF XF, shown
in final assembly
at the Eindhoven
factory in 2003.
DAF's production
doubled from 1996
to 2004.

laboratory in Eindhoven. At the same time, plans were approved to enhance and double the
size of DAF's engine-test laboratory. Hans Staals, DAF Product Manager, noted, "DAF is
enjoying a renaissance of its cabs and power train."

DAF built cab-over-engine (COE) models exclusively, and they proved popular in
international markets, including Australia, where DAF was introduced in 2002. By 2004 it was
represented in Australia by twenty full-service dealerships, nine parts and service dealers, and
two parts-only dealers. DAF entered the Mexican market with the urban delivery LF model
in 2004.

By 2004, DAF was represented by more than a thousand European dealer locations. The
most significant change in dealer relations followed the adoption of new European distribution
laws in 2003 that governed dealer relations with manufacturers and the competition. Until that
time, European manufacturers could have exclusive dealers, and competition between them was
restricted by territory. "If you were going to buy a car, comparison shopping from one country
to another was difficult. You might have a difficult time buying a car in one country and then
moving to another," said PACCAR General Counsel Glen Morie. "But that changed in 2002,
when the European Community adopted a new regulation covering the motor vehicle industry,"
DAF lawyer Duco Zoomer added. "It freed exclusive dealers to represent more than one brand,
and it meant rewriting all of DAF's dealership agreements. The Block Exemption changed the
basic distribution requirements for the automotive industry in Europe. DAF took advantage
of the opportunity to create a Pan-European agreement. This was a different distribution
philosophy, but a great advantage for DAF."

During the 1990s, PACCAR adapted luxury automobile design concepts and materials for truck interior applications. Shown is a 2003 DAF XF interior.

Because of the benefits of local ownership in customer representation, PACCAR preferred independent dealerships. In 2003, however, the prohibitively high cost of entry led the company to open a flagship DAF sales and service center in Berlin, one of the most important markets in Germany. "We were fortunate to have found a management team that had become disillusioned with Scania. They decided to become our employees and to manage the Berlin dealership. Eventually, they will buy the business from us, but we will retain ownership of the property," said Kerry McDonagh, DAF Sales Director.

A significant management change was made in 2004, when Cardillo was promoted to PACCAR as senior vice president. At the same time, Aad Goudriaan was promoted to president of DAF Trucks. Goudriaan had been with DAF since 1987, through its reorganization and later acquisition by PACCAR. "Everybody in and outside the company agreed that DAF was now fully integrated as a proud member of the PACCAR Group of companies and fully benefits from that," wrote DAF Director of Communications Ron den Engelsen. By then DAF had become PACCAR's largest and most profitable division.

— DAF-LEYLAND-FODEN IN THE UNITED KINGDOM —

The Leyland factory, located in the manufacturing heart of England near Preston, Lancashire, had a long relationship with DAF. In 1957, the first engines produced by DAF were manufactured under a licensing agreement with Leyland. DAF acquired Leyland Trucks in 1987, but was forced to sell it in 1993 as part of DAF's bankruptcy. DAF retained a supplier relationship with the plant that was strengthened by PACCAR's acquisition of Leyland in 1998.

Once acquired, the Leyland vehicle brand evolved from Leyland DAF to just the DAF logo. "Leyland in its DAF guise stole the 2001 Brussels Motor Show with the all-new LF45-55," said Leyland Managing Director Stuart Heys. The 600,000-square-foot factory employed a skilled workforce of a thousand that could produce fourteen thousand trucks a year. Many Leyland employees came from a long line of truck-building families. Leyland Trucks was the last of the British Leyland motor transportation empire that once included such legendary nameplates as Range Rover and Jaguar. Heys referred to Leyland as the "sole survivor of the British automotive industry." Leyland's success proved the logic of becoming a part of PACCAR.

In 2000, Leyland was recognized as Britain's Best Engineering Factory by the publication *Management Today* in association with the Cranfield School of Management and the Engineering Employers' Federation. The award was based on the plant's flexibility and efficiency. A year later, Leyland received public recognition during the United Kingdom's Celebration of Innovation. Leyland was also recognized by the U.K.'s Ministry of Commerce for excellence in its training and development of staff, use of information technology, and management of complex manufacturing projects.

In 2001, a 20 percent increase in truck-building capacity at Leyland was attributed to Six Sigma projects. Of the plant's maximum daily production of seventy trucks, about 35 percent were exported, including, by 2004, twenty DAF CF Series a day for European Community

Foden manufacturing was moved to the Leyland factory in 2000. Shown is the Alpha XL, a high-powered COE designed for long-distance operators.

markets. It produced all DAF LF models as well as all CF65 series and a number of CF right-hand-drive models for the United Kingdom and Australia.

Foden's truck production was moved from Sandbach, Cheshire, to the Leyland plant in 2000. The design of Foden trucks was updated, including the all-steel cab Alpha 2000 for construction work and the Alpha 3000 for the highway tractor market. The Alpha XL was a high-roofed COE developed for the long-distance operator. Its cab was enlarged, tripling the storage space of previous models. Foden's market was ultra-strong, high-horsepower trucks for the extractive and construction industries. That year Foden's market share grew by nearly 20 percent. Its dealer network expanded, and the company established Foden Academy, which trained personnel in dealership operations.

The *Defence Suppliers Directory* described the Leyland plant as one of Europe's most advanced truck-assembly facilities. Soon after Foden's production moved to Leyland in 2002, the British Ministry of Defence ordered Foden 6 × 6 trucks for the Army. They joined the Army's fleet of Leyland 4 × 4 general-purpose four-ton vehicles, and more than fifteen hundred Foden DROPS (Demountable Rack Off-loading Pick-up System) vehicles with six-wheel drive and automatic transmissions.

The Foden and DAF supervisory boards made significant contributions to the success of PACCAR in Europe. The boards met quarterly and reviewed the business results of the respective companies. The directors shared their extensive worldwide expertise in a variety of fields, including politics, military, law, finance, and business. Their experience enabled PACCAR to better understand how to integrate its quality and technology initiatives into UK and European manufacturing and marketplaces. The directors' invaluable counsel, advice, and insights were major positive factors in PACCAR's ability to generate 35 percent of its global sales and profits from its European enterprises. In 1994, the Foden Supervisory Board included Sir Anthony Jolliffe, Lord Aldington, Major General Frederick Plaskett, Lord Digby, David Newbigging, Charles Pigott, and Mark Pigott. The DAF Supervisory Board of Directors that served at some time between 1997 and 2004 were Martin Schroder, Herman Santens, Lord MacGregor, Carlo de Swart, Charles Pigott, Walter Hasselkus, David Newbigging, Mark Pigott, Thomas Plimpton, Michael Tembreull, and Kenneth Gangl.

Mark Pigott was awarded the OBE (Officer of the Order of the British Empire) in 2003 in recognition of his exceptional dedication to strengthening business ties between the United Kingdom and the United States. Accepting the honor, Pigott said, "The development of PACCAR's business in the U.K., with the acquisition of Foden Trucks and Leyland Trucks Ltd., has been steadily growing for twenty-four years. The United Kingdom is a major cornerstone of PACCAR's success globally."

— KENWORTH PRODUCT DESIGN EVOLUTION —

After the 1994 introduction of the aerodynamic Kenworth T2000, engineers focused on a series of product updates, with the objective of providing greater strength and reliability, and adding more automotive-like handling, ride, comfort, and conveniences, as well as technology-based improvements. Company engineers employed Pro/E computer workstations, Rapid-Prototype machines, and other advanced technological tools. Their abilities were enhanced when Kenworth opened a 24,000-square-foot research and development center in Renton, Washington, in 2004. The center included an electronics lab, a model shop, a machine shop, and an innovative 3-D design-visualization room.

Quality, comfort, and space were the principal objectives for cab design and construction. Kenworth created options such as an extended day cab for construction and delivery trucks. This cab extension added an extra six inches to the cab's length and three inches to its height. Overall, it added 12 percent more interior room. The driver's seat was mounted farther from the steering wheel, which allowed drivers to push back from the wheel when arranging for the next load or completing paperwork from the last delivery.

Cabs for the long-haul drivers began to resemble the interiors of luxury automobiles. In 1998, Kenworth created an 86-inch Studio AeroCab sleeper for the W900 that contained two full-length closets, a sofa, and a foldout table, connections for a computer and television, and space for a small version of a home entertainment center. The sofa could be made into a 42-inch full-length bed. By 2000 it had been configured for T600 and T800 models. Retired Chief Engineer Larry Orr commented, "Kenworth's product line captures the very best qualities of aerodynamics, efficiency, and luxury."

The T600, T800, and W900 lines were refined and new materials were employed. Metton was an advanced composite material used in W900 hood construction. Metton's surface was more consistent than that of either fiberglass or aluminum, which resulted in a better-painted finish. Metton hoods were 100 pounds lighter than comparable fiberglass or aluminum hoods.

Under the skin, advanced electrical and electronic architecture incorporated multiplexing, which provided greater dashboard gauge reliability. It also facilitated the development of telematics for onboard and remote data communications, as well as safety.

Another weight-saving innovation was the AG380, an advanced proprietary rear axle air suspension system. It saved several hundred pounds over the trailing-arm suspensions that were then common to other heavy-duty trucks. The system also improved the vehicle's ride, handling, and stability.

Kenworth, Peterbilt, and Foden explored the use of engines powered with alternative fuels. Kenworth installed liquid natural gas engines in trucks for testing in California in 1996. Peterbilt manufactured its low-cab-forward Model 320 as a hybrid diesel/natural gas vehicle, primarily used for refuse applications. Foden introduced a dual-fuel engine in 2003 that could run on compressed natural or liquid natural gas in tandem with diesel fuel.

Kenworth trucks set land-speed records on the Bonneville Salt Flats and impressed spectators with their speed and handling during the annual Pikes Peak race in the Class 8 division. "Our customers like it, but primarily it is an engineering exercise," said PACCAR Vice President and General Manager Robert Christensen. "The event attracted attention in the trucking community, and it allowed Kenworth engineers to study vehicle durability, visibility, and the overall strength of the product."

Space and comfort were important aspects of fleet driver retention. Many smaller fleets were longtime Kenworth customers, but larger fleets began to focus on total life-cycle costs and driver-shortage problems. In part because of high resale value, Kenworth received an order for three thousand W900s in 2004, the largest single order in PACCAR history. Gary Moore, Kenworth Sales Manager, said, "This was a great order for Kenworth."

In 2004, Kenworth and Peterbilt had the highest resale value of any Class 8 truck in North America, which was a fundamental advantage for customers.

In 2003, Kenworth's T600, T800, and W900 models shared the 2003 J. D. Power and Associates Award for Customer Satisfaction. "We won the award for the pickup and delivery segment, and that is the segment that uses the T800, T600, and W900," said Christensen. Kenworth's T800 and W900 models shared the 2004 J. D. Power award for the vocational truck segment.

The T800 is regarded as the lowest-operating-cost vehicle in the industry.

Kenworth trucks began competing in the challenging Pikes Peak International Hill Climb, Highway Class/Big Rig Division, in the late 1990s. In 2000, a Kenworth T2000 set a new course record. It won the event again in 2001 and 2002.

Similar attention was given to Kenworth's off-road models. Kenworth had supplied Aramco with the C500 "desert truck" for more than fifty years. Its immense size and brute strength were excellent for the rigorous applications in the desert. Cabs were improved with better soundproofing, heating and cooling, access, and visibility. The C500 was equipped with an in-cab central tire-inflation system that allowed the driver to adjust truck tire pressure for desert sand or highway surfaces. Field results noted improvements in highway speed, maneuverability, comfort, fuel economy, and tire wear.

—FACTORY AND PROCESSES—

Kenworth's North American factories were located in Chillicothe, Ohio, and Renton, Washington. Chillicothe, the larger of the two, was opened in 1974, and its midwestern location provided delivery cost advantages. The Chillicothe plant was equipped with robotic assembly required in the construction of T2000 cabs and in truck production.

The Kenworth Renton factory was opened in 1993 as a single-shift plant with a designed capacity of fifteen to twenty trucks a day, but during peak market periods it produced as many as fifty-six. "We went from fifteen trucks a shift to the point where we could do twenty-eight

trucks per shift," said Operations Manager Tony McQuary. "We have essentially doubled the capacity of the plant without changing its footprint. We have applied DC tools to forty critical joints. This was a significant investment. We know they are always accurate, better than Six Sigma quality."

In its August 14, 2000, edition, *Fortune* magazine named Kenworth's Renton plant one of "America's Elite Factories." In his article about elite factories, Gene Bylinsky cited the plant's ability to produce customized trucks on a moving assembly line. "Automakers talk about the concept largely as a future aspiration," he wrote.

PACCAR International developed worldwide markets for its trucks, including this off-road Kenworth 953, shown at the company's factory in Renton, Washington.

—KENWORTH IN MEXICO AND AUSTRALIA—

PACCAR has more than thirty years in the development of Kenworth Mexicana and PACCAR Australia Pty. Ltd. (Kenworth Australia). Kenworth dominated sales of the Class 8 market in both Mexico and Australia. In 2003 these markets represented 11 percent of PACCAR's total net revenue.

After PACCAR acquired full ownership of Kenworth Mexicana in 1995, that country's market for trucks steadily grew. In 1997, KENMEX produced 5,600 trucks and introduced the U.S.-produced T2000 to the Mexican market. The plant's capacity was increased by 30 percent in

1999, and in 2001 the W900 was reintroduced to Mexico to meet the growing demand for high-horsepower trucks, due in part to increased business generated by NAFTA-driven trade activity and a national program to update Mexico's aging truck fleet.

Demand for quality, comfort, and customer service was equally strong on both sides of the NAFTA border. The AeroCab grew in popularity among truckers who drove the vast expanse of Mexico where truck stops and other conveniences were widely scattered. Customer service was strengthened in 2001, when KENMEX opened a twenty-four-hour Customer Call Center, a system that benefited Kenworth drivers as much as the company's eighty-five dealership locations in Mexico. In 2004, KENMEX introduced DAF LF Trucks to the Mexican urban delivery market, where smaller, more maneuverable vehicles were in demand.

The Australian truck market was radically different from those of Europe, North America, and Mexico. Trucks for Australia were designed to haul heavy loads over vast distances in what was often extremely harsh terrain, which led to the development of a uniquely Australian product range.

Australia is similar in size to the continental United States; climatic conditions vary from cool to tropical, with large areas of desert and semi-arid environments. The road system between remote population centers was challenging, and a high proportion of interstate transport was done over rough, narrow roads.

Loads were longer and heavier in Australia. Typical weights for long-distance on-highway applications ranged from 112,000 up to 475,000 pounds—almost six times typical North American weights. To carry these heavier payloads, two-, three-, and even four-trailer combinations were hauled in configurations known as B Doubles or Road Trains. With highway speeds restricted to 100 kilometers (62 miles) an hour, the amount of available "ram" air needed to cool high-output engines was severely reduced, which in turn necessitated larger and more efficient radiators. Cabs for Australian Kenworth models were raised higher off the chassis for improved engine and in-cab cooling, as well as noise and dust reduction. Maximum fuel capacity for long-distance operations was critical, as were durability and reliability, given the vast distances between refueling and service points.

Australian trucks typically traveled more than 250,000 kilometers (156,000 miles) annually, and some as much as 500,000 kilometers; in four years the average truck traveled one million kilometers.

"Australian Kenworths, like other PACCAR products, are expected to have multiple lives, and the designs of the trucks are such that rebuilds can be achieved readily and affordably," observed PACCAR Australia Managing Director Andrew Wright. "Australian Kenworths command excellent residual value—a testament to their longevity, reliability, and fitness for purpose. On the basis of recent census data, we estimate that over 75 percent of all Kenworths built in Australia over the last thirty-three years are still operating."

Kenworth was the only manufacturer to design and build its entire range of Class 8 trucks in Australia. Models in the range included the K104 COE, one of the largest COEs in the world; the aerodynamically styled T604; and the T904, used for some of the longest road-train combinations where overall length limits were not as restrictive. New models such as the T404SAR, released in 2004, were continually developed to meet the changing needs of the dynamic road-transport industry.

In 2001, a Kenworth road-train image was chosen by Australia Post to represent the road transport industry in a special series of postage stamps commemorating the pivotal role of certain industries in opening up the Australian outback.

—CANADA AND THE CLASS 7—

After a prolonged strike that started in August 1995, PACCAR closed its Ste-Thérèse, Quebec, Canada, plant in 1996, when it was no longer economically feasible to operate. Equipment was removed and the process of selling the site had begun when Quebec officials approached PACCAR in 1997 with an offer to make the site viable. A new plant was built on the site at a cost of $85 million. It was unique in that it was designed to produce both medium- and heavy-duty trucks on the same line. Opened in 1999, the 300,000-square-foot facility could build eighty trucks a day.

The only facility where Kenworth and Peterbilt trucks were manufactured on the same line was in Ste-Thérèse, where PACCAR produced most of its Class 7 trucks for the North American market. The Ste-Thérèse factory had an initial designed annual capacity of twenty thousand medium- and heavy-duty trucks. Kenworth also produced the T300 in Mexicali, Mexico, for the Latin American market.

PACCAR Vice President Richard E. Bangert II described the plant as an "employee-based facility. There are employee-meeting areas all through the plant, not just break areas, but meeting areas. We have computer monitors everywhere for the employees. It's very bright, well air-conditioned and modern, an industrial cathedral." The plant produced T300s for Kenworth, the Model 330 and Model 335 for Peterbilt, and Class 8 Peterbilt day cab models for the Canadian and eastern U.S. markets.

PACCAR's North American Class 7 market share had grown to nearly 10 percent by 2004, due in part to winning the J.D. Power and Associates award for customer satisfaction in 2000, when the Peterbilt Model 330 won the coveted recognition. In 2000, Kenworth received the

Kenworth Australia models haul up to 475,000-pound loads in two-, three-, and even four-trailer road-train configurations called "B Doubles."

Peterbilt and Kenworth Class 7 trucks are produced for the North American market at the Ste-Thérèse plant in Canada. Shown is a Kenworth T300 during final assembly.

Customer Satisfaction award for the T300. Peterbilt received the award in 2001 and 2002, again for the Model 330. The award is based on vehicle quality, engine, transmission, ride, handling, braking, cab interior, exterior design, and styling.

—PETERBILT'S LEADING-EDGE LEGACY—

Peterbilt assured its place in trucking history with the success of the Model 379. Its legacy was long and its following loyal. Some say its root design was the 1949 Model 350, while others mention the legacy begun with Peterbilt's Chief Engineer George Brumbaugh and the Model 351 in 1954. The 351 led to the Model 359 in 1967. The 379, aptly named the Successor, was introduced in 1986.

In February 1999, Peterbilt introduced the Model 387. It was completely new for Peterbilt and was lighter, stronger, and more powerful than competing aerodynamic trucks. It offered more room between the driver and passenger seat and substantially more storage space. In terms of space, it was 17 percent more truck. All dressed up, it weighed within 200 pounds of the 377, Peterbilt's first-generation aero, and delivered industry-leading fuel economy.

In addition to comfort and economy, Peterbilt engineers concentrated on serviceability. They improved forty major service items. "We worked with our suppliers," recalled PACCAR Vice

President and Peterbilt General Manager Daniel Sobic. "If they were making a part guaranteed for five years and 500,000 miles, we asked them to build it so that it could be expected to go seven years and 750,000 miles." The 387 proved to be a remarkably reliable truck. It was also quiet and had excellent ride and handling similar to that of other Peterbilt models.

The 387 was the first PACCAR truck designed solely by computer. The truck's design received the equivalent of twenty million miles of testing at the PACCAR Technical Center. A year after its introduction, Peterbilt received the Parametric Technology Corporation Award for the development of the 387. In its assembly at the Denton, Texas, factory, adhesive bonding technology was used to build the cab structure, adding both strength and durability.

Meanwhile, the classic 379 was updated. Improvements included a 70-inch sleeper that offered 77 cubic feet of storage, 25 percent more than previous sleepers of comparable length. The PACCAR Technical Center's ergonomic laboratory contributed to further improvements in the model.

Heavy Duty Trucking magazine placed the Model 357 construction truck's hood on its Nifty Fifty list of new products in 2003. The hood had been sloped forward to improve forward visibility by about five feet. This was an example of what Peterbilt owners referred to as "purposeful innovation."

The Peterbilt Model 379 has the highest resale value of any truck sold in North America.

Peterbilt introduced the
fuel-efficient Model 387
in 1999.

A Peterbilt Model 335, used in urban applications.

Peterbilt introduced Flex Air, a tandem rear air-suspension system that weighed 400 pounds less than comparable systems, and a clutchless, fully automatic transmission option. The suspension system had been designed by former Peterbilt chief engineer Donald Stephens before his retirement from the PACCAR Technical Center. Flex Air received recognition when it was named one of *Heavy Duty Trucking*'s Nifty Fifty in 2002.

— A COMPANY AND A FAMILY —

Mark Pigott described the one-hundred-year legacy of PACCAR success as being based on "unequivocal integrity and commitment to quality, and profitable growth." This, he said, "sets the benchmark by which we are measured and the standards we will strive to exceed."

PACCAR established benchmarking as a cultural element early in its history. By the 1990s, it had become ingrained in the company's business approach. Which factory was the most efficient? What division was the most innovative? Vice Chairman Mike Tembreull described the evolution of the company's benchmarking: "Early on, we just benchmarked against ourselves, and there was a mind-set that that was enough. Then we started to have field trips." PACCAR managers visited major competitors' and suppliers' factories for insights into process and quality management. By the mid-1990s, PACCAR measured and benchmarked everything from engineering development to credit approvals and inventory turns versus the best practices observed inside and outside the company. Inventory turns increased from twelve to fifty a year, but expectations were still higher. Mark Pigott observed that Dell Computer turned its inventory at much higher levels, so PACCAR began to benchmark its inventory performance against Dell's.

Benchmarks were systematically set. When several seemingly profitable companies failed and their accounting practices were found to be flawed, PACCAR immediately reviewed its own practices. General Counsel Morie advised company management, "There is a difference between those that have all the documentation on the shelves and those that walk the talk." He elaborated at a senior management meeting later that year. "I read excerpts from an ethics code that sounded very good, very convincing, the tenets that every executive would want to subscribe to. Then I pointed out that the excerpts were from a bankrupt company's ethics code. Having a culture that embraces the ethics and sets the standard from the chief executive to all employees in every facility is really what it means to be an ethical company. This is the real foundation of corporate governance at PACCAR."

PACCAR's standards were as much corporate-based as Pigott family–based. In a November 2003 *Business Week* article on family-run companies, the writers found that one-third of the S&P 500 companies had founding families involved in management. Of the one hundred listed companies, only three were as old as PACCAR, and of that group, PACCAR topped the list for average annual stockholder return during the previous decade. "So what is it that gives family companies their edge? In part," reported *Business Week*, "it's having managers with a passion for the enterprise that goes far beyond that of any hired executive, no matter how much they are paid." The writers also suggested that family management often put corporate interests before personal ones.

If the past determines the future, then PACCAR will continue to evolve successfully. Each generation of PACCAR leadership has left a distinctive legacy for the next. Founder William Pigott established the company's basic tenets, including quality and integrity. Acquired by American Car in 1924 and threatened by a severe decline in railcar orders, the company accelerated its innovation of new products. In 1930 it created Carcometal and in 1932 the first Carco winch. Paul Pigott bought back the company in 1934, saving it from the Great Depression's scrap yard. He rebuilt it as a financially sound manufacturer of railcars and winches and entered into the heavy-duty truck business. Charles Pigott envisioned PACCAR as a geographically diverse company and developed its manufacturing capabilities and markets in Canada, Mexico, Australia, and toward the end of his career, Europe. Mark Pigott grew the business so that by 2003, over 50 percent of the company's revenues were generated outside the United States. He rigorously embraced benchmarking and practical information technology, as well as increased quality levels that resulted in record profits and superior return to stockholders within the first decade of his stewardship.

At the beginning of its second century, PACCAR's principal product was technology. In another hundred years, the company's core business might be something unheard of, but its founding values likely won't change. Those values are a matter of culture.

Mark Pigott summarized the company in 2004, noting, "PACCAR is a growth company, a technology company that enjoys building the highest-quality automotive product in the world. We have tremendous personnel, unbelievable financial strength, and a culture of embracing change and technology, which is very important.

"The benefits of geographic diversification, dedicated employees, quality products and service, modern facilities, innovative IT systems, and a strong balance sheet, working in tandem with the best distribution network in the industry, are the fundamental elements that contribute toward this vibrant, dynamic company. Whatever we do, it's the premium quality that is our hallmark. We are always ready to examine additional opportunities. PACCAR is a winner."

PACCAR's quality brands.

PACCAR Inc

Peterbilt

DAF

PACCAR
DIRECTORS AND OFFICERS

Directors

Murray Aitken, 1972–1974
W. S. Bassage, 1934–1935
Weldon G. Bettens, 1937–1941
J. M. Buick, 1924–1926
L. T. Carroll, 1926–1933
Hugh S. Center, 1946–1947
Jack A. Chantrey, 1978–1979
F. W. Chriswell, 1934, 1945
T. S. Clingan, 1914–1936
O. D. Colvin, 1917–1924
O. D. Colvin, Jr., 1936–1941, 1945
Richard P. Cooley, 1991–1996
H. N. Curd, 1930–1945
W. C. Dickerman, 1927–1933
D. E. Douglas, 1953–1963
Joseph M. Dunn, 1986–1990
E. T. Fehnel, 1934
John M. Fluke, Jr., 1984–
Thomas F. Gleed, 1945, 1947–1972
Gerald Grinstein, 1997–2005
Horace Hager, 1926–1933
William M. Hager, 1924–1933
Carl H. Hahn, 1993–1999
C. J. Hardy, 1925–1933
W. J. Harris, 1928–1933
C. L. Havens, 1934
Harold J. Haynes, 1981–1998
Frank P. Helsell, 1934
John G. Holmstrom, 1948–1965
David J. Hovind, 1992–2003
Robert A. Hulbert, 1935–1939
Frank T. Hunter, 1934
B. C. Jameson, 1980
W. Scott Matheson, 1934
John A. McCone, 1967–1973
D. E. McLaughlin,* 1905–1917
T. B. Monson, 1952–1969
David K. Newbigging, 1999–
Robert D. O'Brien, 1957–1977
Stephen F. Page, 2004–
Robert T. Parry, 2004–
Donald F. Pennell, 1966–1971
W. J. Pennington, 1970–1985
Charles M. Pigott, 1961–2001
James C. Pigott, 1972–
M. J. Pigott,* 1905–1917
Mark C. Pigott, 1994–

Paul Pigott, 1934–1959
Robert I. Pigott, 1937–1945
William Pigott,* 1905–1929
William Pigott, Jr., 1934–1944
John W. Pitts, 1964–1999
William G. Reed, 1946–1971
William G. Reed, Jr., 1998–
C. S. Sale, 1924–1933
G. R. Scanland, 1924–1933
F. A. Schidel, 1934
Ferdinand Schmitz, Jr., 1940–1949
J. M. Shields, 1934
N. A. Stancliffe, 1926–1933
Frederick A. Stevenson, 1930–1933
Harry C. Stonecipher, 2001–
E. H. Stuart, 1946
Gordon H. Sweany, 1974–1982
Michael A. Tembreull, 1994–
O. A. Tucker, 1950–1952
James F. Twohy, 1935–1936
James P. Twohy, 1917–1923,
    1928–1929
John Twohy, 1917–1927
Robert E. Twohy, 1917–1924
Harold A. Wagner, 1999–
James H. Wiborg, 1975–1997
E. M. Wilson,* 1905–1917,
    1924, 1926–1927
T. A. Wilson, 1973–1993
H. W. Wolff, 1924–1933

*Founding director

Officers

Murray Aitken, Vice President,
    1970; Senior Vice President,
    1971–1974
David C. Anderson, Vice President/
    General Counsel, 2005–
Ronald E. Armstrong, Vice
    President & Controller, 2002–
Cor G. Baan, Senior Vice President,
    1998–1999
Laurie L. Baker, Vice President,
    1990–2003
Richard E. Bangert II, Vice
    President, 1994–
C. R. Bechtol, Vice President–
    Industrial Relations, 1967–1974

E. A. Black, Vice President,
    1953–1959
J. M. Bodden, Vice President, 1974;
    Senior Vice President, 1975–1978
William E. Boisvert, Senior Vice
    President/CFO, 1988; Executive
    Vice President/CFO, 1989–1995
Diane M. Brown, Secretary, 1982
James G. Cardillo, Vice President,
    1999–2004; Senior Vice President,
    2004–
E. A. Carpenter, Secretary,
    1973–1978, 1983–1984
L. T. Carroll, President, 1924–1933
Louis J. Cattaneo, Vice President,
    1986–1995
Edward Caudill, Vice President,
    1999–2002
Jack A. Chantrey, Vice President/
    Treasurer, 1971–1972; Senior Vice
    President, 1973–1987
Robert J. Christensen, Vice
    President, 2000–
T. S. Clingan, Secretary, 1911–1929
H. N. Curd, Vice President,
    1930–1945
Janice M. D'Amato, Secretary, 1995–
Robert W. Dickey, Vice President/
    General Counsel, 1979–1981;
    Senior Vice President, 1982–1983;
    Executive Vice President, 1984–
    1985; Senior Vice President,
    1986–1987
D. E. Douglas, Secretary/Treasurer,
    1947–1949; Treasurer, 1950–1951;
    Vice President/Treasurer,
    1952–1963
Joseph M. Dunn, Vice President,
    1975–1978; Senior Vice President,
    1979–1984; Executive Vice
    President, 1985; President,
    1987–1990
Patrick F. Flynn, Vice President &
    CIO, 1999–2004
Kenneth R. Gangl, Vice President–
    Financial Services, 1999–
Aad Goudrian, Vice President
    PACCAR/President DAF Trucks,
    2005–

J. W. Grant, General Counsel, 1972–
1975; Vice President/General
Counsel, 1976–1978; Vice
President/Special Counsel, 1979–
1980

William N. Gross, Assistant Vice
President, 1971–1973; Senior Vice
President, 1979–1980; Executive
Vice President, 1981–1985

Leonard A. Haba, Vice President/
Controller, 1972–1981; Senior Vice
President, 1982–1989

William M. Hager, Chairman,
1924–1933

G. Don Hatchel, Vice President/
Controller, 1990–2002

Timothy M. Henebry, Vice
President, 2003–

Ronald R. Hollyoak, Vice President,
1987–1989

John G. Holmstrom, Vice President,
1945–1965

Robert A. Holmstrom, Vice
President, 1974; Senior Vice
President, 1975–1983

David J. Hovind, Vice President,
1985; Senior Vice President, 1986;
Executive Vice President, 1987–
1991; President, 1992–2003; Vice
Chairman, 2003–2004

Donald M. Irwin, Vice President–
Employee Relations, 1974–1983

Reg A. Jackson, Treasurer, 1977–
1982; Vice President, 1983

William D. Jackson, Vice President,
2002–

Paul M. Jacobsen, Vice President,
1950–1962

B. C. Jameson, Vice President,
1968–1970; Senior Vice President,
1971–1980

Richard A. Johnsen, Treasurer,
1985–1990

J. J. Jolley, Vice President/Treasurer,
1973–1976; Vice President, 1977–
1982; Vice President/Treasurer,
1983–1984; Vice President,
1985–1986

H. R. Keele, Vice President,
1983–1985

Henry E. Kiefer, Vice President,
1990–1991

J. E. LeBlanc, Secretary/Treasurer,
1945–1946

Lester Leeman, Controller,
1947–1952

George M. Lhamon, Assistant Vice
President, 1963; Vice President/
Treasurer, 1964–1970; Vice
President–International Finance,
1971–1973; Vice President–
Employee Retirement Benefits,
1974–1978; Vice President/
Secretary, 1979–1981

Thomas A. Lundahl, Vice President,
2002–

James K. Matheson, Assistant Vice
President, 1980–1982

Helene N. Mawyer, Vice President,
2001–

T. B. Monson, Vice President,
1949–1967; Senior Vice President,
1968–1969

Gary S. Moore, Senior Vice
President, 1992–1996; Vice
President, 1996–2002

R. B. Moran, Vice President,
1957–1966

G. Glen Morie, Secretary, 1985–
1995; Vice President/General
Counsel, 1985–2005

T. Ron Morton, Senior Vice
President, 1995–1998

Robert D. O'Brien, Vice President,
1956–1958; Executive Vice
President, 1959; President, 1960–
1964; Chairman of the Board,
1965–1977

M. E. O'Byrne, Controller, 1954–
1963; Vice President/Controller,
1964–1971

Nicholas P. Panza, Vice President,
1999–2003; Senior Vice President,
2003–2004

Donald F. Pennell, Vice President,
1965–1970; Senior Vice President,
1971–1972

W. L. Peterson, Vice President–
Marketing, 1971

Charles M. Pigott, Assistant Vice
President, 1961; Executive Vice
President, 1962–1964; President,
1965–1985; Chairman of the
Board/CEO, 1986–1996;
Chairman Emeritus, 1997–

Mark C. Pigott, Vice President,
1988–1990; Senior Vice President,
1990–1993; Executive Vice
President, 1993–1994; Vice
Chairman, 1995–1996; Chairman
of the Board/CEO, 1997–

Paul Pigott, President, 1934–1960

William Pigott, President, 1905–
1924; Chairman, 1922–1924

William Pigott, Jr., Chairman,
1934–1945

Thomas E. Plimpton, Senior Vice
President, 1996–1998; Executive
Vice President, 1998–2003;
President, 2003–

Jack M. Quinlin, Vice President,
1987–1989

Ronald E. Ranheim, Treasurer,
1996–2003

G. R. Robbins, Vice President, 1980;
Senior Vice President, 1981–1984

John Salathe, Jr., Assistant Vice
President, 1979–1980; Vice
President, 1981–1989

Ferdinand Schmitz, Jr., Vice
President, 1940–1945; Executive
Vice President, 1946–1947;
Vice President, 1948–1949

W. H. Scudder, Secretary, 1950–
1952; Secretary/Assistant
Treasurer, 1953–1963; Secretary/
Assistant Treasurer, 1965–1972

R. J. Sill, Vice President, 1984–1986

Janice Skredsvig, Vice President and
Chief Information Officer, 2005–

Kenneth W. Smith, Sr., Assistant
Vice President, 1978–1985

W. Keith Smith, Executive Vice
President, 1986

Daniel D. Sobic, Vice President,
2003–

Michael A. Tembreull, Senior Vice
President, 1990–1991; Executive
Vice President, 1992–1994; Vice
Chairman, 1995–

O. A. Tucker, Vice President,
1945–1952

John Twohy, Chairman, 1917–1922

John J. Waggoner, Treasurer,
1991–1995

W. D. Wagner, Vice President,
1988–1989

George E. West, Vice President,
1999–

Andrew J. Wold, Treasurer, 2003–

SIGNIFICANT CORPORATE EVENTS

DAF

1928   van Doorne's Aanhangwagenfabriek
1949   First truck produced
1972   International Truck Service (ITS) established
1996   DAF acquired by PACCAR Inc
1998   International Truck of the Year award for DAF 95XF
2002   DAF dealership network established in Australia
      International Truck of the Year award for DAF LF

Dart

1958   Dart Truck Company acquired
1984   Dart Trucks sold

Dynacraft

1968   Dynacraft Division established
1990   Dynacraft Louisville, KY, plant opens

Foden Trucks

1848   Plant & Hancock established, Cheshire, England
1866   Plant & Hancock renamed Hancock & Foden
1870   Hancock & Foden renamed Foden & Hancock
1876   Foden & Hancock becomes Edwin Foden & Son
1902   Fodens Ltd. established
1980   Fodens Ltd. acquired by PACCAR U.K. Ltd.
2000   Foden production transferred from Sandbach to
      the Leyland factory

Kenworth Truck Company

1914   Gerlinger Motor Car Company builds first truck
1915   Gersix Manufacturing Company incorporated
1917   Edgar K. Worthington and Captain Frederick S. Keen
      acquire Gersix Manufacturing Company
1923   Kenworth Motor Truck Company incorporated
1944   Kenworth acquired by Pacific Car and Foundry
1952   Kenworth Mexicana incorporated
1955   Canadian Kenworth Ltd. incorporated
1966   Kenworth Motor Trucks Pty. Ltd. incorporated
      in Australia
1966   Kenworth opens plant in Melbourne, Australia
1973   Kenworth Chillicothe, OH, plant opens
1993   Kenworth Renton, WA, plant opens
2004   Research and Development Center in Renton opens

Leyland Trucks

1896   Lancashire Steam Motor Company founded
1919   Lancashire renamed Leyland Motors Ltd.
1993   Leyland Motors renamed Leyland Trucks Ltd.
1998   Leyland Trucks acquired by PACCAR Inc
2000   Foden production begins in Leyland factory

PACCAR Automotive, Inc.

1987   General Automotive Warehouse Inc. (Al's Auto
      Supply) acquired
1988   Grand Auto, Inc., acquired and merged into General
      Automotive, Inc.
1991   General Automotive renamed PACCAR Automotive,
      Inc.
1999   PACCAR Automotive, Inc., sold to CSK Auto, Inc.

PACCAR Defense Systems

1985   PCF Defense Industries Division established
1986   PCF Defense Industries renamed PACCAR Defense
      Systems
1988   PACCAR Defense Systems closes

PACCAR Financial Services Corporation

1961   Carco Acceptance Corporation formed
1970   Carco Acceptance becomes PACCAR Financial Corp.
1983   PACCAR Financial Sales Limited formed in UK
1993   PACCAR Financial files for $1 billion shelf
      registration
2001   PACCAR Financial Europe (PFE) established
2002   PACCAR Financial Services Corporation formed

PACCAR Foundation

1951   Pacific Car and Foundry Company Foundation
      established
1972   Pacific Car and Foundry Company Foundation
      becomes PACCAR Foundation

PACCAR Inc

1971   PACCAR Inc incorporated
1972   Pacific Car and Foundry merges into PACCAR Inc
1974   Hayes Trucks Ltd. acquired
1974   PACCAR of Canada Ltd. incorporated
1981   VILPAC, S.A., incorporated
1982   PACCAR Australia Pty. Ltd. established
1990   PACCAR U.K. Ltd. Sandbach headquarters opens
1995   Remainder of Kenworth Mexicana, S.A. de C.V., and
      VILPAC, S.A., acquired
1997   Six Sigma initiative established
1999   New Ste-Thérèse plant opens

PACCAR International

1972   PACCAR International Inc. established
1978   First truck sales to China
1995   Licensed assembly plant opens in South Africa

PACCAR ITD

1970   Management Information Systems formed (MIS)
2001   MIS becomes Information Technology Division (ITD)

PACCAR Leasing

1980 PACCAR Leasing Corporation formed
1987 PacLease Limited incorporated in UK
2000 PACCAR Leasing becomes a division of PACCAR Financial Services Corporation

PACCAR Parts

1973 PACCAR Parts Division established
1974 Distribution center opens in Atlanta, GA
1982 Distribution center opens in Lancaster, PA
1986 Kenworth and Peterbilt parts sales and marketing consolidated under PACCAR Parts
1991 Rockford, IL, facility opens
1995 Distribution center opens in Las Vegas, NV
1998 San Luis Potosi, Mexico, distribution center opens
1999 Customer Call Center, North America, opens
2000 DAF Parts is consolidated into PACCAR Parts
2003 Leyland distribution center opens

PACCAR Purchasing Division

1987 Corporate purchasing division formed
1998 PACCAR Purchasing becomes global
2004 North American Transportation System introduced

PACCAR Technical Centers

1982 PACCAR Technical Center opens in Skagit County, WA
1996 DAF Technical Center, Eindhoven

PACCAR Winch Division

1983 Braden, Gearmatic, and Carco merge into PACCAR Winch
1985 Winch Division moves to Broken Arrow, OK
1994 PACCAR Winch purchases Caterpillar Winch product line

Pacific Car and Foundry Company

1905 Seattle Car Manufacturing Company incorporated
1907 Seattle Car Seattle plant destroyed by fire
1908 Seattle Car begins operating at new Renton, WA, plant
1911 Seattle Car Manufacturing Company renamed Seattle Car & Foundry Company
1917 Seattle Car & Foundry Company renamed Pacific Car & Foundry Company
1917 Twohy Brothers Company merges into Pacific Car & Foundry Company
1924 Pacific Car & Foundry Company acquired by American Car and Foundry Company and reincorporated as Pacific Car and Foundry Company
1930 "Carcometal" patented
1932 First Pacific Car and Foundry "Carco" winch introduced
1934 Pacific Car and Foundry Company acquired from American Car and Foundry and reorganized by Pigott family and other stockholders
1936 Pacific Car and Foundry acquires Steel Fabricators, Inc.
1945 Kenworth Motor Truck Company acquired

1958 Dart Truck Company acquired
1958 Peterbilt Motors Company acquired
1960 49 percent of Kenworth Mexicana S.A. de C.V. stock acquired
1963 Gearmatic acquired by Canadian Kenworth Ltd.
1967 Sicard Industries acquired
1969 Pacific Car and Foundry headquarters moves to Bellevue, WA
1972 Sicard Industries sold
1972 Pacific Car and Foundry merges into PACCAR Inc
1975 International Car Company acquired
1977 Braden Winch Company acquired
1984 International Car Company sold
1989 Pacific Car and Foundry and company's railcar fleet sold for $52.4 million

Pacific Car and Foundry—Shipbuilding

1942 Everett Pacific Company incorporated
1944 Everett Pacific stock acquired by Pacific Car and Foundry
1944 Everett Pacific Shipbuilding and Drydock incorporated
1946 Everett Pacific Company dissolved
1951 Everett Pacific shipyard reactivated during Korean conflict
1953 Commercial Ship Repair Company acquired
1955 Everett Pacific shipyard closes
1955 Winslow Marine Railway and Shipyard acquired
1959 Commercial Ship Repair liquidated

Peterbilt Motors Company

1915 Fageol Motor Car Company opens in Oakland, CA
1938 T. A. Peterman acquires Fageol Motor Car from Waukesha Motor Company
1939 First Peterbilt truck manufactured
1940 Peterman Manufacturing Company incorporated
1958 Peterbilt Motors Company acquired by Pacific Car and Foundry
1960 Peterbilt manufacturing and headquarters move to new facilities at Newark, CA
1969 Peterbilt Nashville, TN, plant opens
1980 Peterbilt Denton, TX, plant opens
1986 Peterbilt Newark, CA, plant closes
1993 Peterbilt headquarters moves to Denton, TX

Trico Industries, Inc.

1987 Trico Industries, Inc., acquired
1987 Standard Pump merged into Trico Industries
1994 Hydraulic pumping system products and San Marcos, TX, manufacturing facilities acquired from National-Oilwell
1997 Trico sold to EVI, Inc.

Wagner Mining Equipment Co.

1973 Wagner Mining Equipment Co. acquired
1981 Russel Brothers Ltd. acquired in Canada for manufacture of Wagner Mining equipment
1989 Wagner Mining sold to Atlas Copco
1990 Russel Brothers sold to Leyland Marsh Inc.

PACCAR FINANCIALS
1965–2004

PACCAR Inc

Financial Performance Review

Year	Revenues*	Net Income*	Stockholders Equity*	Adjusted Dividends
1965	$ 295.1	$ 15.1	$ 60.6	$0.01/share
1970	453.1	14.8	126.2	0.02
1975	707.0	20.6	233.7	0.03
1980	1,705.9	81.1	540.5	0.13
1985	2,030.0	72.9	714.6	0.21
1990	2,791.4	63.7	1,019.2	0.19
1995	4,850.4	252.8	1,251.2	0.89
1999	9,021.0	583.6	2,110.6	1.07
2000	7,936.5	441.8	2,249.1	0.98
2001	6,100.5	173.6	2,252.6	0.64
2002	7,218.6	372.0	2,600.7	1.00
2003	8,194.9	526.5	3,246.4	1.37
2004	11,396.3	906.8	3,762.4	2.75

Stock Dividends/Splits

1966, July	3 for 1 split		
1969, September	30% stock dividend	1994, February	15% stock dividend
1971, February	10% stock dividend	1997, May	2 for 1 split
1972, May	200% stock dividend	2002, May	50% stock dividend
1982, February	10% stock dividend	2004, February	50% stock dividend
1983, December	100% stock dividend		
1988, July	100% stock dividend		

PACCAR Financial Services

Financial Performance Review

Year	Assets*	Revenues*	Profits (before tax)*	Profits (after tax)*
1965	$ 26.8	$ 2.7	$ 1.1	$ 0.5
1970	87.2	10.4	2.4	1.2
1975	138.3	17.1	7.1	3.7
1980	407.6	32.2	14.9	8.2
1985	1,048.3	136.8	21.5	11.5
1990	1,671.7	190.7	10.0	6.5
1995	2,744.3	257.5	53.3	34.7
1999	4,582.5	372.8	77.8	50.6
2000	5,114.2	479.1	76.4	49.7
2001	4,758.5	458.8	35.0	22.8
2002	5,112.3	432.6	72.2	46.9
2003	5,605.4	473.8	123.6	80.3
2004	6,980.1	562.6	168.4	109.5

Amounts given in millions

SOURCES

Primary Sources (by subject)

AMERICAN CAR AND FOUNDRY CO. Organization Chart, 1928. Archives of ACF Industries, St. Charles, Missouri

AMERICAN CAR AND FOUNDRY MOTOR CO. Annual reports, 1926–1936. Baker Library, Harvard University, Boston

BASSAGE, W. S. "Car Company History #1." PACCAR Archive, Bellevue

BEEZER, EDWARD "The Pacific Car and Foundry Co., Growth in the Northwest Corner," July 1966. PACCAR Archive, Bellevue

BRADEN WINCH CO. Corporate histories, photographs, files. PACCAR Archive, Bellevue

CANADIAN KENWORTH, LTD. Annual reports, company profiles, files. PACCAR Archive, Bellevue

CARCO ACCEPTANCE CORPORATION Minutes books, company papers. PACCAR vault, Bellevue

CHRISWELL, FREDERICK W. "Sketch of Mr. William Pigott," July 20, 1944. PACCAR Archive, Bellevue

COMMERCIAL SHIP REPAIR CO. Company scrapbook, clippings, photographs. PACCAR Archive, Bellevue

CURD, H. N., AND ALEX FINLAYSON "Report of Trip to Alaska," July 18, 1931. PACCAR Archive, Bellevue

DART TRUCK CO. Company histories, clippings, photographs, letters. PACCAR Archive, Bellevue

EVERETT PACIFIC CO. Minutes books, 1942–1944. PACCAR vault, Bellevue

EVERETT PACIFIC SHIPBUILDING AND DRY DOCK CO. Minutes books, clippings, brochures, employee letter, 1949. PACCAR Archive, Bellevue

INTERNATIONAL CAR CO. "The Caboose Car" and company files. PACCAR Archive, Bellevue

KW-DART CO. Company papers. PACCAR Archive, Bellevue

KENWORTH FINANCE, LTD. Company papers. PACCAR Archive, Bellevue

KENWORTH MANUFACTURING CO. Corporate documents, patents, photographs, files. PACCAR Archive, Bellevue

KENWORTH MOTOR TRUCK CO.
General histories, corporate documents, legal files, photographs, specifications, letters. PACCAR Archive, Bellevue
Class 8. Company Publication. PACCAR Archive, Bellevue

Kenworth Craftsman (company publication). PACCAR Archive, Bellevue
"Kenworth, in the Tradition of Our Founders," 1961. PACCAR Archive, Bellevue

MARPLE, ELLIOT Transcripts and notes of various interviews with Paul Pigott, Thomas Gleed, W. S. Bassage, Charles Linderman, and Charles Pigott, 1948, 1971

NORTHERN PACIFIC RAILWAY CO. *The Northwest and Its Resources*, 1924–1958. University of Washington Libraries, Seattle

PACCAR FINANCIAL CORPORATION Minutes books, company papers. PACCAR vault, Bellevue

PACCAR INC
General histories; correspondence files; legal, financial, corporate files; brochures; photographs, 1972–2004. PACCAR Archive, Bellevue
PACCAR WORLD (company publication), 1972–2004. PACCAR Archive, Bellevue
Profiles (company publication), 1970–1972. PACCAR Archive, Bellevue

PACIFIC CAR AND FOUNDRY CO.
Annual Stockholders Meeting reports, 1932–1933; Board of Directors Meeting reports, 1932–1934; company documents, general histories, clippings, correspondence files, brochures, photographs, 1924–1972. PACCAR Archive, Bellevue
Articles of Incorporation, 1917. PACCAR vault, Bellevue
Correspondence between Paul Pigott and T. S. Clingan. Courtesy of Charles M. Pigott, Bellevue
Financial statements, 1924–1972. PACCAR Archive, Bellevue
Minutes books, 1917–1972. PACCAR vault, Bellevue
Carco Comments (company publication). PACCAR Archive, Bellevue
Carco Craftsman (company publication). PACCAR Archive, Bellevue
"Carco Winch Products," 1978. PACCAR Archive, Bellevue
"Highlights," August 1963. PACCAR Archive, Bellevue
Management News Letter
"Military Vehicles." PACCAR Archive, Bellevue
Renegotiation reports—U.S. Army, 1945, 1953. PACCAR Archive, Bellevue
Russian Railway Agreement, November 3, 1917. PACCAR Archive, Bellevue

PACIFIC CAR AND FOUNDRY CO.—STRUCTURAL STEEL DIVISION

Company files, clippings, photographs, scrapbooks, 1936–1972. PACCAR Archive, Bellevue

"Searching Constantly," 1964. PACCAR Archive, Bellevue

"World Trade Center," 1967. PACCAR Archive, Bellevue

PACIFIC COAST STEEL CO.

William Pigott's correspondence files, 1903–1929. Charles M. Pigott, Bellevue

William Pigott's correspondence files, published and unpublished reports, metallurgical and business studies, photographs. Joseph Daniels Collection, Manuscripts and University Archives Division, University of Washington Libraries, Seattle

Carrigan, M. J. "Prospectus of the Seattle Iron and Steel Co.," 1904. Joseph Daniels Collection, Manuscripts and University Archives Division, University of Washington Libraries, Seattle

Carrigan, M. J. "Iron Manufacture of the Pacific Coast," 1904. Joseph Daniels Collection, Manuscripts and University Archives Division, University of Washington Libraries, Seattle

Daniels, Joseph. "Analysis of Charcoal Pig Iron Made at Irondale, Washington," 1901. Manuscripts and University Archives Division, University of Washington Libraries, Seattle

———. "History of Pig Iron Manufacture of the Pacific Coast," November 30, 1925. Manuscripts and University Archives Division, University of Washington Libraries, Seattle

———. "The Pacific Coast Steel Company," April 17, 1916. Joseph Daniels Collection, Manuscripts and University Archives Division, University of Washington Libraries, Seattle

———. "Western Steel Corporation," November 19, 1910. Joseph Daniels Collection, Manuscripts and University Archives Division, University of Washington Libraries, Seattle

PETERBILT MOTORS CO. General histories, correspondence files, published and unpublished reports, financial and corporate files. PACCAR Archive, Bellevue

PIGOTT, PAUL Clingan, T. S. Letter of May 1, 1934. Charles M. Pigott, Bellevue

PIGOTT, WILLIAM

Ames, Edwin. Letters. Edwin Ames Collection, Manuscripts and University Archives Division, University of Washington Libraries, Seattle

Ault, Harry E. B. Letters. Harry E. B. Ault Collection, Manuscripts and University Archives Division, University of Washington Libraries, Seattle

SEATTLE CAR AND FOUNDRY CO. General histories, corporate documents, legal files, photographs, printed materials, 1911–1917. PACCAR Archive, Bellevue

SEATTLE CAR MANUFACTURING CO.

General histories, corporate documents, legal files, photographs, correspondence, printed materials, 1905–1911. PACCAR Archive, Bellevue

Minutes books, 1907–1911. PACCAR vault, Bellevue

President's statement, March 25, 1907. PACCAR Archive, Bellevue

Stock subscriptions list, December 30, 1905; bond holders; financial statements. PACCAR Archive, Bellevue

SEATTLE STEEL COMPANY Stock certificates, stock book, corporate documents. PACCAR Archive, Bellevue

SICARD, LTD. Correspondence files, reports, clippings, scrapbooks, photographs. PACCAR Archive, Bellevue

TEXAS KENWORTH CO. General corporate documents, legal files, printed materials. PACCAR vault, Bellevue

TRINIDAD ROLLING MILL CO. Partnership Agreement, July 1, 1892. PACCAR Archive, Bellevue

TRUCK ACCEPTANCE CORP. Corporate documents, legal files, financial records. PACCAR vault, Bellevue

TWOHY BROTHERS CO. Corporate papers, 1924. PACCAR Archive, Bellevue

WAGNER MINING EQUIPMENT COMPANY

Publications, correspondence, sales brochures. PACCAR Archive, Bellevue

Holbrook, N. A. "History of Wagner Mining Equipment Co.," 1972. PACCAR Archive, Bellevue

WILLIAM PIGOTT COMPANY

Stock subscription, minutes books, September 1925–1929. PACCAR Archive, Bellevue

Secondary Sources (by author)

Binns, Archie. *Northwest Gateway: The Story of the Port of Seattle.* Garden City, N.Y.: Doubleday, Doran & Company, 1941.

Clark, Norman Harold. *Milltown: Social History of Everett, Washington.* Seattle: University of Washington Press, 1970.

Corman, Edwin Truman, Jr., and Helen M. Gibbs. *Time, Tide and Timber: A Century of Pope & Talbot.* Stanford: Stanford University Press, 1949.

Grant, Frederick James. *History of Seattle, Washington.* New York: American Publishing and Engraving Co., 1891.

Hidy, Ralph Willard, Frank Ernest Hill, and Allan Nevins. *Timber and Men: The Weyerhaeuser Story.* New York: Macmillan Company, 1963.

Ingram, Arthur. *Leyland Lorries.* Nynehead, England: Roundoak Publishing, 1996.

Mallonee, R. "History of Kenworth Truck Co.," 1981.

Morgan, Murray Chromwell. *The Last Wilderness.* Seattle: University of Washington Press, 1976.

———. *Puget's Sound: A Narrative of Early Tacoma and the Southern Sound.* Seattle: University of Washington Press, 1979.

———. *Skid Road: An Informal Portrait of Seattle.* New
York: Ballantine Books, 1960.

Nelson, Gerald B. *Seattle: The Life and Times of an
American City.* New York: A. Knopf, 1977.

Sale, Roger. *Seattle: Past to Present.* Seattle: University
of Washington Press, 1976.

Slauson, Morda C., and Ethel Telbaw. *Renton: From Coal
to Jets.* Renton, Wash.: Renton Historical Society,
1976.

Trade Periodicals

Airport World & Aviation System Management
Canadian Geographical Journal
Columbia River and Oregon Timberman
The Engineer
Iron Age
Marine Digest
New Seattle Chamber of Commerce Record
Pacific Lumber Trade Journal
Railway and Marine News
Timberman
The Washington Historical Quarterly
West Coast Lumberman
Western Machinery and Steel World

General Periodical Articles

Argus (1898–1958)
The Atlantic Monthly (1930–1932)
Barron's (1924–1933)
Business Week (1942–1948, November 2003)
Business Wire (March, July 2004)
CBS MarketWatch (October 2003, August 2004)
Commercial and Financial Chronicle (1924–1933)
Daily Journal American (1977–1979)
Daily Journal of Commerce (1934–1972)
Everett Herald (1941–1953)
Forbes (July–November 1980, 2002)
Fortune (1945, 1980, 2000, 2002, 2004)
J.D. Power and Associates Reports (2000–2004)
Life (1942–1945)
Mainliner (1980)
Marple's Business Roundup (1959–1976)
Marple's Pacific Northwest Letter (1976–2004)
The Nation (1930–1932)
National Business (1964–1969, 1974–1976)
New York Times (July–November 1980)
New York Times Magazine (December 2, 1951)
Newsweek (November 2, 1953)
Seattle Business (1929–1979)
Seattle Post-Intelligencer (1940–2004)
Seattle Times (1905–2004)
TRUCK magazine (June 2004)
Wall Street Journal (November 3, 1980)
Washington CEO (December 2000, January 2004)

Recorded Reminiscences and Oral Histories of PACCAR Inc from the PACCAR Archive, Bellevue, Washington

Aitken, Murray
Armstrong, Ronald E.
Bangert, Richard E., II
Baugh, Douglas
Brown, Wallace
Cannon, John
Cardillo, James G.
Chantrey, Jack A.
Christensen, Robert J.
Chriswell, F.W.
Czarniecki, John
Douglas, D.E.
Dunn, Joseph M.
Elliott, Ken
Engstrom, Adolph W.
Fetterman, Paul
Flynn, Patrick F.
Gangl, Kenneth R.
Gilligan, Stephen P.
Grant, J.W.
Gross, William N.
Hahn, J.E.
Hatchel, G. Don
Henebry, Timothy M.
Hickey, H.R.
Holmstrom, Robert A.
Hovind, David J.
Jackson, William D.
Lhamon, George M.
Lundahl, Thomas A.
Marple, Elliot
Mawyer, Helene N.

McCone, John A.
McCone, Theiline Pigott
Miller, Emmett
Moore, Gary S.
Moran, R.B.
Morie, G. Glen
Newell, Richard
Norrie, Robert
O'Brien, Robert D.
'Over the Hill Gang'*
Pacific Car and Foundry
   Executives**
Panza, Nicholas P.
Pennell, Donald F.
Pennington, W.J.
Pigott, Charles M.
Pigott, James C.
Pigott, Mark C.
Poff, James
Reed, William G., Sr.
Robbins, G.R.
Rowe, Keith
Schmitz, Ferdinand, Jr.
Shepard, Hil B.
Sobic, Daniel D.
Southern, Robert
Tembreull, Michael A.
West, George E., Jr.
White, Marion
White, Priscilla
Wrightson, Ron

*Group of retired PACCAR and Kenworth senior executives
**Senior and/or retired Pacific Car and Foundry Co. executives

INDEX

Page numbers in **boldface** type refer to illustrations.